W9-AWF-903

Handbook of
Usability Testing

Handbook of
Usability Testing
Second Edition

How to Plan, Design, and Conduct Effective Tests

Jeff Rubin
Dana Chisnell

WILEY

Wiley Publishing, Inc.

Handbook of Usability Testing, Second Edition: How to Plan, Design, and Conduct Effective Tests

Published by
Wiley Publishing, Inc.
10475 Crosspoint Boulevard
Indianapolis, IN 46256

Copyright © 2008 by Wiley Publishing, Inc., Indianapolis, Indiana

Published simultaneously in Canada

ISBN: 978-0-470-18548-3

Manufactured in the United States of America

10 9 8 7 6 5

For general information on our other products and services or to obtain technical support, please contact our Customer Care Department within the U.S. at (800) 762-2974, outside the U.S. at (317) 572-3993 or fax (317) 572-4002.

Library of Congress Cataloging-in-Publication Data is available from the publisher.

Dedicated to those for whom usability and user-centered design is a way of life and their work a joyful expression of their genuine concern for others.

— Jeff

To my parents, Jan and Duane Chisnell, who believe me when I tell them that I am working for world peace through user research and usability testing.

— Dana

About the Authors

Jeff Rubin has more than 30 years experience as a human factors/usability specialist in the technology arena. While at the Bell Laboratories' Human Performance Technology Center, he developed and refined testing methodologies, and conducted research on the usability criteria of software, documentation, and training materials.

During his career, Jeff has provided consulting services and workshops on the planning, design, and evaluation of computer-based products and services for hundreds of companies including Hewlett Packard, Citigroup, Texas Instruments, AT&T, the Ford Motor Company, FedEx, Arbitron, Sprint, and State Farm. He was cofounder and managing partner of The Usability Group from 1999–2005, a leading usability consulting firm that offered user-centered design and technology adoption strategies. Jeff served on the Board of the Usability Professionals Association from 1999–2001.

Jeff holds a degree in Experimental Psychology from Lehigh University. His extensive experience in the application of user-centered design principles to customer research, along with his ability to communicate complex principles and techniques in nontechnical language, make him especially qualified to write on the subject of usability testing.

He is currently retired from usability consulting and pursuing other passionate interests in the nonprofit sector.

Dana Chisnell is an independent usability consultant and user researcher operating UsabilityWorks in San Francisco, CA. She has been doing usability research, user interface design, and technical communications consulting and development since 1982.

Dana took part in her first usability test in 1983, while she was working as a research assistant at the Document Design Center. It was on a mainframe office system developed by IBM. She was still very wet behind the ears. Since then, she has worked with hundreds of study participants for dozens of clients to learn about design issues in software, hardware, web sites, online services, games, and ballots (and probably other things that are better forgotten about). She has helped companies like Yahoo!, Intuit, AARP, Wells Fargo, E*TRADE, Sun Microsystems, and RLG (now OCLC) perform usability tests and other user research to inform and improve the designs of their products and services.

Dana's colleagues consider her an expert in usability issues for older adults and plain language. (She says she's still learning.) Lately, she has been working on issues related to ballot design and usability and accessibility in voting.

She has a bachelor's degree in English from Michigan State University. She lives in the best neighborhood in the best city in the world.

Credits

Executive Editor
Bob Elliott

Development Editor
Maureen Spears

Technical Editor
Janice James

Production Editor
Eric Charbonneau

Copy Editor
Foxxe Editorial Services

Editorial Manager
Mary Beth Wakefield

Production Manager
Tim Tate

Vice President and Executive Group Publisher
Richard Swadley

Vice President and Executive Publisher
Joseph B. Wikert

Project Coordinator, Cover
Lynsey Stanford

Proofreader
Nancy Bell

Indexer
Jack Lewis

Cover Image
Getty Images/Photodisc/McMillan Digital Art

Acknowledgments

From Jeff Rubin

From the first edition, I would like to acknowledge:

- Dean Vitello and Roberta Cross, who edited the entire first manuscript.
- Michele Baliestero, administrative assistant extraordinaire.
- John Wilkinson, who reviewed the original outline and several chapters of the manuscript.
- Pamela Adams, who reviewed the original outline and most of the manuscript, and with whom I worked on several usability projects.
- Terri Hudson from Wiley, who initially suggested I write a book on this topic.
- Ellen Mason, who brought me into Hewlett Packard to implement a user-centered design initiative and allowed me to try out new research protocols.

For this second edition, I would like to acknowledge:

- Dave Rinehart, my partner in crime at The Usability Group, and co-developer of many user research strategies.
- The staff of The Usability Group, especially to Ann Wanschura, who was always loyal and kind, and who never met a screener questionnaire she could not master.
- Last, thanks to all the clients down through the years who showed confidence and trust in me and my colleagues to do the right thing for their customers.

From Dana Chisnell

The obvious person to thank first is Jeff Rubin. Jeff wrote *Handbook of Usability Testing*, one of the seminal books about usability testing, at a time when it was very unusual for companies to invest resources in performing a reality check on the usability of their products. The first edition had staying power. It became such a classic that apparently people want more. For better or worse, the world still needs books about usability testing. So, a thousand thank-yous to Jeff for writing the first edition, which helped many of us get started with usability testing over the last 14 years. Thanks, too, Jeff, for inviting me to work with you on the second edition. I am truly honored. And thank you for offering your patience, diligence, humor, and great wisdom to me and to the project of updating the *Handbook*.

Ginny Redish and Joe Dumas deserve great thanks as well. Their book, *A Practical Guide to Usability Testing*, which came out at the same time as Jeff's book, formed my approach to usability testing. Ginny has been my mentor for several years. In some weird twist of fate, it was Ginny who suggested me to Jeff. The circle is complete.

A lot of people will be thankful that this edition is done, none of them more than I. But Janice James probably comes a close second. Her excellent technical review of every last word of the second edition kept Jeff and me honest on the methodology and the modern realities of conducting usability tests. She inspired dozens of important updates and expansions in this edition.

So did friends and colleagues who gave us feedback on the first edition to inform the new one. JoAnn Hackos, Linda Urban, and Susan Becker all gave detailed comments about where they felt the usability world had changed, what their students had said would be more helpful, and insights about what they might do differently if it were their book.

Arnold Arcolio, who also gave extensive, specific comments before the revising started, generously spot-checked and re-reviewed drafts as the new edition took form.

Sandra Olson deserves thanks for helping me to develop a basic philosophy about how to recruit participants for user research and usability studies. Her excellent work as a recruiting consultant and her close review informed much that is new about recruiting in this book.

Ken Kellogg, Neil Fitzgerald, Christy Wells, and Tim Kiernan helped me understand what it takes to implement programs within companies that include usability testing and that attend closely to their users' experiences.

Other colleagues have been generous with stories, sources, answers to random questions, and examples (which you will see sprinkled throughout the book), as well. Chief among them are my former workmates at Tec-Ed, especially Stephanie Rosenbaum, Laurie Kantner, and Lori Anschuetz.

Jared Spool of UIE has also been encouraging and supportive throughout, starting with thorough, thoughtful feedback about the first edition and continuing through liberal permissions to include techniques and examples from his company's research practice in the second edition.

Thanks also go to those I've learned from over the years who are part of the larger user experience and usability community, including some I have never met face to face but know through online discussions, papers, articles, reports, and books.

To the clients and companies I have worked with over 25 years, as well as the hundreds of study participants, I also owe thanks. Some of the examples and stories here reflect composites of my experiences with all of those important people.

Thanks also go to Bob Elliott at Wiley for contacting Jeff about reviving the *Handbook* in the first place, and Maureen Spears for managing the "developmental" edit of a time-tested resource with humor, flexibility, and understanding.

Finally, I thank my friends and family for nodding politely and pouring me a drink when I might have gone over the top on some point of usability esoterica (to them) at the dinner table. My parents, Jan and Duane Chisnell, and Doris Ditner deserve special thanks for giving me time and space so I could hole up and write.

Contents

Foreword

Hey! I know you!

Well, I don't know you personally, but I know the type of person you are. After all, I'm a trained observer and I've already observed a few things.

First off, I observed that you're the type of person who likes to read a quality book. And, while you might appreciate a book about a dashing anthropology professor who discovers a mysterious code in the back of an ancient script that leads him on a globetrotting adventure that endangers his family and starts to topple the world's secret power brokers, you've chosen to pick up a book called *Handbook of Usability Testing, Second Edition*. I'm betting you're going to enjoy it just as much. (Sorry, there is no secret code hidden in these pages — that I've found — and I've read it four times so far.)

You're also the type of person who wonders how frustrating and hard to use products become that way. I'm also betting that you're a person who would really like to help your organization produce designs that delight its customers and users.

How do I know all these things? Because, well, I'm just like you; and I have been for almost 30 years. I conducted my first usability test in 1981. I was testing one of the world's first word processors, which my team had developed. We'd been working on the design for a while, growing increasingly uncomfortable with how complex it had become. Our fear was that we'd created a design that nobody would figure out.

In one of the first tests of its kind, we'd sat a handful of users down in front of our prototype, asked each to create new documents, make changes, save the files, and print them out. While we had our hunches about the design confirmed (even the simplest commands were hard to use), we felt exhilarated by the amazing feedback we'd gotten directly from the folks who would be using our design. We returned to our offices, changed the design, and couldn't wait to put the revised versions in front of the next batch of folks.

Since those early days, I've conducted hundreds of similar tests. (Actually, it's been more than a thousand, but who's counting?) I still find each test as fascinating and exhilarating as those first word processor evaluations. I still learn something new every time, something (I could have never predicted) that, now that we know it, will greatly improve the design. That's the beauty of usability tests — they're never boring.

Many test sessions stand out in my mind. There was the one where the VP of finance jumped out of his chair, having come across a system prompt asking him to "Hit Enter to Default", shouting "I've never *defaulted* on anything before, I'm not going to start now." There was the session where each of the users looked quizzically at the icon depicting a blood-dripping hatchet, exclaiming how cool it looked but not guessing it meant "Execute Program". There was the one where the CEO of one of the world's largest consumer products companies, while evaluating an information system created *specifically for him*, turned and apologized to me, the session moderator, for ruining my test — because he couldn't figure out the design for even the simplest tasks. I could go on for hours. (Buy me a drink and I just might!)

Why are usability tests so fascinating? I think it's because you get to see the design through the user's eyes. They bring something into the foreground that no amount of discussion or debate would ever discover. And, even more exciting, is when a participant turns to you and says, "I love this — can I buy it right now?"

Years ago, the research company I work for, User Interface Engineering, conducted a study to understand where usability problems originate. We looked at dozens of large projects, traipsing through the myriad binders of internal documentation, looking to identify at what point usability problems we'd discovered had been introduced into the design. We were looking to see if we could catalogue the different ways teams create problems, so maybe they could create internal processes and mechanisms to avoid them going forward.

Despite our attempts, we realized such a catalogue would be impossible, not because there were too many causes, but because there were too few. In fact, there was only one cause. Every one of the hundreds of usability problems we were tracking was caused by the same exact problem: someone on the design team was missing a key piece of information when they were faced with an important design decision. Because they didn't have what they needed, they'd taken a guess and the usability problem was born. Had they had the info, they would've made a different, more informed choice, likely preventing the issue.

So, as fun and entertaining as usability testing is, we can't forget its core purpose: to help the design team make informed decisions. That's why the amazing work that Jeff and Dana have put into this book is so important.

They've done a great job of collecting and organizing the essential techniques and tricks for conducting effective tests.

When the first edition of this book came out in 1994, I was thrilled. It was the first time anyone had gathered the techniques into one place, giving all of us a single resource to learn from and share with our colleagues. At UIE, it was our bible and we gave hundreds of copies to our clients, so they'd have the resource at their fingertips.

I'm even more thrilled with this new edition. We've learned a ton since '94 on how to help teams improve their designs and Dana and Jeff have captured all of it nicely. You'll probably get tired of hearing me recommend this book all the time.

So, read on. Learn how to conduct great usability tests that will inform your team and provide what they need to create a delightful design. And, look forward to the excitement you'll experience when a participant turns to you and tells you just how much they love your design.

— Jared M. Spool, Founding Principal, User Interface Engineering

P.S. I think there's a hint to the secret code on page 114. It's down toward the bottom. Don't tell anyone else.

Preface to the Second Edition

Welcome to the revised, improved second edition of *Handbook of Usability Testing*. It has been 14 long years since this book first went to press, and I'd like to thank all the readers who have made the *Handbook* so successful, and especially those who communicated their congratulations with kind words.

In the time since the first edition went to press, much in the world of usability testing has changed dramatically. For example, "usability," "user experience," and "customer experience," arcane terms at best back then, have become rather commonplace terms in reviews and marketing literature for new products. Other notable changes in the world include the Internet explosion, (in its infancy in '94) the transportability and miniaturization of testing equipment, (lab in a bag anyone?), the myriad methods of data collection such as remote, automated, and digitized, and the ever-shrinking life cycle for introducing new technological products and services. Suffice it to say, usability testing has gone mainstream and is no longer just the province of specialists. For all these reasons and more, a second edition was necessary and, dare I say, long overdue.

The most significant change in this edition is that there are now two authors, where previously, I was the sole author. Let me explain why. I have essentially retired from usability consulting for health reasons after 30 plus years. When our publisher, Wiley, indicated an interest in updating the book, I knew it was beyond my capabilities alone, yet I did want the book to continue its legacy of helping readers improve the usability of their products and services. So I suggested to Wiley that I recruit a skilled coauthor (if it was possible to find one who was interested and shared my sensibilities for the discipline) to do the heavy lifting on the second edition. It was my good fortune to connect with Dana Chisnell, and she has done a superlative job, beyond my considerable expectations, of researching, writing, updating, refreshing, and improving the

Handbook. She has been a joy to work with, and I couldn't have asked for a better partner and usability professional to pass the torch to, and to carry the *Handbook* forward for the next generation of readers.

In this edition, Dana and I have endeavored to retain the timeless principles of usability testing, while revising those elements of the book that are clearly dated, or that can benefit from improved methods and techniques. You will find hundreds of additions and revisions such as:

- Reordering of the main sections (see below).
- Reorganization of many chapters to align them more closely to the flow of conducting a test.
- Improved layout, format, and typography.
- Updating of many of the examples and samples that preceded the ascendancy of the Internet.
- Improved drawings.
- The creation of an ancillary web site, www.wiley.com/go/usabilitytesting, which contains supplemental materials such as:
  - Updated references.
  - Books, blogs, podcasts, and other resources.
  - Electronic versions of the deliverables used as examples in the book.
  - More examples of test designs and, over time, other deliverables contributed by the authors and others who aspire to share their work.

Regarding the reordering of the main sections, we have simplified into three parts the material that previously was spread among four sections. We now have:

- **Part 1: Overview of Testing**, which covers the definition of key terms and presents an expanded discussion of user-centered design and other usability techniques, and explains the basics of moderating a test.
- **Part 2: Basic Process of Testing**, which covers the how-to of testing in step-by-step fashion.
- **Part 3: Advanced Techniques**, which covers the who?, what?, where?, and how? of variations on the basic method, and also discusses how to extend one's influence on the whole of product development strategy.

What hasn't changed is the rationale for this book altogether. With the demand for usable products far outpacing the number of trained professionals available to provide assistance, many product developers, engineers, system designers, technical communicators, and marketing and training specialists have had to assume primary responsibility for usability within their organizations. With little formal training in usability engineering or user-centered design, many are being asked to perform tasks for which they are unprepared.

This book is intended to help bridge this gap in knowledge and training by providing a straightforward, step-by-step approach for evaluating and improving the usability of technology-based products, systems, and their accompanying support materials. It is a "how-to" book, filled with practical guidelines, realistic examples, and many samples of test materials.

But it is also intended for a secondary audience of the more experienced human factors or usability specialist who may be new to the discipline of usability testing, including:

- Human factors specialists
- Managers of product and system development teams
- Product marketing specialists
- Software and hardware engineers
- System designers and programmers
- Technical communicators
- Training specialists

A third audience is college and university students in the disciplines of computer science, technical communication, industrial engineering, experimental and cognitive psychology, and human factors engineering, who wish to learn a pragmatic, no-nonsense approach to designing usable products.

In order to communicate clearly with these audiences, we have used plain language, and have kept the references to formulas and statistics to a bare minimum. While many of the principles and guidelines are based on theoretical and practitioner research, the vast majority have been drawn from Dana's and my combined 55 years of experience as usability specialists designing, evaluating, and testing all manner of software, hardware, and written materials. Wherever possible, we have tried to offer explanations for the methods presented herein, so that you, the reader, might avoid the pitfalls and political landmines that we have discovered only through substantial trial and error. For those readers who would like to dig deeper, we have included references to other publications and articles that influenced our thinking at www.wiley.com/go/usabilitytesting.

Caveat

In writing this book, we have placed tremendous trust in the reader to acknowledge his or her own capabilities and limitations as they pertain to user-centered design and to stay within them. Be realistic about your own level of knowledge and expertise, even if management anoints you as the resident usability expert. Start slowly with small, simple studies, allowing yourself time to acquire the necessary experience and confidence to expand further. Above all, remember that the essence of user-centered design is clear (unbiased) seeing, appreciation of detail, and trust in the ability of your future customers to guide your hand, if you will only let them.

— Jeff Rubin

PART

I

Usability Testing:
An Overview

What Makes Something Usable?

What makes a product or service usable?

Usability is a quality that many products possess, but many, many more lack. There are historical, cultural, organizational, monetary, and other reasons for this, which are beyond the scope of this book. Fortunately, however, there are customary and reliable methods for assessing where design contributes to usability and where it does not, and for judging what changes to make to designs so a product can be usable enough to survive or even thrive in the marketplace.

It can *seem* hard to know what makes something usable because unless you have a breakthrough usability paradigm that actually drives sales (Apple's iPod comes to mind), usability is only an issue when it is lacking or absent. Imagine a customer trying to buy something from your company's e-commerce web site. The inner dialogue they may be having with the site might sound like this: *I can't find what I'm looking for. Okay, I have found what I'm looking for, but I can't tell how much it costs. Is it in stock? Can it be shipped to where I need it to go? Is shipping free if I spend this much?* Nearly everyone who has ever tried to purchase something on a web site has encountered issues like these.

It is easy to pick on web sites (after all there are so very many of them), but there are myriad other situations where people encounter products and services that are difficult to use every day. Do you know how to use all of the features on your alarm clock, phone, or DVR? When you contact a vendor, how easy is it to know what to choose in their voice-based menu of options?

What Do We Mean by "Usable"?

In large part, what makes something usable is the *absence of frustration* in using it. As we lay out the process and method for conducting usability testing in this book, we will rely on this definition of "usability;" when a product or service is truly usable, *the user can do what he or she wants to do the way he or she expects to be able to do it, without hindrance, hesitation, or questions.*

But before we get into defining and exploring usability *testing*, let's talk a bit more about the concept of usability and its attributes. To be usable, a product or service should be useful, efficient, effective, satisfying, learnable, and accessible.

Usefulness concerns the degree to which a product enables a user to achieve his or her goals, and is an assessment of the user's willingness to use the product at all. Without that motivation, other measures make no sense, because the product will just sit on the shelf. If a system is easy to use, easy to learn, and even satisfying to use, but does not achieve the specific goals of a specific user, it will not be used even if it is given away for free. Interestingly enough, usefulness is probably the element that is most often overlooked during experiments and studies in the lab.

In the early stages of product development, it is up to the marketing team to ascertain what product or system features are desirable and necessary before other elements of usability are even considered. Lacking that, the development team is hard-pressed to take the user's point of view and will simply guess or, even worse, use themselves as the user model. This is very often where a system-oriented design takes hold.

Efficiency is the quickness with which the user's goal can be accomplished accurately and completely and is usually a measure of time. For example, you might set a usability testing benchmark that says "95 percent of all users will be able to load the software within 10 minutes."

Effectiveness refers to the extent to which the product behaves in the way that users expect it to and the ease with which users can use it to do what they intend. This is usually measured quantitatively with error rate. Your usability testing measure for effectiveness, like that for efficiency, should be tied to some percentage of total users. Extending the example from efficiency, the benchmark might be expressed as "95 percent of all users will be able to load the software correctly on the first attempt."

Learnability is a part of effectiveness and has to do with the user's ability to operate the system to some defined level of competence after some prede-termined amount and period of training (which may be no time at all). It can also refer to the ability of infrequent users to relearn the system after periods of inactivity.

Satisfaction refers to the user's perceptions, feelings, and opinions of the product, usually captured through both written and oral questioning. Users are more likely to perform well on a product that meets their needs and provides satisfaction than one that does not. Typically, users are asked to rate and rank products that they try, and this can often reveal causes and reasons for problems that occur.

Usability goals and objectives are typically defined in measurable terms of one or more of these attributes. However, let us caution that making a product usable is never simply the ability to generate numbers about usage and satisfaction. While the numbers can tell us whether a product "works" or not, there is a distinctive qualitative element to how usable something is as well, which is hard to capture with numbers and is difficult to pin down. It has to do with how one interprets the data in order to know *how* to fix a problem because the behavioral data tells you *why* there is a problem. Any doctor can measure a patient's vital signs, such as blood pressure and pulse rate. But interpreting those numbers and recommending the appropriate course of action for a specific patient is the true value of the physician. Judging the several possible alternative causes of a design problem, and knowing which are especially likely in a particular case, often means looking beyond individual data points in order to design effective treatment. There exist these little subtleties that evade the untrained eye.

Accessibility and usability are siblings. In the broadest sense, accessibility is about having access to the products needed to accomplish a goal. But in this book when we talk about accessibility, we are looking at what makes products usable by people who have disabilities. Making a product usable for people with disabilities — or who are in special contexts, or both — almost always benefits people who do not have disabilities. Considering accessibility for people with disabilities can clarify and simplify design for people who face temporary limitations (for example, injury) or situational ones (such as divided attention or bad environmental conditions, such as bright light or not enough light). There are many tools and sets of guidelines available to assist you in making accessible designs. (We include pointers to accessibility resources on the web site that accompanies this book (see www.wiley.com/go/usabilitytesting for more information.) You should acquaint yourself with accessibility best practices so that you can implement them in your organization's user-centered design process along with usability testing and other methods.

Making things more usable and accessible is part of the larger discipline of user-centered design (UCD), which encompasses a number of methods and techniques that we will talk about later in this chapter. In turn, user-centered design rolls up into an even larger, more holistic concept called *experience design*. Customers may be able to complete the purchase process on your web site, but how does that mesh with what happens when the product is delivered, maintained, serviced, and possibly returned? What does your organization do to support the research and decision-making process leading up to the purchase? All of these figure in to experience design.

Which brings us back to usability.

True usability is invisible. If something is going well, you don't notice it. If the temperature in a room is comfortable, no one complains. But usability in products happens along a continuum. How usable is your product? Could it be more usable *even though* users can accomplish their goals? Is it worth improving?

Most usability professionals spend most of their time working on eliminating design problems, trying to minimize frustration for users. This is a laudable goal! But know that it is a difficult one to attain for every user of your product. And it affects only a small part of the user's experience of accomplishing a goal. And, though there are quantitative approaches to testing the usability of products, it is impossible to measure the usability of something. You can only measure how *un*usable it is: how many problems people have using something, what the problems are and why.

By incorporating evaluation methods such as usability testing throughout an iterative design process, it is possible to make products and services that are useful and usable, and possibly even delightful.

What Makes Something Less Usable?

Why are so many high-tech products so hard to use?

In this section, we explore this question, discuss why the situation exists, and examine the overall antidote to this problem. Many of the examples in this book involve not only consumer hardware, software, and web sites but also documentation such as user's guides and embedded assistance such as on-screen instructions and error messages. The methods in this book also work for appliances such as music players, cell phones, and game consoles. Even products, such as the control panel for an ultrasound machine or the user manual for a digital camera, fall within the scope of this book.

Five Reasons Why Products Are Hard to Use

For those of you who currently work in the product development arena, as engineers, user-interface designers, technical communicators, training specialists, or managers in these disciplines, it seems likely that several of the reasons for the development of hard-to-use products and systems will sound painfully familiar.

- Development focuses on the machine or system.
- Target audiences change and adapt.
- Designing usable products is difficult.
- Team specialists don't always work in integrated ways.
- Design and implementation don't always match.

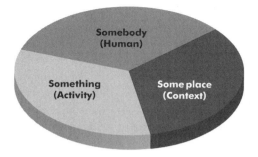

Figure 1-1 Bailey's Human Performance Model

Reason 1: Development Focuses on the Machine or System

During design and development of the product, the emphasis and focus may have been on the machine or system, not on the person who is the ultimate end user. The general model of human performance shown in Figure 1-1 helps to clarify this point.

There are three major components to consider in any type of human performance situation as shown in Bailey's Human performance model.

- The human
- The context
- The activity

Because the development of a system or product is an attempt to improve human performance in some area, designers should consider these three components during the design process. All three affect the final outcome of how well humans ultimately perform. Unfortunately, of these three components, designers, engineers, and programmers have traditionally placed the greatest emphasis on the *activity* component, and much less emphasis on the human and the context components. The relationship of the three components to each other has also been neglected. There are several explanations for this unbalanced approach:

- There has been an underlying assumption that because humans are so inherently flexible and adaptable, it is easier to let them adapt themselves to the machine, rather than vice versa.

- Developers traditionally have been more comfortable working with the seemingly "black and white," scientific, concrete issues associated with systems, than with the more gray, muddled, ambiguous issues associated with human beings.

- Developers have historically been hired and rewarded not for their interpersonal, "people" skills but for their ability to solve technical problems.

- The most important factor leading to the neglect of human needs has been that in the past, designers were developing products for end users who were much like themselves. There was simply no reason to study such a familiar colleague. That leads us to the next point.

Reason 2: Target Audiences Expand and Adapt

As technology has penetrated the mainstream consumer market, the target audience has expanded and continues to change dramatically. Development organizations have been slow to react to this evolution.

The original users of computer-based products were enthusiasts (also known as early adopters) possessing expert knowledge of computers and mechanical devices, a love of technology, the desire to tinker, and pride in their ability to troubleshoot and repair any problem. Developers of these products shared similar characteristics. In essence, users and developers of these systems were one and the same. Because of this similarity, the developers practiced "next-bench" design, a method of designing for the user who is literally sitting one bench away in the development lab. Not surprisingly, this approach met with relative success, and users rarely if ever complained about difficulties.

Why *would* they complain? Much of their joy in using the product was the amount of tinkering and fiddling required to make it work, and enthusiast users took immense pride in their abilities to make these complicated products function. Consequently, a "machine-oriented" or "system-oriented" approach met with little resistance and became the development norm.

Today, however, all that has changed dramatically. Users are apt to have little technical knowledge of computers and mechanical devices, little patience for tinkering with the product just purchased, and completely different expectations from those of the designer. More important, *today's user is not even remotely comparable to the designer in skill set, aptitude, expectation, or almost any attribute that is relevant to the design process.* Where in the past, companies might have found Ph.D. chemists using their products, today they will find high-school graduates performing similar functions. Obviously, "next-bench" design simply falls apart as a workable design strategy when there is a great discrepancy between user and designer, and companies employing such a strategy, even inadvertently, will continue to produce hard-to-use products.

Designers aren't hobbyist enthusiasts (necessarily) anymore; most are trained professionals educated in human computer interaction, industrial design, human factors engineering, or computer science, or a combination of these. Whereas before it was unusual for a nontechnical person to use electronic or computer-based equipment, today it is almost impossible for the average person *not to use* such a product in either the workplace or in private life. The overwhelming majority of products, whether in the workplace or the home, be they cell phones, DVRs, web sites, or sophisticated testing equipment, are intended for this less technical user. Today's user wants a tool, not another hobby.

Reason 3: Designing Usable Products Is Difficult

The design of usable systems is a difficult, unpredictable endeavor, yet many organizations treat it as if it were just "common sense."

While much has been written about what makes something usable, the concept remains maddeningly elusive, especially for those without a background in either the behavioral or social sciences. Part art, part science, it seems that *everyone* has an opinion about usability, and how to achieve it — that is, until it is time to evaluate the usability of a product (which requires an operational definition and precise measurement).

This trivializing of usability creates a more dangerous situation than if product designers freely admitted that designing for usability was not their area of expertise and began to look for alternative ways of developing products. Or as Will Rogers so aptly stated "It's not the things that we don't know that gets us into trouble; it's the things we do know that ain't so." In many organizations usability engineering has been approached as if it were nothing more than "common sense."

When this book was first published in 1994, few systems designers and developers had knowledge of the basic principles of user-centered design. Today, most designers have some knowledge of — or at least exposure to — user-centered design practices, whether they are aware of them or not. However, there are still gaps between awareness and execution. Usability principles are still not obvious, and there is still a great need for education, assistance, and a systematic approach in applying so-called "common sense" to the design process.

Reason 4: Team Specialists Don't Always Work in Integrated Ways

Organizations employ very specialized teams and approaches to product and system development, yet fail to integrate them with each other.

To improve efficiency, many organizations have broken down the product development process into separate system components developed independently. For example, components of a software product include *the user interface, the help system,* and *the written materials.* Typically, these components are developed by separate individuals or teams. Now, there is nothing inherently wrong with specialization. The difficulty arises when there is little integration of these separate components and poor communication among the different development teams.

Often the product development proceeds in separate, compartmentalized sections. To an outsider looking on, the development would be seen as depicted in Figure 1-2.

Figure 1-2 Nonintegrated approach to product development

Each development group functions independently, almost as a silo, and the final product often reflects this approach. The help center will not adequately support the user interface or it will be organized very differently from the interface. Or user documentation and help will be redundant with little cross-referencing. Or the documentation will not reflect the latest version of the user interface. You get the picture.

The problem occurs when the product is released. The end user, upon receiving this new product, views it and expects it to work as a single, integrated product, as shown in Figure 1-3. He or she makes no particular distinction among the three components, and each one is expected to *support and work seamlessly with the others*. When the product does not work in this way, it clashes with the user's expectations, and whatever advantages accrue through specialization are lost.

Even more interesting is how often organizations unknowingly exacerbate this lack of integration *by usability testing each of the components separately*. Documentation is tested separately from the interface, and the interface separately from the help. Ultimately, this approach is futile, because it matters little if each component is usable within itself. Only if the components work well together will the product be viewed as usable and meeting the user's needs.

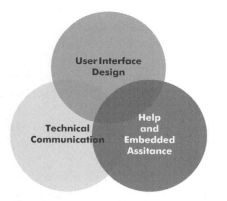

Figure 1-3 Integrated approach to product development

Fortunately, there have been advances in application development methodologies in recent years that emphasize iterated design and interdisciplinary teams. Plus there are great examples of cutting-edge products and services built around usability advantages that are dominating their markets, such as Netflix, eBay, Yahoo!, and the iPod and iPhone, as well as Whirlpool's latest line of home appliances. Their integration of components is a key contributor to their success.

Reason 5: Design and Implementation Don't Always Match

The *design* of the user interface and the technical *implementation* of the user interface are different activities, requiring very different skills. Today, the emphasis and need are on design skills, while many engineers possess the mind-set and skill set for technical implementation.

Design, in this case, relates to how the product communicates, whereas implementation refers to how it works. Previously, this dichotomy between design and implementation was rarely even acknowledged. Engineers and designers were hired for their *technical expertise* (e.g., programming and machine-oriented analysis) rather than for their *design expertise* (e.g., communication and human-oriented analysis). This is understandable, because with early generation computer languages the great challenge lay in simply getting the product to work. If it communicated elegantly as well, so much the better, but that was not the prime directive.

With the advent of new-generation programming languages and tools to automatically develop program code, the challenge of technical implementation has diminished. The challenge of design, however, has increased dramatically due to the need to reach a broader, less sophisticated user population and the rising expectations for ease of use. To use a computer analogy, the focus has moved from the inside of the machine (how it works) to the outside where the end user resides (how it communicates).

This change in focus has altered the skills required of designers. This evolution toward design and away from implementation will continue. Someday, perhaps skills such as programming will be completely unnecessary when designing a user interface.

These five reasons merely brush the surface of how and why unusable products and systems continue to flourish. More important is the common theme among these problems and misperceptions; namely that too much emphasis has been placed on the product itself and too little on the desired effects the product needs to achieve. Especially in the heat of a development process that grows shorter and more frenetic all the time, it is not surprising that the user continues to receive too little attention and consideration.

It is easy for designers to lose touch with the fact that they are not designing products per se, but rather they are designing the *relationship* of product and human. Furthermore, in designing this relationship, designers must allow the human to focus on the task at hand — help the human attain a goal — not on the means with which to do that task. They are also designing the relationship of the various product components to each other. This implies excellent communication among the different entities designing the total product and those involved in the larger experience of using the product in a life or work context. What has been done in the past simply will not work for today's user and today's technologies.

What is needed are methods and techniques to help designers change the way they view and design products — methods that work from the outside in, from the end user's needs and abilities to the eventual implementation of the product is *user-centered design* (UCD). Because it is only within the context of UCD that usability testing makes sense and thrives, let's explore this notion of user-centered design in more detail.

What Makes Products More Usable?

User-centered design (UCD) describes an approach that has been around for decades under different names, such as human factors engineering, ergonomics, and usability engineering. (The terms *human factors engineering* and *ergonomics* are almost interchangeable, the major difference between the two having more to do with geography than with real differences in approach and implementation. In the United States, human factors engineering is the more widely used term, and in other countries, most notably in Europe, ergonomics is more widely used.) UCD represents the techniques, processes, methods, and procedures for designing usable products and systems, but just as important, it is the philosophy that places the user at the center of the process.

Although the design team must think about the technology of the product first (can we build what we have in mind?), and then what the features will be (will it do what we want it to do?), they must also think about what the user's experience will be like when he or she uses the product. In user-centered design, development starts with the user as the focus, taking into account the abilities and limitations of the underlying technology and the features the company has in mind to offer.

As a design process, UCD seeks to support how target users actually work, rather than forcing users to change what they do to use something. The International Organization for Standardization (ISO) in standard 13407 says that UCD is "characterized by: the active involvement of users and a clear understanding of user and task requirements; an appropriate allocation of function between users and technology; the iteration of design solutions; multidisciplinary design."

Going beyond user-centered design of a product, we should be paying attention to the whole user experience in the entire cycle of user ownership of a product. Ideally, the entire process of interacting with potential customers, from the initial sales and marketing contact through the entire duration of ownership through the point at which another product is purchased or the current one upgraded, should also be included in a user-centered approach. In such a scenario, companies would extend their concern to include all prepurchase and postpurchase contacts and interactions. However, let's take one step at a time, and stick to the design process.

Numerous articles and books have been written on the subject of user-centered design (UCD) (for a list of our favorites, see the web site that accompanies this book, www.wiley.com/go/usabilitytesting). However, it is important for the reader to understand the basic principles of UCD in order to understand the context for performing usability testing. Usability testing is not UCD itself; it is merely one of several techniques for helping ensure a good, user-centered design.

We want to emphasize these basic principles of user-centered design:

- Early focus on users and their tasks
- Evaluation and measurement of product usage
- Iterated design

An Early Focus on Users and Tasks

More than just simply identifying and categorizing users, we recommend direct contact between users and the design team throughout the development lifecycle. Of course, your team needs training and coaching in how to manage these interactions. This is a responsibility that you can take on as you become more educated and practiced, yourself.

Though a goal should be to institutionalize customer contact, be wary of doing it merely to complete a check-off box on one's performance appraisal form. What is required is a systematic, structured approach to the collection of information from and about users. Designers require training from expert interviewers before conducting a data collection session. Otherwise, the results can be very misleading.

Evaluation and Measurement of Product Usage

Here, emphasis is placed on behavioral measurements of ease of learning and ease of use very early in the design process, through the development and testing of prototypes with actual users.

Iterative Design and Testing

Much has been made about the importance of design iteration. However, this is not just fine-tuning late in the development cycle. Rather, true iterative design allows for the complete overhaul and rethinking of a design, through early testing of conceptual models and design ideas. If designers are not prepared for such a major step, then the influence of iterative design becomes minimal and cosmetic. In essence, true iterative design allows one to "shape the product" through a process of design, test, redesign, and retest activities.

Attributes of Organizations That Practice UCD

User-centered design demands a rethinking of the way in which most companies do business, develop products, and think about their customers. While currently there exists no cookie-cutter formula for success, there are common attributes that companies practicing UCD share. For example:

- Phases that include user input
- Multidisciplinary teams
- Concerned, enlightened management
- A "learn as you go" perspective
- Defined usability goals and objectives

Phases That Include User Input

Unlike the typical phases we have all seen in traditional development methodologies, a user-centered approach is based on receiving user feedback or input during each phase, prior to moving to the next phase. This can involve a variety of techniques, usability testing being only one of these.

Today, most major companies that develop technology-based products or systems have product lifecycles that include some type of usability engineering/human factors process. In that process, questions arise. These questions and some suggested methods for answering them appear in Figure 1-4.

Within each phase, there will be a variety of usability engineering activities. Note that, although this particular lifecycle is written from the viewpoint of the human factors specialist's activities, there are multiple places where collaboration is required among various team members. This leads to our next attribute of organizations practicing UCD.

A Multidisciplinary Team Approach

No longer can design be the province of one person or even of one specialty. While one designer may take ultimate responsibility for a product's design, he

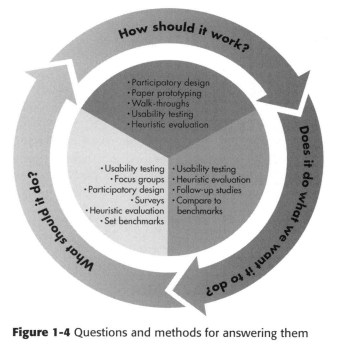

Figure 1-4 Questions and methods for answering them

or she is not all-knowing about how to proceed. There are simply too many factors to consider when designing very complex products for less technical end users. User-centered design requires a variety of skills, knowledge, and, most importantly, information about the intended user and usage. Today, teams composed of specialists from many fields, such as engineering, marketing, training, user-interface design, human factors, and multimedia, are becoming the norm. In turn, many of these specialists have training in complementary areas, so cross-discipline work is easier and more dynamic than ever before.

Concerned, Enlightened Management

Typically, the degree to which usability is a true corporate concern is the degree to which a company's management is committed to following its own lifecycle and giving its guidelines teeth by holding the design team accountable. Management understands that there are financial benefits to usability and market share to be won.

A "Learn as You Go" Perspective

UCD is an evolutionary process whereby the final product is shaped over time. It requires designers to take the attitude that the optimum design is acquired through a process of trial and error, discovery, and refinement. Assumptions about how to proceed remain assumptions and are not cast in concrete until evaluated with the end user. The end user's performance and preferences are the final arbiters of design decisions.

Defined Usability Goals and Objectives

Designing a product to be useful must be a structured and systematic process, beginning with high-level goals and moving to specific objectives. You cannot achieve a goal — usability or otherwise — if it remains nebulous and ill-conceived. Even the term *usability* itself must be defined with your organization. An operational definition of what makes your product usable (tied to successful completion criteria, as we will talk about in Chapter 5) may include:

- Usefulness
- Efficiency
- Effectiveness
- Satisfaction
- Accessibility

Thus bringing us full circle to our original description of what makes a product usable. Now let's review some of the major techniques and methods a usability specialist uses to ensure a user-centered design.

What Are Techniques for Building in Usability?

UCD comprises a variety of techniques, methods, and practices, each applied at different points in the product development lifecycle. Reviewing the major methods will help to provide some context for usability testing, which itself is one of these techniques. Please note that the order in which the techniques are described is more or less the order in which they would be employed during a product's development lifecycle.

Ethnographic Research

Ethnographic research borrows techniques from anthropology. It involves observing users in the place where they would normally use the product (e.g., work, home, coffee bar, etc.) to gather data about who your target users are, what tasks and goals they have related to your planned product (or enhancements), and the context in which they work to accomplish their goals. From this qualitative research, you can develop user profiles, personas (archetype users), scenarios, and task descriptions on which you and the design team can base design decisions throughout the development lifecycle.

Participatory Design

Less a technique and more an embodiment of UCD, participatory design employs one or more representative users on the design team itself. Often used for the development of in-house systems, this approach thrusts the end user into the heart of the design process from the very commencement of the project by tapping the user's knowledge, skill set, and even emotional reactions to the design. The potential danger is that the representative users can become *too* close to the design team. They begin to react and think like the others, or by virtue of their desire to avoid admonishing their colleagues, withhold important concerns or criticism.

A variation on this technique is to arrange short, individual workshops where users, designers, and developers work together on an aspect of design. For example, users, designers, and engineers using workable models, work together to determine the best size and shape for the product.

Focus Group Research

Use focus group research at the very early stages of a project to evaluate preliminary concepts with representative users. It can be considered part of "proof of concept" review. In some cases it is used to identify and confirm the characteristics of the representative user altogether. All focus group research employs the simultaneous involvement of more than one participant, a key factor in differentiating this approach from many other techniques.

The concepts that participants evaluate in these group sessions can be presented in the most preliminary form, such as paper-and-pencil drawings, storyboards, and/or more elaborate screen-based prototypes or plastic models. The objective is to identify how acceptable the concepts are, in what ways they are unacceptable or unsatisfactory, and how they might be made more acceptable and useful. The beauty of the focus group is its ability to explore a few people's judgments and feelings in great depth, and in so doing learn something about how end users think and feel. In this way, focus groups are very different from — and no substitute for — usability tests. A focus group is good for general, qualitative information but not for learning about performance issues and real behaviors. Remember, people in focus groups are reporting what they feel like telling you, which is almost always different from what they actually do. Usability tests are best for observing behaviors and measuring performance issues, while perhaps gathering some qualitative information along the way.

Surveys

By administering surveys you can begin to understand the preferences of a broad base of users about an existing or potential product. While the survey cannot match the focus group in its ability to plumb for in-depth responses and rationale, it can use larger samples to generalize to an entire population. For example, the Nielsen ratings, one of the most famous ongoing surveys, are used to make multimillion-dollar business decisions for a national population based on the preferences of about 1500 people. Surveys can be used at any time in the lifecycle but are most often used in the early stages to better understand the potential user. An important aspect of surveys is that their language must be crystal clear and understood in the same way by all readers, a task impossible to perform without multiple tested iterations and adequate preparation time. Again, asking people about what they do or have done is no substitute for observing them do it in a usability test.

Walk-Throughs

Once you have a good idea who your target users are and the task goals they have, walk-throughs are used to explore how a user might fare with a product by envisioning the user's route through an early concept or prototype of the product. Usually the designer responsible for the work guides his or her colleagues through actual user tasks (sometimes even playing the role for the user), while another team member records difficulties encountered or concerns of the team. In a structured walk-through, as first developed by IBM to perform code reviews, the participants assume specific roles (e.g., moderator, recorder) and follow explicit guidelines (e.g., no walk-through longer than two hours) to ensure the effectiveness of the effort. Rather than the designer taking on the role of the user, you may want to bring in a real user, perhaps someone from a favored client.

Open and Closed Card Sorting

Use card sorting to design in "findability" of content or functionality. This is a very inexpensive method for getting user input on content organization, vocabulary, and labeling in the user interface. You can either give participants cards showing content without titles or categories and have the users do the naming (an open card sort), or give participants preliminary or preexisting categories and ask participants to sort content or functions into those (a closed sort).

Paper Prototyping

In this technique users are shown an aspect of a product on paper and asked questions about it, or asked to respond in other ways. To learn whether the flow of screens or pages that you have planned supports users' expectations, you may mock up pages with paper and pencil on graph paper, or create line drawings or wireframe drawings of screens, pages, or panels, with a version of the page for each state. For example, if the prototype is for a shopping cart for an e-commerce web site, you can show the cart with items, as items are being changed, and then with shipping and taxes added. (Or, you may simply decide to have the participant or the "computer" fill these items in as the session progresses.)

To learn whether the labels help users know what to expect next, and if the categories you have planned reflect how users think and talk about tasks, you can show the top-level navigation. As the participant indicates the top-level choice, you then show the next level of navigation for that choice. The process continues until the user has gone as deeply into the navigation as you have designed and prepared for the sessions.

Or, you may simply ask participants about the prototype you have created. The questions can range from particular attributes, such as organization and layout, to where one might find certain options or types of information.

The value of the paper prototype or paper-and-pencil evaluation is that critical information can be collected quickly and inexpensively. One can ascertain those functions and features that are intuitive and those that are not, *before one line of code has been written*. In addition, technical writers might use the technique to evaluate the intuitiveness of their table of contents before writing one word of text. The technique can be employed again and again with minimal drain on resources.

Expert or Heuristic Evaluations

Expert evaluations involve a review of a product or system, usually by a usability specialist or human factors specialist who has little or no involvement in the project. The specialist performs his or her review according to accepted usability principles (heuristics) from the body of research, human factors literature, and previous professional experience. The viewpoint is that of the specific target population that will use the product.

A "double" specialist, that is, someone who is an expert in usability principles or human factors as well as an expert in the domain area (such as healthcare, financial services, and so on, depending on the application), or in the particular technology employed by the product, can be more effective than one without such knowledge.

Usability Testing

Usability testing, the focus of this book, employs techniques to collect empirical data while observing representative end users using the product to perform realistic tasks. Testing is roughly divided into two main approaches. The first approach involves formal tests conducted as true experiments, in order to confirm or refute specific hypotheses. The second approach, a less formal but still rigorous one (and the one we emphasize in this book), employs an iterative cycle of tests intended to expose usability deficiencies and gradually shape or mold the product in question.

Follow-Up Studies

A follow-up study occurs after formal release of the product. The idea is to collect data for the next release, using surveys, interviews, and observations. Structured follow-up studies are probably the truest and most accurate appraisals of usability, because the actual user, product, and environment are all in place and interacting with each other. That follow-up studies are so rare is unfortunate because designers would benefit immensely from learning what happened to the product that they spent two years of their lives perfecting. Sales figures, while helpful, add nothing to one's knowledge of the product's strengths and weaknesses.

This is not a definitive list of methods by any means, and it is meant merely to provide the reader with an appreciation for the wealth of techniques available and the complexity involved in implementing a UCD approach. It is a rare organization that performs all of these techniques, and just as few conduct them in their pure form. Typically, they are used in altered and combined form, as the specific needs and constraints of a project dictate. For more about these techniques, check out our list of resources on the web site that accompanies this book at www.wiley.com/go/usabilitytesting.

Now let's take a closer look at one of the most renowned techniques of all the ones discussed, and the focus of this book, usability testing, in Chapter 2.

What Is Usability Testing?

The term *usability testing* is often used rather indiscriminately to refer to *any* technique used to evaluate a product or system. Many times it is obvious that the speaker is referring to one of the other techniques discussed in Chapter 1. Throughout this book we use the term *usability testing* to refer to a process that employs people as testing participants who are representative of the target audience to evaluate the degree to which a product meets specific usability criteria. This inclusion of representative users eliminates labeling as usability testing such techniques as expert evaluations, walk-throughs, and the like that do not require representative users as part of the process.

Usability testing is a research tool, with its roots in classical experimental methodology. The range of tests one can conduct is considerable, from true classical experiments with large sample sizes and complex test designs to very informal qualitative studies with only a single participant. Each testing approach has different objectives, as well as different time and resource requirements. The emphasis of this book is on more informal, less complex tests designed for quick turnaround of results in industrial product development environments.

Why Test? Goals of Testing

From the point of view of some companies, usability testing is part of a larger effort to improve the profitability of products. There are many aspects to doing so, which in the end also benefits users greatly: design decisions are informed by data gathered from representative users to expose design issues so they can be remedied, thus minimizing or eliminating frustration for users.

Informing Design

The overall goal of usability testing is to inform design by gathering data from which to identify and rectify usability deficiencies existing in products and their accompanying support materials prior to release. The intent is to ensure the creation of products that:

- Are useful to and valued by the target audience
- Are easy to learn
- Help people be effective and efficient at what they want to do
- Are satisfying (and possibly even delightful) to use

Eliminating Design Problems and Frustration

One side of the profitability coin is the ease with which customers can use the product. When you minimize the frustration of using a product for your target audience by remedying flaws in the design ahead of product release, you also accomplish these goals:

- Set the stage for a positive relationship between your organization and your customers.
- Establish the expectation that the products your organization sells are high quality and easy to use.
- Demonstrate that the organization considers the goals and priorities of its customers to be important.
- Release a product that customers find useful, effective, efficient, and satisfying.

Improving Profitability

Goals or benefits of testing for your organization are:

- **Creating a historical record of usability benchmarks for future releases.**   By keeping track of test results, a company can ensure that future products either improve on or at least maintain current usability standards.
- **Minimizing the cost of service and support calls.**   A more usable product will require fewer service calls and less support from the company.
- **Increasing sales and the probability of repeat sales.**   Usable products create happy customers who talk to other potential buyers or users. Happy customers also tend to stick with future releases of the product, rather than purchase a competitor's product.

- **Acquiring a competitive edge because usability has become a market separator for products.**   Usability has become one of the main ways to separate one's product from a competitor's product in the customer's mind. One need only scan the latest advertising to see products described using phrases such as "simple" and "easy" among others. Unfortunately, this information is rarely truthful when put to the test.

- **Minimizing risk.**   Actually, all companies and organizations have conducted usability testing for years. Unfortunately, the true name for this type of testing has been "product release," and the "testing" involved trying the product in the marketplace. Obviously, this is a very risky strategy, and usability testing conducted *prior* to release can minimize the considerable risk of releasing a product with serious usability problems.

Basics of the Methodology

The basic methodology for conducting a usability test has its origin in the classical approach for conducting a controlled experiment. With this formal approach, often employed to conduct basic research, a specific hypothesis is formulated and then tested by isolating and manipulating variables under controlled conditions. Cause-and-effect relationships are then carefully examined, often through the use of the appropriate inferential statistical technique(s), and the hypothesis is either confirmed or rejected. Employing a true experimental design, these studies require that:

- **A hypothesis must be formulated.**   A hypothesis states what you expect to occur when testing. For example, "Help as designed in format A will improve the speed and error rate of experienced users more than help as designed in format B." It is essential that the hypothesis be as specific as possible.

- **Randomly chosen (using a very systematic method) participants must be assigned to experimental conditions.**   One needs to understand the characteristics of the target population, and from that larger population select a representative random sample. Random sampling is often difficult, especially when choosing from a population of existing customers.

- **Tight controls must be employed.**   Experimental controls are crucial or else the validity of the results can be called into question, regardless of whether statistical significance is the goal. All participants should have nearly the identical experience as each other prior to and during the test.

In addition, the amount of interaction with the test moderator must be controlled.

■ **Control groups must be employed.**   In order to validate results, a control group must be employed; its treatment should vary only on the single variable being tested.

■ **The sample (of users) must be of sufficient size to measure statistically significant differences between groups.**   In order to measure differences between groups statistically, a large enough sample size must be used. Too small a sample can lead to erroneous conclusions.

The preceding approach is the basis for conducting classical experiments, and when conducting basic research, it is the method of choice. *However, it is not the method expounded in this book for the following reasons.*

■ It is often impossible or inappropriate to use such a methodology to conduct usability tests in the fast-paced, highly pressurized development environment in which most readers will find themselves. It is impossible because of the many organizational constraints, political and otherwise. It is inappropriate because the purpose of usability testing is not necessarily to formulate and test specific hypotheses, that is, conduct research, but rather to make informed decisions about design to improve products.

■ The amount of prerequisite knowledge of experimental method and statistics required in order to perform these kinds of studies properly is considerable and better left to an experienced usability or human factors specialist. Should one attempt to conduct this type of tight research without the appropriate background and training, the results can often be very misleading, and lead to a worse situation than if no research had been conducted.

■ In the environment in which testing most often takes place, it is often very difficult to apply the principle of randomly assigning participants because one often has little control over this factor. This is especially true as it concerns the use of existing customers as participants.

■ Still another reason for a less formal approach concerns sample size. To achieve generalizable results for a given target population, one's sample size is dependent on knowledge of certain information about that population, which is often lacking (and sometimes the precise reason for the test). Lacking such information, one may need to test 10 to 12 participants *per condition* to be on the safe side, a factor that might require one to test 40 or more participants to ensure statistically significant results.

■ Last, and probably most important, the classical methodology is designed to obtain quantitative proof of research hypotheses that one design is better than another, for example. It is not designed to obtain qualitative information on how to fix problems and redesign products. We assume that most readers will be more concerned with the latter than the former.

The approach we advocate is a more informal, iterative approach to testing, albeit with experimental rigor at its core. As the reader will see in later chapters of this book, experimental rigor is essential for *any* study that one conducts.

Much can be achieved by conducting *a series* of quick, pointed studies, beginning early in the development cycle. It is the intent of this book to present the basics of conducting this type of less formal, yet well-designed test that will identify the specific usability deficiencies of a product, their cause, and the means to overcome them. The basics of this approach are described in the sections that follow.

Basic Elements of Usability Testing

■ Development of research questions or test objectives rather than hypotheses.

■ Use of a representative sample of end users which may or may not be randomly chosen.

■ Representation of the actual work environment.

■ Observation of end users who either use or review a representation of the product.

■ Controlled and sometimes extensive interviewing and probing of the participants by the test moderator.

■ Collection of quantitative and qualitative performance and preference measures.

■ Recommendation of improvements to the design of the product.

We detail the "how-to" of this approach in the chapters that follow.

Limitations of Testing

Now, having painted a rather glorified picture of what usability testing is intended to accomplish, let's splash a bit of cold water on the situation. Testing is neither the end-all nor be-all for usability and product success, and it is important to understand its limitations. Testing does not guarantee success or even prove that a product will be usable. Even the most rigorously conducted formal test cannot, with 100 percent certainty, ensure that a product will be usable when released. Here are some reasons why:

- **Testing is always an artificial situation.**   Testing in the lab, or even testing in the field, still represents a depiction of the actual situation of usage and not the situation itself. The very act of conducting a study can itself affect the results.

- **Test results do not prove that a product works.**   Even if one conducts the type of test that acquires statistically significant results, this still does not prove that a product works. Statistical significance is simply a measure of the probability that one's results were not due to chance. It is not a guarantee, and it is very dependent upon the way in which the test was conducted.

- **Participants are rarely fully representative of the target population.**   Participants are only as representative as your ability to understand and classify your target audience. Market research is not an infallible science, and the actual end user is often hard to identify and describe.

- **Testing is not always the best technique to use.**   There are many techniques intended to evaluate and improve products, as discussed in Chapter 1 and Chapter 13. For example, in some cases it is more effective both in terms of cost, time, and accuracy to conduct an expert or heuristic evaluation of a product rather than test it. This is especially true in the early stages of a product when gross violations of usability principles abound. It is simply unnecessary to bring in many participants to reveal the obvious.

However, in spite of these limitations, usability testing, when conducted with care and precision, for the appropriate reasons, at the appropriate time in the product development lifecycle, and as part of an overall user-centered design approach, is an almost infallible indicator of potential problems and the means to resolve them. It minimizes the risk considerably of releasing an unstable or unlearnable product. In almost every case, and this is an underlying theme of this book: *it is better to test than not to test*.

The next chapter covers the basics for conducting four types of specific tests and then provides a hypothetical case study employing all four tests in the course of a development cycle.

CHAPTER 3

When Should You Test?

Some type of usability testing fits into every phase of a development lifecycle. The type of testing is distinguished by the research questions asked, the state of the completeness of the product, and the time available for implementing solutions to problems revealed in testing. This chapter outlines four types of tests that fit into the general phases that any product development cycle goes though (see Figure 3-1).

Our Types of Tests: An Overview

The literature is filled with a variety of testing methodologies, each with a slightly different purpose. Often, different terms are used to describe identical testing techniques. Needless to say, this can be extremely confusing. In deciding which tests to discuss and emphasize, the most beneficial approach might be to use the product development lifecycle as a reference point for describing several different types of tests. Associating a test with a particular phase in the lifecycle should help you understand the test's purpose and benefits.

We discuss three tests — exploratory (or formative), assessment (or summative), and validation (or verification) tests — at a high level, according to the approximate point in the product development lifecycle at which each would be administered. The fourth type of test, the comparison test, can be used as an integral part of any of the other three tests and is not associated with any specific lifecycle phase.

The basic methodology for conducting each test is roughly the same and is described in detail in Chapter 5. However, each test will vary in its emphasis on qualitative vs. quantitative measures, and by the amount of interaction

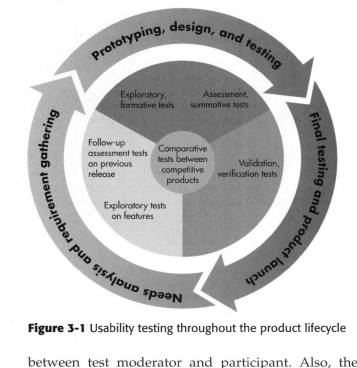

Figure 3-1 Usability testing throughout the product lifecycle

between test moderator and participant. Also, the tests expounded here are definitely biased toward an environment of tight deadlines and limited resources, and chosen with a keen eye on the bottom line.

Our other purpose for presenting the test types in terms of the product development lifecycle has to do with the power of iterative design. Usability testing is most powerful and most effective when implemented as part of an iterative product development process. That is, a cycle of design, test and measure, and redesign throughout the product development lifecycle has the greatest probability of concluding with a usable product. Even if important product flaws or deficiencies are missed during one test, another testing cycle offers the opportunity to identify these problems or issues.

An iterative design and testing approach also allows one to make steady and rapid progress on a project, to learn through empirical evidence, and to "shape" the product to fit the end users' abilities, expectations, and aptitude. We feel very strongly that such an approach provides the value when resources are limited, and that one will obtain the best results by conducting a series of short, precise tests that build one upon the other.

However, while the tests we are about to describe lend themselves to an iterative design process, one need not be concerned about applying the tests at *exactly* the correct moment. Rather, consider what it is that you need to understand about your product, and let that drive your test objectives and the appropriate application of a particular test method. Also, do not be put off if you are unable to conduct multiple tests. One test is almost always better than none, and it is better to focus on what you *can* do than on what you cannot do.

The first three tests, exploratory (or formative), assessment (or summative), and validation (or verification), are shown in Figure 3-1 next to the approximate points in the lifecycle at which they are most effectively conducted. Now let's review each in turn.

Exploratory or Formative Study

When

The exploratory study is conducted quite early in the development cycle, when a product is still in the preliminary stages of being defined and designed (hence the reason it is sometimes called "formative"). By this point in the development cycle, the user profile and usage model (or task analysis) of the product will have (or should have) been defined. The project team is probably wrestling with the functional specification and early models of the product. Or perhaps the requirements and specifications phase is completed, and the design phase is just about to begin.

Objective

The main objective of the exploratory study is to examine the effectiveness of preliminary design concepts. If one thinks of a user interface or a document as being divided into a high-level aspect and a more detailed aspect, the exploratory study is concerned with the former.

For example, designers of a Web application interface would benefit greatly knowing early on whether the user intuitively grasps the fundamental and distinguishing elements of the interface. For example, designers might want to know how well the interface:

- Supports users' tasks within a goal.
- Communicates the intended workflow.
- Allows the user to navigate from screen to screen and within a screen.

Or, using the task-oriented user guide of a software product as an example, technical writers typically might want to explore the following high-level issues:

- Overall organization of subject matter
- Whether to use a graphic or verbal approach
- How well the proposed format supports findability

- Anticipated points of assistance and messaging
- How to address reference information

The implications of these high-level issues go beyond the product, because you are also interested in verifying your assumptions about the *users*. Understanding one is necessary to define the other. Some typical user-oriented questions that an exploratory study would attempt to answer might include the following:

- What do users conceive and think about using the product?
- Does the product's basic functionality have value to the user?
- How easily and successfully can users navigate?
- How easily do users make inferences about how to use this user interface, based on their previous experience?
- What type of prerequisite information does a person need to use the product?
- Which functions of the product are "walk up and use" and which will probably require either help or written documentation?
- How should the table of contents be organized to accommodate both novice and experienced users?

The importance of this type of *early* analysis and research cannot be over emphasized, for this is the point in time when critical design decisions set the stage for all that will follow. If the project begins with wrong assumptions and faulty premises about the user, the product is almost guaranteed to have usability problems later. Similarly to building a house, once you lay the foundation for one type of model, you cannot simply build a totally different model without first ripping out the existing framework. The underlying structure determines all that will follow.

Overview of the Methodology

Exploratory tests usually dictate extensive interaction between the participant and test moderator to establish the efficacy of preliminary design concepts. One way to answer very fundamental questions, similar to those listed previously, is to develop preliminary versions of the product's interface and/or its support materials for evaluation by representative users. For software, this would typically involve a prototype simulation or mockup of the product that represents its basic layout, organization of functions, and high-level operations. Even prior to a working prototype, one might use static screen representations or even paper drafts of screens. For hardware representations, one might use two-dimensional or three-dimensional foamcore, clay, or plastic models. For user support materials, one might provide very rough layouts of manuals, training materials, or help screens.

When developing a prototype, one need not represent the entire functionality of the product. Rather, one need only show enough functionality to address the particular test objective. For example, if you want to see how the user responds to the organization of your pull-down menus, you need only show the menus and one layer of options below. If the user proceeds deeper than the first layer, you might show a screen that reads, "Not yet implemented," or something similar and ask what the participant was looking for or expecting next.

This type of prototype is referred to as a "horizontal representation," since the user can move left or right but is limited in moving deeper. However, if your test objective requires seeing how well a user can move down several menu layers, you will need to prototype several functions "vertically," so users can proceed deeper. You might achieve both objectives with a horizontal representation of *all* major functions, and a vertical representation of two of the functions.

During the test of such a prototype, the user would attempt to perform representative tasks. Or if it is too early to perform tasks, then the user can simply "walk through" or review the product and answer questions under the guidance of a test moderator. Or, in some cases, the user can even do both. The technique depends on the point in the development cycle and the sophistication of the mockups.

The testing process for an exploratory test is usually quite informal and almost a collaboration between participant and test moderator, with much interaction between the two. Because so much of what you need to know is cognitive in nature, an exploration of the user's thought process is vital. The test moderator and participant might explore the product together, with the test moderator conducting an almost ongoing interview or encouraging the participant to "think aloud" about his or her thought process as much as possible. Unlike later tests where there is much less interaction, the test moderator and participant can sit side by side as shown in Figure 3-2.

Ask participants for their ideas about how to improve confusing areas. Unlike later tests where there is more emphasis on measuring *how well* the user is able to perform by collecting quantitative data, here you strive to understand *why* the user performs as he or she does by collecting qualitative data. Regardless of whether you use a working prototype, static screens, early manuals, or whether the user performs tasks or simply "walks through" a product with the test moderator, the distinguishing feature of the exploratory test is its emphasis on discussion and examination of high-level concepts and thought processes, thus helping to form the final design.

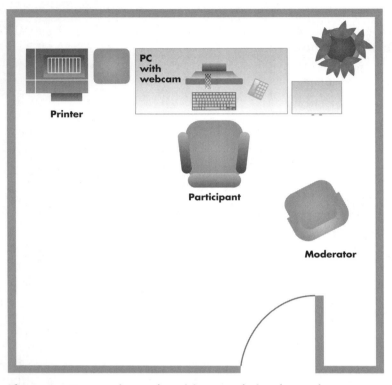

Printer

PC with webcam

Participant

Moderator

Figure 3-2 Test monitor and participant exploring the product

Example of Exploratory Study

Because the nature of the exploratory test is often somewhat abstract, let's review how a typical exploration might proceed for a product, such as a web site. Assume that you are exploring the home page of a web site, which employs options in the left navigation, each revealing further choices when the user mouses over it. Assume also that this is a very early stage of development, so the user interface simply consists of a single screen without any underlying structure or connections. However, the navigation menus function, so the user can view the menu options underneath each menu heading, as shown in Figure 3-3.

Now let's look at Figure 3-4, which contains an excerpt of a test script for conducting an exploratory test, to see how the test might proceed. You might continue in this vein, having the user attempt to accomplish realistic tasks with much discussion about assumptions and thought process. Alternatively, though, if the web page is in such a preliminary stage that the navigation does

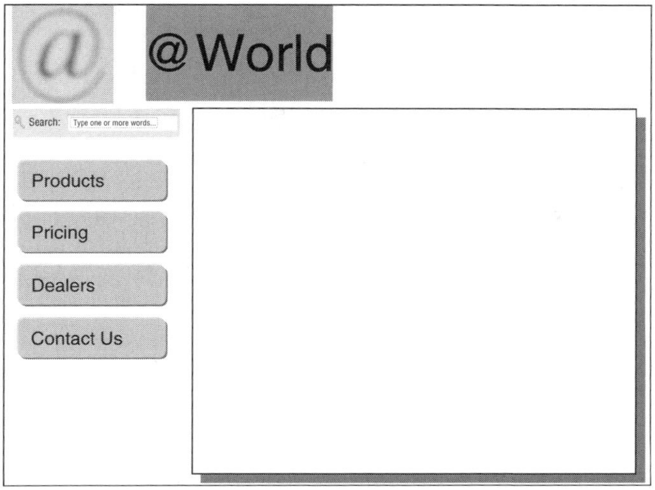

Figure 3-3 Web page navigation interface

The purpose of our session today is to review the design for a new web site and get your opinions about it. As we review this design together, I will be asking you a series of questions about what you see and how you expect things to work. Please feel free to ask any questions and offer any observations during the session. There are no wrong answers or stupid questions. This product is in a very preliminary stage; do not be concerned if it acts in unexpected ways.

Let's begin with a hypothetical situation. You would like to understand just what it is that this company offers.

(*User indicates how the task would be attempted, or attempts to do the task if the navigation works.*)

You would like to calculate the cost for offerings from this company. How do you start?

(*User indicates how the task would be attempted, or attempts to do the task if the navigation works.*)

Okay, you've found the pricing page. What does it tell you?

(*User discusses the information on the page, describing what is useful, clear (or not), and where there could be more detail.*)

Figure 3-4 A Portion of an exploratory test script

not work, and you wanted to evaluate the effectiveness of the organization of the navigation, you might ask the user to simply point to the navigation label under which he or she would expect to accomplish a particular task, similarly to a paper-and-pencil evaluation. This approach would establish which tasks were harder to initiate and less intuitive.

Exploratory tests are often conducted as comparison tests, with different prototypes matched against each other. This prevents the project team from committing too early to one design, only to find out later that the design has serious flaws and liabilities. An example of this type of test is shown later in this chapter.

The important point of exploratory tests is that you can be extremely creative in simulating early versions of the product. Paper screens, prototypes with limited functionality, and so on all help to acquire important high-level information before the design is cast in concrete. It is never too early to learn how the user perceives the product and its fundamental presentation.

The benefits of using exploratory research to establish the soundness of high-level design *prior* to fleshing out all the details are innumerable. The time saved alone makes early research well worth doing. Explore very basic ideas and concepts as soon as you are able to simulate how they will work to users. Do not wait to take action until a very well thought-out, full-blown design takes shape.

Assessment or Summative Test

When

The assessment test is probably the most typical type of usability test conducted. Of all the tests, it is probably the simplest and most straightforward for the novice usability professional to design and conduct. Assessment tests are conducted either early or midway into the product development cycle, usually after the fundamental or high-level design or organization of the product has been established.

Objective

The purpose of the assessment test is to expand the findings of the exploratory test by evaluating the usability of lower-level operations and aspects of the product. If the intent of the exploratory test is to work on the skeleton of the product, the assessment test begins to work on the meat and the flesh. Assuming that the basic conceptual model of the product is sound, this test seeks to examine and evaluate how effectively the concept has been implemented. Rather than just exploring the intuitiveness of a product, you are interested in seeing how well a user can actually perform full-blown realistic tasks and in identifying specific usability deficiencies in the product.

Overview of the Methodology

Often referred to as an information-gathering or evidence-gathering test, the methodology for an assessment test is a cross between the informal exploration of the exploratory test and the more tightly controlled measurement of the validation test. Unlike the exploratory test:

- The user will always *perform* tasks rather than simply walking through and commenting upon screens, pages, and so on.
- The test moderator will lessen his or her interaction with the participant because there is less emphasis on thought processes and more on actual behaviors.
- Quantitative measures will be collected.

Validation or Verification Test

When

The validation test, also referred to as the verification test, is usually conducted late in the development cycle and, as the name suggests, is intended to measure usability of a product against established benchmarks or, in the case of a verification test, to confirm that problems discovered earlier have been remedied and that new ones have not been introduced. Unlike the first two tests, which take place in the middle of a very active and ongoing design cycle, the validation test typically takes place much closer to the release of the product.

Objective

The objective of the validation test is to evaluate how the product compares to some predetermined usability standard or benchmark, either a project-related performance standard, an internal company or historical standard, or even a competitor's standard of performance. The intent is to establish that the product meets such a standard prior to release, and if it does not, to establish the reason(s) why. The standards usually originate from the usability objectives developed early in the project. These in turn come from previous usability tests, marketing surveys, interviews with users, or simply educated guesses by the development team.

Usability objectives are typically stated in terms of performance criteria, such as efficiency and effectiveness, or how well and how fast the user can perform various tasks and operations. Or the objectives can be stated in terms of preference criteria, such as achieving a particular ranking or rating from users. A verification test has a slightly different flavor. The objective here is to ensure that usability issues identified in earlier tests have been addressed and corrected appropriately.

It only makes sense then that the validation test itself can be used to *initiate* standards within the company for future products. Verification can accomplish the same thing. For example, if one establishes that a setup procedure for a software package works well and can be conducted within 5 minutes with no more than one error, it is important that future releases of the product perform to that standard or better. Products can then be designed with this benchmark as a target, so that usability does not degrade as more functions are added to future releases.

Another major objective of the validation test is to evaluate, sometimes for the first time, how all the components of a product work together in an end-to-end study. For example, how documentation, help, and software/hardware are integrated with each other, or all the steps in a longer process or workflow. The importance of an integrated validation test cannot be overstated. Because components are often developed in relative isolation from each other, it is not unusual that they do not work well together. It behooves an organization to discover this prior to release because, from the user's viewpoint, it is all one product and it is expected to perform that way.

Still another objective of the validation test, or really any test conducted very late in the development cycle, has become known in the trade as "disaster or catastrophe insurance." At this late stage, management is most concerned with the risk of placing into the marketplace a new product that contains major flaws or that might require recall. If such a flaw is discovered, slipping the schedule may be preferable to recalling the product or having to send out "fixes" to every user. Even if there is no time to make changes before release, you are always at an advantage if you can anticipate a major deficiency in the product. There will be time to prepare a solution, train the support team, and even prepare public-relation responses. Even so, with all these advantages, there are companies that would rather not know about problems that exist in a product.

Overview of the Methodology

The validation test is conducted in similar fashion to the assessment test with three major exceptions.

- Prior to the test, benchmarks or standards for the tasks of the test are either developed or identified. This can be specific error or time measures, or as simple as eliminating the problems identified in earlier exploratory tests.

- Participants are given tasks to perform with either very little or no interaction with a test moderator. (And they are probably not asked to "think aloud.")

- The collection of quantitative data is the central focus, although reasons for substandard performance are identified.

Because you are measuring user performance against a standard, you also need to determine beforehand how adherence to the standard will be measured, and what actions will be taken if the product does not meet its standards. For example, if the standard for a task addresses "time to complete," must 70 percent of participants meet the standard, or will you simply compare the standard to the average score of all participants? Under what conditions will the product's schedule be postponed? Will there be time to retest those tasks that did not meet the standard? These are all questions that should be addressed and resolved *prior* to the test.

Compared to an assessment test, a validation test requires more emphasis on experimental rigor and consistency, because you are making important quantitative judgments about the product. Make sure that members of the design team have input and buy-in into developing the standards used during the test. That way they will not feel as if the standards were overly difficult or unattainable.

Comparison Test

When

The comparison test is not associated with any specific point in the product development lifecycle. In the early stages, it can be used to compare several radically different interface styles via an exploratory test, to see which has the greatest potential with the proposed target population. Toward the middle of the lifecycle, a comparison test can be used to measure the effectiveness of a single element, such as whether pictorial buttons or textual buttons are preferred by users. Toward the end of the lifecycle, a comparison test can be used to see how the released product stacks up against a competitor's product.

Objective

The comparison test is the fourth type of test and can be used in conjunction with any of the other three tests. It is used to compare two or more designs, such as two different interface styles, or the current design of a manual with a proposed new design, or to compare your product with a competitor's. The comparison test is typically used to establish which design is easier to use or learn, or to better understand the advantages and disadvantages of different designs.

Overview of the Methodology

The basic methodology involves the side-by-side comparison of two or more clearly different designs. Performance data and preference data are collected for each alternative, and the results are compared. The comparison test can be conducted informally as an exploratory test, or it can be conducted as a tightly controlled classical experiment, with one group of participants serving as a control group and the other as the experimental group. The form used is dependent on your goals in testing. If conducted as a true experiment designed to acquire statistically valid results, the alternatives should vary along a single dimension — for example, keeping the content and functionality constant, but altering the visual design or the navigation scheme — and the expected results of the test should be formulated as a hypothesis.

If conducted less formally as a more observational, qualitative study, the alternatives may vary on many dimensions. One needs to ascertain why one alternative is favored over another, and which aspects of each design are favorable and unfavorable. Inevitably, when comparing one or more alternatives in this fashion, one discovers that there is no "winning" design per se. *Rather, the best design turns out to be a combination of the alternatives, with the best aspects of each design used to form a hybrid design.*

For exploratory comparison tests, experience has shown that the best results and the most creative solutions are obtained by including wildly differing alternatives, rather than very similar alternatives. This seems to work because:

- The design team is forced to stretch its conceptions of what will work rather than just continuing along in a predictable pattern. With the necessity for developing very different alternatives, the design team is forced to move away from predictable ways of thinking about the problem. Typically, this involves revisiting fundamental premises about an interface or documentation format that have been around for years. The result is often a design that redefines and improves the product in fundamental ways.

- During the test, the participant is forced to really consider and contemplate why one design is better and which aspects make it so. It is easier to compare alternatives that are very similar, but harder to compare very different ones. Why? Similar alternatives share the same framework and conceptual model, with only the lower-level operations working differently. Very different alternatives, however, are often based on different conceptual models of how each works and may challenge the user, especially one experienced with the product, to take stock of how the tasks are actually performed.

Iterative Testing: Test Types through the Lifecycle

Now, having reviewed the basics of each type of test, let us explore how a series of tests might in fact work. Let's suppose that your company is developing a web-based software application and its associated documentation. The software is a personal information manager, consisting of calendar, contact, and task management functionality. You intend to conduct three usability tests at three different times in the product development lifecycle. Following is a hypothetical series of tests on this product throughout the lifecycle, complete with hypothetical outcomes at the end of each test. Understand the details have been greatly simplified to provide an overview of iterative design in action.

Test 1: Exploratory/Comparison Test

The situation

Two early prototypes of the interface have been developed (see Figures 3-5 and 3-6). The interfaces use the same underlying architecture, programming languages, and functionality, although the layout of their navigation is considerably different from each other.

The prototypes have very limited working functionality (e.g., about 30 to 40 percent of the proposed functions work). There is no documentation, but

Figure 3-5 Left navigation interface

Figure 3-6 Top navigation interface

during the test, a technical expert will be available to reveal limited but crucial information needed to use the product. (See the gradual disclosure technique in Chapter 13 for an explanation of how to use a technical expert in this way.) Primitive help topics, available on paper only, will be provided to the participant on demand; that is, when the participant clicks the appropriate prompt or asks a question, the test moderator will provide what would normally be embedded assistance, instruction prompts, or messages on paper as they would appear on the screen.

Main Research Questions

- Which of the two interface styles/concepts is the most effective? In which is the user better able to remain oriented within the program?
- What are the best and worst features of each approach?
- What are the main stumbling blocks for the user?
- After some period of initial learning, which style has the greatest potential for the power user?
- For which tasks will users need help, further instructions, or supporting documentation?

- What types of written information will be required?
  - Prerequisite
  - Theoretical or conceptual
  - Procedural
  - Examples
  - Training

Brief Summary of Outcome

The test was conducted. As is typical of comparison tests at this point, there was no "winner" per se. Rather, the result was an interface with the best attributes of both prototypes. The navigation schema employing the navigation on the left was most efficient and effective, but some of the options available did not seem to belong with the others and so will remain in a navigation bar across the top of the main work area. Apparently, the options to remain in the top navigation are done less frequently.

There were many advanced features for use in a corporate setting that users needed additional information about. Because this personal information manager will be used throughout a large company, some functionality was added to support work group collaboration, which added complexity to the product. To remedy the complexity issue, the first line of defense is to develop a documentation set that includes, at minimum, a guide for setting up preferences, some self-paced training on interface operations, and a procedural user guide for more advanced, less frequent tasks.

Test 2: Assessment Test

The Situation

Time has passed. A single prototype has now been expanded to approximately 60 to 80 percent of its eventual functionality. There are comprehensive help topics for working functions in a separate section of the web site. A first draft, of simplified documentation, on 8 1/2" by 11" bond paper is available for the test, with a table of contents, but no index.

Main Test Objectives

- Confirm whether the findings of the original test adequately match interface operations with the user's workflow.
- Expose all major usability deficiencies and their causes for the most common tasks.

- Determine if there is a seamless connection of help topics, embedded assistance, and messaging with the functionality and user interface. Does the software give support at the right moments? Is the help center organized in a way that answers participants' questions?

- Is the documentation being utilized as designed? Is it accessible? Are graphics understood and at the appropriate level of detail? Are certain sections not read at all? Are additional sections required? Is all terminology clear? Are there areas that require more explanation?

- Where do participants still have questions? What are their questions?

Brief Summary of Test Outcome

Many difficulties in operations were identified, but the users' workflow matched that employed by the design team for the product's interface operations. Essentially, the high-level interface "works," and the lower-level details remain to be implemented and refined. The help information was accurate and helpful, but users rarely invoked it unless prompted. There was a strong preference for trial and error with this particular user audience. When users were prompted to try the help, it was found that the organization of the help topics needs to be extensively revamped and made more task-oriented. Even more theoretical, contextual information needs to be included for the most advanced users. This last issue turned out to be very controversial because designers felt it was not their responsibility to force particular operational approaches on corporate working groups. It is possible that an interactive primer for users may be required for infrequent but important tasks.

Test 3: Verification Test

The Situation

Some weeks have passed. For this last test, a fully functional product with comprehensive help topics has been prepared. All sections of the documentation have been through one draft, with half of the sections undergoing a second draft. The documentation has a rough index for the test. A small "tour" for users about quarterly and semi-annual tasks was developed. For the major tasks of the product, specified measurable time and accuracy criteria have been developed. For example, one criterion reads:

Using the setup guide, a user will be able to correctly implement View and Network preferences within 10 minutes, with no more than two attempts required.

Unbelievably, and for only the first time in the recorded history of software development, there actually *will* be time to make minor modifications before release.

Test Objectives

- Verify that 70 percent of participants can meet established successful completion criteria for each major task scenario.

  (The 70 percent benchmark is something that Jeff has personally evolved toward over time, and that Dana has used effectively. It provides a reasonably challenging test while still leaving the design team some work to do before product release to move that number toward a more acceptable and traditional 95 percent benchmark. A benchmark of 100 percent is probably not realistic except for tasks involving danger or damage to the system or possible loss of life, and should never be used lightly. In the 1960s NASA found that achieving 100 percent performance cost as much as 50 times the cost of achieving 95 percent performance. It is likely that such costs have gone down over 40 years, but the point is that you should only use the higher benchmark if you are willing to pay the piper.)

- Identify any tasks and areas of the product that risk dire consequences (e.g., are unusable, contain destructive bugs) if the product is released as is.

- Identify all usability deficiencies and sources of those problems. Determine which deficiencies must be repaired before release and which, if there is not time within the schedule, can be implemented in the next release.

Brief Summary of Test Outcome

Every major task passed the 70 percent successful completion criteria with the exception of two. The team felt that the problems associated with those tasks could be corrected prior to release, and wanted to schedule a very quick test to confirm. Twenty recommendations from the test were identified for implementation prior to release, and at least fifteen recommendations were diverted to future releases.

Providing a "tour" of advanced features prior to the test proved to be a stroke of genius. Participants loved it, and some even insisted on taking it back to their current jobs. One user suggested the company market it or a longer virtual seminar as a separate product for customers, and that is already in the works.

The revamped organization of the user guide was much more in tune with users' expectations than the previous set, although the index proved difficult to use. More task-oriented items must be added to the index to improve accessibility.

As you can tell from this condensed series of tests, the product evolved over time and reflected each test's findings. We strongly advocate such an iterative approach, but again, do not be discouraged if you can manage only one test to begin. Now let's talk about what it takes to be a good test moderator.

CHAPTER 4

Skills for Test Moderators

The role of the test moderator or test administrator is the most critical of all the test team members, presuming that you even have the luxury of a test team. In fact, the moderator is the one team member that you absolutely must have in order to conduct the test. The moderator is ultimately responsible for all preparations including test materials, participant arrangements, and coordination of the efforts of other members of the test team.

During the test, the moderator is responsible for all aspects of administration, including greeting the participant, collecting data, assisting and probing, and debriefing the participant. After the test, he or she needs to collate the day's data collection, meet with and debrief other team members, and ensure that the testing is tracking with the test objectives. If the usability test were an athletic contest, the moderator would be the captain of the team. As such, he or she has the potential to make or break the test. An ineffective moderator can seriously negate test results and even waste much of the preliminary preparation work. This chapter discusses several alternatives for acquiring test moderators from inside and outside your organization, as well as the desired characteristics of an effective test moderator. Chapter 9 includes guidelines for moderating test sessions, including information about when and how to intervene, and the advantages and disadvantages of using a "think-aloud" protocol.

Who Should Moderate?

One of the basic tenets of usability testing — and of this book — is that it is almost impossible to remain objective when conducting a usability test of your own product. There is simply too strong a tendency to lead participants in a direction that you want the results to go, rather than acting as a neutral enabler of the process. This is even true for experienced test moderators who conduct the test from an external control room. In fact, asking someone to test his or her own product is like asking parents to objectively evaluate the abilities of their child. It is an impossible endeavor.

Having said that, if there is only you available to test your product, do so. In almost every case, it is still better to test than not to test, even if you must do the testing yourself. However, for the long term, you would want to be out of the self-testing business as soon as possible.

Imagine that you want to conduct a test on a product for which you have primary responsibility, and if possible you would like someone less involved with the product to conduct the test. You can help develop the test materials, make arrangements, and select participants, but you need a more objective person to handle the actual test moderating. Suppose also that your organization currently has no in-house testing staff and does not plan to introduce one shortly. To whom should you look for help?

The following sources represent a number of areas from which you can find candidates who possess the requisite skills to conduct a test, or who could head up the beginnings of an internal testing group. They may or may not already be working on your product.

Human Factors Specialist

A human factors specialist is the most likely candidate to conduct a usability test. This type of person typically has an advanced degree in psychology, industrial engineering, or similar discipline, and is familiar with experimental methodology and test rigor. Just as important, the human factors specialist is grounded in the basics of information processing, cognitive psychology, and other disciplines related to the development of usable products, systems, and support materials. This grounding is crucial in differentiating the important from the superficial usability factors in a product and ultimately in designing and conducting the test.

With the current focus on usability engineering and testing, it is highly probable that human factors specialists within your organization are already involved with testing in one form or another.

Marketing Specialist

A marketing specialist is typically customer-oriented, user-oriented, or both, has good interpersonal and communication skills, and would be very interested in improving the quality of products. This type of specialist may already be involved with your product, but usually not to the detailed level that would tend to disqualify him or her from conducting the testing.

Technical Communicator

Technical communicators, including technical writers and training specialists, often make wonderful test moderators. Many technical communicators already serve as user advocates on projects, and their profession requires them to think as a user in order to design, write, and present effective support materials.

Rotating Team Members

Let's suppose that no one from the disciplines listed previously is available to help on your project, and you are still determined not to test your own materials. Another alternative is to draw upon colleagues of similar disciplines, who are *not* working on the same product. An example of this approach is for technical communicators to test each other's manuals or for software engineers to test each other's program modules.

In such a scenario, the person whose product is being tested could help prepare many of the test materials and make the pretest arrangements, then turn over the actual moderating of the test to a colleague. One of the advantages of this approach is that two (or more) heads are better than one, and it is always beneficial to have someone other than yourself help prepare the test. The person acting as the test moderator would need time to become familiar with the specific product being tested and to prepare to test it in addition to the time required to actually moderator the test.

Should you decide to implement this approach, you must plan ahead in order to build the test into your mutual schedules. You cannot expect your colleague to drop everything he or she is working on to help you. Of course, you would reciprocate and serve as test moderator for your colleague's product.

External Consultant

Another option is to hire an external consultant. Many human factors, industrial design, market research, and usability engineering firms now offer usability testing as one of their services, including the use of their test laboratories. You may simply want to outsource the usability test to such a firm, or use such a firm to "kick off" a testing program in your organization.

Using an external consulting company guarantees the objectivity that testing requires. Even some organizations that employ internal human factors specialists to work on the design and development of products still outsource the testing work for the greater sense of impartiality it provides.

If you know your organization is committed to eventually forming a long-term testing program on site, then seek out a consulting company that will work with you to transfer the knowledge of testing into your organization.

Even if you are unsure about the long-term prospects for testing in your company, it still might be easier to have outside help with an initial test. Just make sure that if you conduct the test off-site, its location is physically close enough to allow development team members to attend the test sessions. Do not simply farm out the test to a remote location. (Although, in a pinch, team members could observe tests from their remote locations via Morae, Camtasia, or other electronic monitoring tools.) Viewing tests in person is much more effective than watching or listening to a recording, especially for those who are skeptical about the value of testing.

Characteristics of a Good Test Moderator

Regardless of who conducts the test, either yourself or internal or external staff, and regardless of the background of that person, there are several key characteristics that the most effective test moderators share. These key characteristics are listed and described in the paragraphs that follow. If you are personally considering taking on the role of test moderator in your organization, use these key characteristics as a checklist of the skills you need to acquire. If you are considering using either an internal person or hiring an external person to perform this role, use these key characteristics to help evaluate the person's capabilities.

Grounding in the Basics of User-Centered Design

Grounding in the basics of human information processing, cognitive psychology, and user-centered design (essentially the domain of the human factors specialist) helps immensely because it enables the test moderator to sense, even before the test begins, which interactions, operations, messages, or instructions are liable to cause problems. Test moderators with this background have a knowledge of which problems can be generalized to the population at large and which are more trivial. This helps to ascertain when to probe further and what issues need to be explored thoroughly during the debriefing session. Additionally, this background can also prevent the need to test situations that are known to cause problems for users, such as the inappropriate use of color or the incorrect placing of a note in a manual. Lastly, a strong background in usability engineering helps the test moderator to focus on fixing the important issues after a test is complete.

Quick Learner

An effective test moderator need not be expert in the intricacies of the specific product being tested. For example, if the product is a database management system, the moderator need not be an expert in database management.

However, he or she must be able to absorb new concepts quickly and to integrate these concepts into his or her thinking and vocabulary. The moderator also needs to absorb all the peripheral issues surrounding a product, such as its positioning in the marketplace, competitors, and historical problems. During the test itself, the moderator must be able to understand the actions and comments of the participant quickly, as well as the implications behind those actions and comments. Being a quick learner enables the moderator to probe and question effectively.

Instant Rapport with Participants

Bringing in participants to evaluate your product is an auspicious and very opportune point in the development cycle that should not be squandered. If for some reason a participant is not at ease and is not able to function as he or she normally would, it represents a lost opportunity and potentially misleading results. If you are able to test only five participants, one uneasy participant represents a potential loss of 20 percent of your test data. The test moderator's ability to quickly size up each participant's personality, make friends, and put the person at ease is essential to getting the most from the testing process. Some participants need coddling, some need stroking, and some are businesslike and require a more formal approach. Whichever the case, the test moderator must make each person feel comfortable and secure.

Excellent Memory

Some might believe that because usability test sessions are recorded, the test moderator need not rely on memory for conducting and evaluating a test session. Actually, memory is called into play well before a test session has ended. Because a test session can be rather long, the test moderator needs to remember behaviors or comments that took place earlier in the session in order to cross-check and probe those behaviors later in the session. For example, a participant may attempt to perform the same task in two or three different ways, and the test moderator may want to probe to understand why the participant performed the task differently each time.

  Memory is also required to recall the results of a test session after its completion. Because there is often very little time to devote to searching the videotapes after a test, except as insurance against missing some point entirely, the test moderator often must rely heavily on memory and notes.

Good Listener

Listening skills involve the test moderator's ability to hear with "new ears" during each session and to lay aside personal biases and strong opinions about what he or she is seeing and hearing. The test moderator needs to understand both the content and the implication of a participant's comments, as there are often mixed messages of all kinds during testing. The test moderator must pick up on the subtle nuances of speech and emphasis, as a participant's comments are often indirect and less than forthcoming. It is so important to understand the rationale behind the participant's behavior, because the rationale often signals whether a change in the product is required or not.

Comfortable with Ambiguity

Usability is not a precise science consisting of formulas and black and white answers. Even if a usability test is conducted under the most rigorous conditions, which is atypical, you are still not assured that all of the results are valid and generalizable to your entire user population. Instead, usability testing can often be an imprecise, ambiguous enterprise, with varying and sometimes conflicting observations, not surprising for any venture that has human beings as its focus. A test moderator, then, must understand and be comfortable with ambiguity.

For example, prior to testing you may think that there are only two ways to perform a particular task. During testing though, you discover that the participants have found *four other ways* to perform the same task. Or, you discover that you are no closer to a clear-cut resolution of a product's problems after a week of testing than you were before you began. Or, when testing multiple versions of a product, no clear winner emerges. The versions are all equally bad or, if you are lucky, equally good. These situations require patience, perseverance, and very often skill at negotiation. Without tolerance for ambiguity and the patience to persevere, the test moderator tends to rationalize and to blame the participants for making unplanned choices during the test.

Flexibility

Another related characteristic of an effective test moderator is flexibility, which has to do with knowing when to deviate from the test plan (we discuss this further in Chapter 9). There are times when a particular participant does not have the expected skills or simply views the task in a completely different way than was originally intended. Jeff conducted a test when the entire high-level design of an interface became questionable after testing only two participants. He could see immediately that the premise for the design was flawed. At that time, he recommended that the company halt testing and go back to the drawing board. To continue ferreting out minor problems with the product would have been a waste of everyone's time. While this is an extreme case, the point is that one needs to be prepared for the unexpected, even if that has serious consequences.

Long Attention Span

Experienced test moderators share a secret: Usability testing can be tedious and boring. There are long stretches when seemingly nothing is happening, when participants are reading and absorbing, thinking, and sometimes just resting. The moderator cannot possess the type of personality that needs new stimulation every 5 to 10 minutes. The moderator must be able to pay attention for long periods of time because there is no predicting when a gem of a discovery will arise during a test session. In addition, because the moderator may view up to 10, 15, or 20 sessions, all of which involve observing the same or similar tasks, the ability to stay focused is extremely vital.

Empathic "People Person"

Participants will relate more readily to a test moderator who is an empathic individual. This may not be all that critical during the test session itself, especially if the session requires little probing or exploration on the part of the test moderator. However, empathy can play a major part during the debriefing session when the test moderator is trying to elicit a participant's innermost thoughts and feelings about the previous two hours of work. Participants will tend to hold back if they feel that the test moderator cannot relate to their particular situation, this being especially true if the session was unusually frustrating or difficult.

"Big Picture" Thinker

There is so much data collected during a usability test, and there is so much data that *could* be collected during a test that it is very easy to lose sight of the forest for the trees. The test moderator must be able to weed out the significant from the insignificant, and this ability takes two concrete forms.

- The ability to draw together all of the various inputs, comments, and data from a *single* test to form a cohesive picture of a participant's performance.
- The ability to draw together the varied inputs from different test sessions and focus on the most important and critical findings.

It is very easy to get lost in the details and focus on trivial observations. It is also easy to be influenced by the last participant and forget all that has come before.

An effective test moderator, however, avoids these difficulties by staying focused on the big picture.

Good Communicator

Good communication skills are essential in usability testing. The test moderator must communicate with individual members of the development team, participants, observers, and other individuals who may be helping to administer the test in one way or another. The test moderator must be skillful at persuading others to make changes that are in their best interest, and he or she must be able to explain the implications behind the test results. Good writing skills are also essential because the test report is often the sole means of communicating test results to those who did not attend the test sessions. The written report is also the important historical document that is relied upon months or years later to review or revisit the test results.

Good Organizer and Coordinator

A usability test is a project within a project. Even a simple test requires the management of an astonishing number of small details, events, and milestones. Ensuring that equipment is in running order, getting all participants to the site on time, and making sure that the product is ready for testing are ultimately the responsibility of the test moderator. In addition, the test moderator is the focal point for the other test team members, and must coordinate their activities as well as those of any outside consultants into a unified effort. Therefore, the test moderator should be a good organizer and coordinator.

Getting the Most out of Your Participants

Let's explore some things that the test moderator can do to enhance the process. One of the best things a test moderator can do is to develop increased sensitivity to the plight of the participants. What does it feel like to be in the testing hot seat? Figure 4-1 shows a hypothetical example of one participant's point of view compiled from many of the participants observed over the years. While it is written tongue in cheek, its point is not. Participants are often placed in awkward, stressful situations where they have little control over events. The more you put them at ease, the greater are your chances for accurate results that are applicable to real-world situations. You should become familiar with the codes of ethics of the Usability Professionals' Association and the Human Factors and Ergonomics Society. The links for each are available on the web site that accompanies this book (www.wiley.com/go/usabilitytesting).

A Day in the Life of the Participant

Well, today's the day. I received a confirmation email yesterday and I am supposed to report to some building over on Montgomery Street, some sort of research facility.

I feel kind of intimidated when someone watches me do things over my shoulder. Technology can be really befuddling. It's always been that way, ever since I can remember. I can't touch-type, which makes using a computer slow for me. And now this person wants me to perform with some people watching me. Well, it's an easy 75 bucks, I guess, and seeing as how I don't know these people it can't be too embarrassing.

So, I head over to the building where I'm supposed to report and a man greets me at the front door. He ushers me into a room, hands me a questionnaire, and begins asking me the same questions I answered on the phone. I guess they want to make sure I'm really not some kind of ringer. I'm starting to get that nervous feeling in the middle of my stomach. That same feeling I used to get when I took those tests in fifth grade with Mrs. Harmer. That kind of feeling that I'm going to be put on the spot and I'm not quite sure how this is going to pan out. My palms are really starting to sweat. Maybe I should have stayed home and painted the garage floor.

I'm probably being silly, so I complete the questionnaire and begin making small talk with some of the people in the room. I'm just starting to relax when I'm ushered into another room. The room is empty, and I begin to wonder where everybody is. I just assumed there would be a lot of people watching. The room is large, with a table, a desk, computer, and a piece of equipment I've never seen before. I'm told to sit down. That's when somebody else comes into the room and begins to explain that I'll be working in this room by myself and some people on the other side of the glass will be watching me.

Now my palms *really* begin sweating. They can see me but I can't see them? This is definitely worse than with Mrs. Harmer. What if I can't do this? What if I totally bomb? What if I'm the first person that has ever tried this that can't use it? Oh boy, if one more person tells me, "Remember, we're not testing you," I'm going to walk out. The next thing I know, they'll be telling me this is for my own good. Well, at least I still have my sense of humor and I'm $75.00 to the richer.

Figure 4-1 A Day in the Life of the Participant

Choose the Right Format

Keeping in mind the research questions you are working with, the location of the test sessions, the time you have available, and the types of participants involved, you must consider the best way to get data from the people you have brought in to help you evaluate the product.

Sit-By Sessions versus Observing from Elsewhere

When the practice of usability testing started, most sessions were conducted in a highly clinical style, with the moderator seated in a control room to observe and collect data. Over the years, a less formal, "sit-by" style of conducting sessions has developed for circumstances under which one would want to be near participants during usability testing, including most of the types of tests we describe in this book. For example, being with the participant in the testing room is advantageous for exploratory situations in which one wants to be able to gather the first impressions of participants about the design or functionality of a product. Doing so allows the moderator to be able to ask follow-up questions easily in a more cooperative session.

Additionally, if there is very quick interaction that must be observed closely or if you are conducting paper prototyping sessions, the moderator must be with the participant to mimic the computer actions.

However, if there is a chance in an assessment or validation test that the moderator's presence may bias the data, or if the emphasis is on gathering quantitative rather than qualitative data, set the test up to let the participant work by him- or herself while you manage the sessions from another room. For a deeper discussion of the physical arrangements for testing and observation rooms, see Chapter 6.

"Think-Aloud" Advantages and Disadvantages

Some participants will naturally verbalize what they are going through as they work through a usability test session. These people are gold; having a running commentary (something researchers call a "verbal protocol") from participants as they "think aloud" while they perform tasks offers many insights to why a problem exists and how someone tries to work around it. Asking participants to think aloud during their sessions also reveals important clues about how they are thinking about the product or system they are using and whether the way it works matches up with the way it was designed.

Participants always filter to some extent, however, so they may consciously or unconsciously leave things out as they talk. Likewise, it is impossible to know *everything* that is going through a participants' mind during the session (it is of course likely that you don't want to know everything, just what pertains to your product, anyway). Thinking aloud can also help participants think through the design problem and form ideas for recovering. While this isn't always what they would do in real life, their doing so will give you ideas about how to remedy design problems.

One important reason to avoid asking participants to think aloud is when you are measuring time on tasks. Thinking aloud slows performance significantly.

Retrospective Review

An alternative to having participants think aloud is to replay the test with the participant after all of the tasks are done. As the moderator, you will have noted where during tasks the participant had issues, questions, or concerns. After the tasks are done, you can toggle to the point in the recordings where you want the participant to discuss what issues he or she was having, what the thought processes were, and how the workarounds were arrived at. Review can be a good tool to use with participants for whom talking and working might be difficult, such as small children, very old adults, and people with cognitive disabilities.

A serious drawback to performing a review is the time it takes to do. You have completed a full slate of tasks and now must spend more time reviewing the session from the beginning. It can take as much time as or more time than the main part of the session actually took. Some practitioners also avoid retrospective review because it gives some participants opportunity to revise and rationalize their behavior rather than simply reporting on what happened and why.

Give Participants Time to Work through Hindrances

Keeping in mind that the participant may be very nervous is the first step. Skillfully working with the person's sense of frustration is the next step. There will be times when the participant becomes exceedingly frustrated during the course of a test. When you see that this is occurring, recognize this as a critical point that can be advantageous. Many test moderators, at the first sign of user frustration, will immediately tell the participant to give up and go on to the next task. They do this in order to avoid confrontation, keep things on an even keel, and maintain the participant's interest. However, because the frustration is usually related to a critical deficiency in the product, moving on too quickly misses an important opportunity. *The participant's behavior at this point can be more revealing than at any other time* and can help the test team to understand how the participant learns to use the product. It is important to encourage the participant to continue rather than cutting the task short too quickly. The trick is to find just that point when the participant is frustrated but is still willing to try.

Offer Appropriate Encouragement

Another reason for encouraging the participant to keep trying is to show designers and developers watching the usability test the dire consequences of certain difficulties experienced by participants. It is important to let them see just how painful and frustrating the process of using their product can be. Actually seeing the participant struggle and get very frustrated and observing the serious consequences firsthand will do more to convince a designer to revise a product than weeks of discussions and negotiations. Sometimes just that extra amount of human struggle will convince a product designer that a change is needed and that the product should not be released as is.

So how should you encourage the participant? One way is to empathize with the participant and provide an end goal or end time frame. For example, you might say, "I can sense you're getting frustrated, but this is a particularly crucial part of the software/documentation, would you please try a little bit longer?"

You might try stating that other participants in the past have also had their share of difficulty. While this runs the risk of slightly biasing the participant, you may lose the participant in any case, if he or she has already experienced great difficulty. You might say, "I see you're having a difficult time with this. This isn't the first time that I've seen someone experience some difficulty here. Would you please continue on for five more minutes?"

The most skilled test moderator can encourage a participant to work with a smile. Make it seem like you and the participant are in this together, and that what is happening in the test is not a reflection of the participant's abilities. Often, the frustration level builds due to a sense of self-consciousness and a loss of self-esteem on the part of the participant. The test moderator can help immensely by deflecting the problem back to the product. For example, the test moderator might say, "Boy this sure is turning out to be a tough section. I really appreciate your efforts in trying to get through this." Don't be afraid to encourage the participant to verbalize what's happening. Very often, if a participant is allowed to vent while performing, frustration can be minimized. It is up to the test moderator to gauge that fine line between rescuing the participant too early and pushing him or her beyond the point at which continuing the test is no longer possible. Through practice and experience, one can find the middle road between pushing too hard and giving up too early in order to get the best results.

Troubleshooting Typical Moderating Problems

Now that you have reviewed some of the important characteristics that a test moderator should possess, as well as some pointers for moderating the smoothest possible sessions with test participants, let's review some of the behaviors that test moderators should avoid. We describe the most common "errors" that test moderators make while conducting a test, many of which we have learned from experience. Consider it a list of "what not to do." Even experienced test moderators can benefit from taking a few moments just prior to testing to review this list. As with the previous list of characteristics, you can use this list to evaluate and improve your own performance or to evaluate the performance of someone you hire to conduct usability testing for you.

Leading Rather Than Enabling

Behavior that leads rather than enables is usually caused by the test moderator being too close to the product and unintentionally providing cues to the participant about correct performance. The test moderator's tone of voice, a nod of the head, cutting short tasks when the participant struggles, even the type of question the test moderator asks can all influence the participant and the test results. This potential problem is the main reason why assessment and validation testing is often conducted from a control room, although subtle hints are still possible even from there. To avoid the problem of leading rather than enabling, remember that you are there to collect data and to ensure that the test environment remains as neutral as possible.

Too Involved with the Act of Data Collection

While the purpose of the test is to collect as much information as possible, the act of collecting that information should not interfere with direct observation of what is occurring. The test moderator needs to stay aware of what the participant is doing at all times, even if that means that every aspect of the participant's behavior is not written down. That's one purpose of recording the test, of developing coding categories, and of having others help with the more rote collection of such things as timings and number of references to an index or online help. All of these aids help ensure that the test moderator does not become so engrossed in the collection process that he or she misses important behaviors.

Acting Too Knowledgeable

This problem occurs when the test moderator and participant are in the same room during the test. Participants will tend to defer to the test moderator and ask many questions if they feel that the test moderator knows all the answers. Being too knowledgeable can also intimidate a participant who may be somewhat nervous and self-conscious about his or her abilities.

One simple way to counteract the problem of acting too knowledgeable is for the test moderator to "play dumb." That is, the test moderator downplays any knowledge of the product and takes on the role of a research technician who is simply collecting data. Participants then change their entire demeanor when it becomes clear that they were not going to receive any assistance from the test moderator. They begin to try harder and to behave as if they were alone in their own home or office.

Too Rigid with the Test Plan

An experienced test moderator will know when to deviate from the test plan. It is important for the moderator to sense when the test design is not achieving its objectives and is not exposing the product's deficiencies to the fullest extent. At those times, it is up to the moderator to make the appropriate changes so that a participant's time and efforts are not wasted. Sometimes a participant with a different background than what was expected will appear. Sometimes the tasks are the wrong ones for addressing the research questions. Whatever the case, it is up to the moderator to revise the plan accordingly.

Not Relating Well to Each Participant

Participants come in all shapes, sizes, and demeanors. Regardless of whether a particular participant is shy, arrogant, moody, intimidated, self-conscious, or whatever, the test moderator needs to adjust his or her style in order to allow the participant to be comfortable and at ease. The test moderator should not get involved with battling, belittling, or in any way making a participant feel like anything but a guest. As far as the test moderator is concerned, the participant is always right.

Jumping to Conclusions

Inexperienced test moderators tend to overreact to early results. This can cause other members of the test team to act on the data prematurely. It is up to the test moderator to maintain a cool, steady demeanor and remind everyone to avoid forming conclusions until all of the results are in. One of the reasons for testing multiple participants is just for that purpose: to get a rounded, comprehensive view of the product through the eyes of different types of people with different types of backgrounds. While it is important for the test moderator to pick up patterns in the behavior of participants as early as possible, this does not necessarily mean reacting to that behavior. Avoiding premature conclusions helps to keep members of the test team from making major product changes before all the data is in.

How to Improve Your Session-Moderating Skills

Conducting a usability test is an extremely challenging and worthwhile endeavor on a variety of levels. On the most ordinary level, you are working very closely with people in an attempt to design a product for maximum utility and benefit. On a deeper level, it is a very profound experience that forces you to confront your own mind and its tendency to be biased, distracted, and flighty.

Monitoring a test puts you on the spot and forces you to be extremely mindful and disciplined. You spend long periods of time maintaining concentration while observing people, all the time being as unobtrusive as possible. We both have found it to be delightful, frustrating, boring, and exhausting, and sometimes these feelings result from working with *just the first participant*.

If you are seriously considering acting as a test moderator on a regular basis in either some official or unofficial capacity, know that it can be a very rewarding and enlightening experience. Let's look at some ways for growing into this job.

Learn the Basic Principles of Human Factors/Ergonomics

Learn the basic principles of human information processing, experimental psychology, cognitive psychology, statistics, interface design, and usability engineering. Subscribe to and read the proceedings from the major societies (listed in Chapter 14). Attend seminars and study basic psychology courses. Many universities and community colleges offer certificate programs in usability testing or human factors. Attend conferences hosted by professional societies. (See Chapter 14 for a list.)

Learn from Watching Others

Watching other test moderators is a key to success. When you have an opportunity to watch an experienced test moderator at work, you get to see what works and what doesn't firsthand. If the opportunity presents itself, ask the test moderator why he or she uses a particular technique that caught your interest. Take notes about particular techniques, behaviors, and so forth that seem particularly effective and try them out yourself. Again, do not let your concern for making mistakes prevent you from exploring new techniques.

Watch Yourself on Tape

One of the benefits of recording your test sessions is that you have an ideal medium for reviewing your own performance. Take advantage of this technology by reviewing your sessions with the intent of improving your skills. Take notes on what you do well and on behaviors that need improvement. That way you will remember to work on those aspects the next time you moderate a test.

Work with a Mentor

Work closely with an experienced test moderator. Help the test moderator work on a test and have that moderator do the same for you. If it is a test with many participants, perhaps you can conduct some of the sessions. Have your mentor watch you and critique your performance. If you hire a consultant to help conduct a test, arrange for the consultant to work closely with you in a mentor/coaching relationship, so that you can learn faster than by just observing.

Practice Moderating Sessions

Start with the right attitude. Do not be a perfectionist. You are going to make mistakes, bias participants, reveal information you should not, and invent new ways to invalidate a test session's results. This is just par for the course. Usability testing has a twofold saving grace — testing multiple participants and iterative design. Testing multiple participants means that if you invalidate something in one session, there is always another opportunity to do it right. Iterative design also makes up for any mistakes you might make, because you have several chances throughout the product development lifecycle to catch problems with the product. The important thing is not to get discouraged. Continue to practice, continue to learn, continue to improve. Even the most experienced test moderators make mistakes.

Learn to Meditate

Meditation practice, specifically the type of meditation that fosters mindfulness and awareness, can be a valuable aid in learning to see clearly and in observing subtle nuances in behavior. This type of discipline is based on the belief that to understand another's mind, you first have to master your own.

Meditation practice or mindfulness training involves setting aside a period of time to sit down on a cushion and practice a simple breathing technique, while at the same time acknowledging thoughts that arise and letting them be. Over time, the result of this practice is a very personal and heartfelt recognition of how everything we perceive is filtered and biased by our version of things. Through continual practice, one's thoughts become more transparent, which in turn frees one to perceive more clearly and directly. During a test session, this is exactly what an excellent test moderator attempts to do; observe the participant's behavior free from the tyranny of his or her own expectations and biases.

Don't take up meditation strictly to become a better test moderator; that would be missing the point. However, if you are already inclined toward a discipline to quiet the mind and gain a clearer perception, meditation practice is a natural complement to the testing discipline.

Practice "Bare Attention"

"Bare attention" practice is an adjunct to meditation practice, except that it is done within one's normal daily routine. Practicing "bare attention" can heighten your ability to concentrate during test sessions. To practice "bare attention," set aside a period of time (15–30 minutes is more than enough to begin) when you intentionally and very deliberately heighten your awareness of whatever you happen to be doing and of your surroundings. For example, if you are working at a computer, experience very deliberately the sense of your fingers hitting the keys, of your eyes looking from the paper to the screen, of your thought process. Notice when (and how often) your mind wanders from what you are doing, and when it does, gently bring it back to the present task at hand. The intent is to stay in the present moment 100 percent of the time. Try it sometime just to see how difficult it is. This practice, as with the previously described meditation practice, helps to foster mindfulness and awareness.

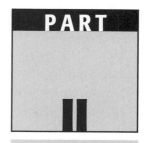

PART

II

The Process for Conducting a Test

Develop the Test Plan

The test plan is the foundation for the entire test. It addresses the how, when, where, who, why, and what of your usability test. Under the sometimes unrelenting time pressure of project deadlines, there could be a tendency to forgo writing a detailed test plan. Perhaps, feeling that you have a good idea of what you would like to test in your head, you decide not to bother writing it down. This informal approach is a mistake, and it invariably will come back to haunt you.

Why Create a Test Plan?

A sound approach is to start writing the test plan as soon as you know you will be testing. Then, as the project proceeds, continue to refine it, get feedback, buy-in, and so forth. Of course, there is a limit to flexibility, so prior to the test you need to set a reasonable deadline after which the test plan may not change. Let that date also serve as the point at which the product can no longer change until after the test. You may find that the test plan is the only concrete milestone at that point in time in the development cycle and, as such, serves an important function.

Once you reach the cutoff date, do all that you can to freeze the design of the product you will be testing. Additional revisions may invalidate the test design you have chosen, the questions you ask, even the way you collect data. If you are pressured to revise the test after the cutoff date, make sure that everyone understands the risks involved. The test may be invalidated, and the product may not work properly with changes made so close to the test date.

The following are some important reasons why it is necessary to develop a comprehensive test plan, as well as some ways to use it as a communication vehicle among the development team.

It Serves as a Blueprint for the Test

Much as the blueprint for a house describes exactly what you will build, the test plan describes exactly how you will go about testing your product. Just as you don't want your building contractor to "wing it" when building your house, so the exact same logic applies here. The test plan sets the stage for all that will follow. You do not want to have any loose ends just as you are about to test your first participant.

It Serves as the Main Communication Vehicle

The test plan serves as the main communication vehicle among the main designer and developer, the test moderator, and the rest of the team. The test plan is the document that all involved members of the development team, as well as management (if it is interested and involved), should review in order to understand how the test will proceed and to see whether their particular needs are being met. You use it to get buy-in and feedback from other members to ensure that everyone agrees on what will transpire. Because projects are dynamic and change from day to day and from week to week, you do not want someone to say at the end of the test that his or her particular agenda was not addressed. Especially when your organization is first starting to test, everyone who is directly affected by the test results should review the test plan. This makes good business sense and political sense as well.

It Defines or Implies Required Resources

The test plan describes or implies required resources, both internal and external. Once you delineate exactly what will happen and when, it is a much easier task to foretell what you will need to accomplish with your test. Either directly or by implication, the test plan should communicate the resources that are required to complete the test successfully.

It Provides a Focal Point for the Test and a Milestone

Without the test plan, details get fuzzy and ambiguous, especially under time pressure. The test plan forces you to approach the job of testing systematically, and it reminds the development team of the impending dates. Having said all that, it is perfectly acceptable, and highly probable, that the test plan will be developed in stages as you gradually understand more of the test objectives and talk to the people who will be involved. Projects are dynamic, and the best laid plans will change as you begin to approach testing. By developing the test plan in stages, you can accommodate changes. For example, as your time and resource constraints become clearer, your test may become less ambitious and simpler. Or, perhaps you cannot acquire as many qualified participants as you thought. Perhaps not all modules or sections of the document will be ready in time. Perhaps your test objectives are too imprecise and need to be simplified and focused. These are all real-world examples that force you to revise the test and the test plan.

NOTE Remember to keep the end user in mind as you develop the test plan. If you are very close to the project, there is a tendency to forget that you are not testing the product, you are testing its relationship to a human being with certain specific characteristics.

The Parts of a Test Plan

Test plan formats will vary according to the type of test and the degree of formality required in your organization. However, the following are the typical sections to include, along with a description of each one. At the end of this chapter is a sample test plan.

- Purpose, goals, and objectives of the test
- Research questions
- Participant characteristics
- Method (test design)
- Task list
- Test environment, equipment, and logistics
- Test moderator role
- Data to be collected and evaluation measures
- Report contents and presentation

These parts are discussed in detail in the following sections, with the exception of the role of the test moderator, which gets its own chapter, Chapter 4, because it merits a special discussion.

Review the Purpose and Goals of the Test

For this part of the document, you need to describe at a high level the reasons for performing this test at this time. You need not provide the very specific objectives or problems to be explored here — rather, the major focus or impetus is the key point, often from the viewpoint of your organization. For example:

- Is the test attempting to resolve problems that have been reported by the company's call center or support desk?
- Have server logs or web usage statistics shown that visitors to your company's web site leave the site at a particular point in a process that leaves a transaction incomplete?
- Has a new policy recently been instituted stating that all products must be tested before release?
- Does management feel it is critical for the development team to see real users at this time?

It is okay if the test purpose remains at a high level, because the research questions and problem statements will reduce the goal(s) to measurable statements. The important point is that the testing be tied to business goals within the organization and that testing is the most appropriate technique for addressing the problem or opportunity.

When Not to Test

Following are some rather vague, inappropriate reasons for usability testing a product. These are rarely placed on paper but are usually communicated via word of mouth. They are *not* sound reasons for testing, and invariably they often come back to sabotage the project.

- You can improve the user experience (you may be able to test one part of the customer experience but not all the touch points your company has with customers).
- Everyone else has a usability testing program (everyone else has many things).
- The meeting rooms used for testing are available the third week of the month (so is the cafeteria every evening).
- Lou just went to the latest ACM SIGCHI (Association for Computing Machinery Special Interest Group on Computer-Human Interaction) conference and learned about this really neat testing technique (let Lou promote the technique's benefits to the organization first).
- You want to see if there is a need for this type of product in the marketplace (backwards logic; a focus group or survey is a more appropriate technique early on).

You might say to yourself, especially if you are eager to begin usability testing, "As long as we test, I don't care what the reasons are. We'll worry about the consequences later." And for the short term, there is no problem with any of the reasons stated previously. However, in the long term, if you want testing to become an integral part of the way your organization develops products, you must tie testing to the needs of the product and to the organization's overall business needs. Otherwise, you run the risk of your testing becoming one more fad, one more of the latest approaches that come and go with the seasons.

Good Reasons to Test

The following list gives some more rational reasons for conducting a test, which should result in successful outcomes and pave the way for future tests.

- You want to understand whether both of your major types of users can use the product equally well.
- You want to know whether or not the documentation is able to compensate for some acknowledged problems with the interface.
- You have received numerous complaints associated with using the product. You are interested in determining the exact nature of the problem and how you will fix it within your development budget for this year.

Figure 5-1 shows one example of purpose and goals for a usability test of a hotel reservations web site.

Communicate Research Questions

This section is the single most important one in the test plan, because it describes the issues and questions that need to be resolved and focuses the research, as well as the rest of the activities associated with planning, designing, and conducting the test. It is essential that the research questions be as precise, accurate, clear, and measurable (or observable) as possible. Even when conducting exploratory testing in the early stages of developing a product, which is typically less structured, you still need to accurately describe what you hope to learn.

Without a clear succinct research question(s), you might find yourself in the unenviable position of conducting a wonderful test that neglects to answer the

---

Overall objectives for the study

We will gather baseline data about the overall effectiveness of H.com. The goals of this study are to:

- Assess the overall effectiveness of www.H.com for different types of users performing basic, common tasks.
- Identify obstacles to completing room reservations on the site.
- Create a repeatable usability study protocol.

Figure 5-1 Sample purpose and goals for a usability test

key concern of developers on the project team. Or, you might find yourself with a test whose development bogs down in controversy because no one can agree on what to test. Speaking from experience, we have seen test preparations move in circles and the test itself result in controversy because the test objectives were never committed to paper.

The following are two examples of unfocused and vague research questions.

■ **EXAMPLE 1.**   Is the current product usable?

■ **EXAMPLE 2.**   Is the product ready for release or does it need more work?

The difficulty with these questions is *not* that they do not make sense. Rather, they are incomplete and vague. They neither state nor imply how to measure or quantify the results. A test based on these statements will invariably bias the results favorably. Why? If those involved cannot agree on what problems or issues need to be resolved, how do you know when you have found one? Of course, in those circumstances, the tendency will be *not* to find any problems.

The table below shows an example of several more appropriately focused research questions for several types of products. The research question(s) should originate with discussions with the development team or with individual developers, technical writers, marketing personnel, and so on. Do not be surprised if they have difficulty in pinning down the test objectives and if they can communicate only the most general questions or objectives. This may be an indication that:

■ They are not quite ready to test.

■ They need a greater understanding and education of the goals, intent, and process of testing.

■ They need help in formulating their objectives into research questions that can be measured or observed. Do not be afraid to jump in and help.

If you find that you are having unusual difficulty designing the test and/or appropriate measures, or deciding on the appropriate end users, or even designing the data collection form, you might return to the research questions to see if they are clear or need further clarification.

PRODUCT	RESEARCH QUESTIONS
Web sites	How easily do users understand what is clickable?
	How easily and successfully do users find the products or information they are looking for?
	How easily and successfully do users register for the site?
	Where in the site do users go to find Search? Why?
	How easily can users return to the home page?

(continued)

PRODUCT	RESEARCH QUESTIONS
Small interfaces	How easily do users switch between modes on multi-purpose buttons?
	How well do users understand the symbols and icons? Which ones are problematic? Why?
	How easily do users download updates and features?
	How quickly can users perform common tasks?
Hardware	How easily and successfully can users use all buttons on the control panel?
	Can users use the control panel without assistance or training?
	How easily can users find the correct input and output ports?
	How easily can users change settings in the menus?
Online and written documentation	Do users go to online help when they encounter error messages?
	How easily do users find topics they are looking for in the online help? How well do the topic titles reflect what users are looking for?
	How well do they understand the content of the topics they find?
	How helpful is the topic content?
	Which parts of each topic do users pay attention to?
	Can users easily switch between reading the online help and interacting with the interface to complete the task?
Software	How closely does the flow of the software reflect how the user thinks of the work flow?
	How easily and successfully do users find the tools or options they want?
	Do users use the toolbar icons or the standard menus? Why?
	Is the response time a cause of user frustration or errors?
General	What obstacles prevent users from completing installation and set up?
	Can users perform common tasks within established benchmarks?
	What are the major usability flaws that prevent users from completing the most common tasks?
	How does ease-of-use compare in the planned release to the last release?
	How does ease-of-use compare between our product and the competition?
	Is there an appropriate balance of ease of use and ease of learning?

Research questions

In addition, in this study will try to answer these questions:

- How easily and successfully do travelers get started with making a reservation on the site?
- Does the starting point make any difference in whether travelers are successful in reaching their goal on H.com? If so, what are the differences?
- What paths do travelers take to completing a booking?
- How well does the site support the paths and goals of the travelers? That is, how closely does the organization and flow of the site match travelers' expectations?
- What obstacles do travelers encounter on the way to completing a booking, whether using a credit card or rewards?
- What questions do travelers ask as they work through their reservation?
- How do travelers feel about how long it takes them to complete an online booking, both the perceived of time and the number of steps?

Figure 5-2 Sample research questions

Figure 5-2 shows an example of research questions from a usability test of a hotel reservations web site.

Summarize Participant Characteristics

This section of the test plan describes the characteristics of the end user(s) of the product/document that you will be testing. It is important to work closely with others in your organization to determine the characteristics of the target users. For detailed procedures on how to establish the user profile and acquire participants, see Chapter 7. A basic example of participant characteristics for a usability test of a hotel reservations web site appears in Figure 5-3.

One thing to remember when describing the participant characteristics is to use the right number of participants. When it comes to selecting the number of participants to employ for a test, the overriding guideline is "You cannot have too many participants." When thinking about achieving statistically valid results, small sample sizes lack the statistical power to identify significant differences between groups. For a true experimental design, you must use a minimum of 10 to 12 participants per condition. However, for the purpose of conducting a less formal usability test, research has shown that four to five participants who represent one audience cell will expose about 80 percent of the usability deficiencies of a product for that audience, and that this 80 percent will represent most of the major problems. Of course, if you have the time and resources to study more than four or five participants, by all means do so. It is possible that the additional 20 percent of deficiencies you might find could be important for your product.

We have conducted many tests that held true to the preceding principle. In one, Jeff tested eight participants and discovered about 80 percent of the problems within the first four participants. However, participant 8, the last one, performed a particularly grievous error on one task that would have required a service call for the product. This would never have been uncovered

Characteristic	Desired number of participants
Participant type	
pilot	1
regular	12
backup	2
Total number of participants	14
Travel frequency	
infrequently: 1–5 trips per year	4
moderately often: 6–12 trips per year	4
very often: 13 or more trips per year	4
Types of travel	
mostly business	6
mostly leisure	6
Booking experience	
book their own trips and accommodations	all
book online most of the time	6
book on the phone or other method	6
Age	
21–30	2–3
31–40	4–5
41–50	4–5
51–60	2–3
Gender	
female	6
male	6

Figure 5-3 Sample participant characteristics and desired mix

had we only tested four participants. Until you become experienced at testing, employing more participants decreases the probability you will miss an important problem, while providing additional opportunities to practice your moderating skills.

If you find you have very limited time and budget, you may want to institute a practice of "discount" usability testing, in which you would run several small, iterated usability tests over time. That is, conduct a test with 4 or 5 participants from one cell and one or two conditions, incorporate the findings into the interface, and then conduct another test with a similar set of participants and conditions. Over three or four tests, you end up with a large sample of participants, but the development team is able to accommodate changes in between tests.

Describe the Method

This section of the test plan is a detailed description of how you are going to carry out the research with the participants, and how the test session will unfold. Essentially, it is a synopsis of your test design. It should provide an overview of each facet of the test from the time the participants arrive until the time they leave, in enough detail so that someone observing the test will know roughly what to expect. If you are questioning why this amount of detail is necessary in the test plan, the following reasons should satisfy your curiosity.

- It enables others to understand and visualize what will happen so that they can comment and make suggestions accordingly.

- It enables you as the test developer to focus on what has to be done and the types of materials that have to be developed before participants arrive.

- It reveals the need to communicate your plans to additional resources whom you might have forgotten, such as a receptionist who will greet the participants in a corporate lobby when they first arrive.

- It allows multiple test moderators (if that is required by the test design) to conduct the test in as similar a manner to each other as possible.

Test design is one of the more highly specialized skills required of a usability professional, often requiring knowledge of experimental design and method and basic statistical analysis. Designing a test requires one to clearly identify and understand the test objectives, and then to select the test design that will effectively ferret out the answers to the questions posed. If the test design is flawed or if the test is carried out with little attention to experimental rigor, then the results will be suspect. Not only can this result in faulty recommendations, but it also sabotages the progress of usability engineering per se within the organization. Therefore, the first few times that you conduct a usability test, get advice and feedback on your test design from someone more experienced than you.

The test design is mainly predicated upon your test objectives — what you need to learn about the product and its audience. The design will be greatly affected by your resources, your constraints, and your creativity. Constraints are time, money, management backing, development team support, ability to acquire participants, and other real-world concerns. The following sections give examples of test designs for some of the most common situations you will face. Following that, we present some guidelines for ensuring experimental rigor.

The simplest test design, shown in the table in the next section, consists of testing several different users, all from one type of user group (e.g., older adults), and having them perform a series of representative tasks on different parts of the web site.

Independent Groups Design or Between Subjects Design

This is called an independent groups design because each part of the web site is tested by a unique set of users. For our example, shown in the table below, this design requires 15 participants and mitigates the potential transfer of learning effects caused by doing one set of tasks prior to performing other similar tasks. In other words, performing Task A may help one to perform Task B, and mask any usability problems associated with Task B. You can also use this design if the tasks are extremely lengthy and there is a possibility that the participants may become fatigued.

TASK A SIGN UP TO BECOME A MEMBER	TASK B FIND ONLINE CLASSES TO TAKE	TASK C FIND VOLUNTEER OPPORTUNITIES
Terry	Pat	Tracy
Lesley	Michael	Dana
Lisa	Andrea	Duane
Kim	Erin	Aaron
Blair	Paula	Janet

Within-Subjects Design

Perhaps testing 15 participants is simply out of the question. Instead of 15, you could get by with only five participants by having each one perform all three modules as shown in the table below. This is called a *within-subjects* design. However, you have the same problem of transfer of learning effects to consider. To mitigate these effects, you must use a technique called *counterbalancing*, whereby the order of tasks is either randomized or balanced out. By varying the order of the presentation of tasks, you can limit the effects of learning transfer.

TASK A SIGN UP TO BECOME A MEMBER	TASK B FIND ONLINE CLASSES TO TAKE	TASK C FIND VOLUNTEER OPPORTUNITIES
Terry	Terry	Terry
Lesley	Lesley	Lesley
Lisa	Lisa	Lisa
Kim	Kim	Kim
Blair	Blair	Blair

To counterbalance, you vary the presentation order of modules as shown in the table below, with each participant performing modules in a different order. By randomizing the order of the modules, you minimize the transfer effects while requiring only four participants. However, there are still some issues to resolve. If the order of modules would normally be sequential in real life (e.g., the modules required to set up a piece of hardware), then you have an important decision. Is it more critical to provide a realistic task order for users and possibly mask some usability problems on later tasks (possibly measuring whether participants learn as they progress through the modules), or is it more crucial to provide a random order of tasks (which is possible in the lab) and risk confusing and alienating the participant? Most would argue that you should retain the sequential order. If you decide to do so, you will still need to address possible transfer effects, possibly by using prerequisite training to equalize participants' experience before performing. In addition, you may need to conduct each session with breaks to allow participants to rest.

PARTICIPANT	TASK SEQUENCE
Terry	A, B, C
Lesley	B, C, A
Lisa	C, A, B
Kim	B, A, C
Blair	C, B, A

Testing Multiple Product Versions

Now let's look at another common situation. Suppose that you want to compare two different versions of a product, Version A and Version B, to see which one shows more promise as your ultimate design. (These are known as different "conditions.") Additionally, you want to see whether performance varies for either of two user groups, call them supervisors and technicians. This will result in a 2 × 2 matrix design as shown in the following table.

GROUP	VERSION A	VERSION B
Supervisors	4	4
Technicians	4	4

If you use an *independent groups* design whereby each cell in the table you use to describe your test design is populated by a different set of participants, then this design will require 16 participants to satisfy the four different conditions: Four supervisors will use Version A and four technicians will use Version A, and so on. Suppose though that you only want to use eight participants. You could simply populate each cell with only two participants, but that is increasing the risk that the data for any one group will be meaningless. Instead, let each person in the two groups, supervisors and technicians, try each of the versions, one after the other, as shown in the table below. As with the previous example, there may be an unfair advantage for the version that is tested last, because the participant may learn to perform the tasks while using the first version. On the other hand, it may even reverse the effect; the participant may learn the first version and have difficulty adapting to the second version because it is so different. In either case, your results may be biased.

SUPERVISORS	VERSION	TECHNICIANS	VERSION
Ginny	A, B	Laurie	A, B
Stephanie	B, A	Janice	B, A
Ken	A, B	Arnold	A, B
James	B, A	Andrew	B, A

To account for these potential differences, you will again counterbalance the order of presentation of the versions. As shown in the table above, for eight participants, some participants will do Version A first, and others will do Version B first. Note that each version is performed as many times in the first position as it is in the last position, which negates the potential biasing effects.

Testing Multiple User Groups

Now let's look at a slightly more complex, yet realistic scenario. Suppose your user profile consists of two different user groups, managers and clerks, who will be using your product. One of your test objectives is to see if there are differences in ability to use the product between or among user groups. In addition, you also want to see if there are differences in novice and experienced users within each group. You will therefore need to vary experience and job type, each of which will have two levels. Once again, you will use a matrix design, as shown below.

GROUP	NOVICE	EXPERIENCED
Managers	4	4
Clerks	4	4

Each one of the four conditions or cells shown in the table above will be populated with a different set of participants. If you want to acquire at least four participants per cell, as shown, you will need a total of 16 participants. If this is too many participants for your budget and time, (four participants is about the bare minimum per group required to evaluate group differences), then you *cannot* simply apply a within-subjects design. Instead, you will either have to limit each cell to fewer participants or simplify the study. Remember, limiting a cell to less than four participants severely limits the conclusions you can draw about each group. You will probably need to simplify the research to exclude a study of group differences (see Figure 5-4).

Methodology

This usability study will be somewhat exploratory but will also gather assessment data about the effectiveness of www.H.com. Participants will fall into three groups by the starting point they use to perform the main task, which is to reserve a room. We will collect data about error and success rates as well as qualitative data about participants' experiences using the site.

We will use a between-subjects design

In this between-subjects study, each participant will work through one task path (in a within-subjects study, each participant would try all paths in counterbalanced order). I will conduct up to 30 individual 45-minute usability study sessions. Each participant will perform one of three major task "paths" using www.H.com. I'll use 15 minutes of each session to explain the session to the participant, review basic background information with the participant, and then conduct a post-test debriefing interview. During the middle 30 minutes of the session, participants will work to reserve a room at an H property in a major U.S. city.

Session outline and timing

The test sessions will be 45 minutes long. I will use 15 minutes of each session for pre-test introductions and post-test debriefing interviews. The sessions will take place at Shugoll Research in Bethesda.

Pre-test arrangements

Have the participant:

- Review and sign nondisclosures and recording permissions.
- Fill out a background questionnaire (with the same questions as the screener).

Introduction to the session (2 minutes)

Discuss:

- Participant's experience with usability studies and focus groups.
- Importance of their involvement in the study.
- Moderator's role.
- Room configuration, recording systems, observers, etc.
- The protocol for the rest of the session.
- Thinking aloud.

Background interview (3 minutes)

Discuss the participant's:

- Experiences booking their own travel.
- Reasons for booking their own travel.

Tasks (30 minutes)

Participants will start at one of three points to reserve a room at an H hotel in a major U.S. city where H has multiple properties.

Post-test debriefing (10 minutes)

- Ask broad questions to collect preference and other qualitative data.
- Follow up on any particular problems that came up for the participant.

Figure 5-4 High-level description of a test method

NOTE If you are new to the game and are not confident that you can conduct a test with experimental rigor, then by all means keep the test simple. The more straightforward the test, the easier it is to keep everything consistent from session to session. It is better to attain meaningful results from a smaller, simpler study than to acquire a wealth of meaningless data from a larger study. Do some usability testing as early and often as possible. It need not be elaborate to be useful or cost-effective.

List the Tasks

The task list comprises those tasks that the participants will perform during the test. The list should consist of tasks that will ordinarily be performed during the course of using the product, documentation, and so on.

There are two stages to developing these tasks. In the early stages of developing the test, the task list description is intended only for members of the project team and not for eventual participants. You need to supply only enough detail so that reviewers of the test plan can judge whether the tasks are the correct ones and are being exercised properly.

Later, you will expand the tasks into full-blown task scenarios, which are presented to the participants. The scenarios will provide the realistic details and context that enable the participants to perform tasks with little intervention from the test moderator. Expanding the initial tasks into task scenarios is covered in Chapter 8. For now, your task list need only include the following.

Parts of a Task for the Test Plan

For the test plan, you need only touch on four main components of each task:

A brief Description of the Task

Include only enough detail at this time to communicate the task to the project team. A one-line description is usually enough.

The Materials and Machine States Required to Perform the Task

Context is everything in usability testing. As the test moderator, you may actually be providing these materials or simulating the machine states if the product is in an early stage. For example, if you were testing a web site before the screens are coded or prototyped, you might provide printed wireframe drawings of the pages. Or if the page were available in a file on the computer but not hooked up as part of a working prototype yet, you (or the participant) might open that file on the screen for viewing at the appropriate time.

Or, perhaps parts of the test will be performed with documentation, while other sections will not. For example, if you are testing how well instructions work for installing a wireless network, and the later tasks will be done without documentation, such as specifying drive designations on the new network, you need to specify this. If it is appropriate and helpful, your task list might also include components of the product that are being exercised for that particular task. If, for example, a task asks a participant to enter a customer name into an online form, you might specify the screens or web pages that the participant will navigate during task completion. This helps to give you a sense of whether the full system is being exercised or not.

A Description of Successful Completion of the Task

How will you measure success? It is amazing how much disagreement there will be over this question and how often developers have differing opinions on what represents successful completion of a task. When you include *successful completion criteria* (SCC) with the task description, you add precision to what you are measuring and how you view the task. SCC define the boundaries of your task and help to clarify test scoring. When you have difficulty ascertaining the SCC, it reflects the development team's confusion about the product design. Establishing and documenting the SCC is a good exercise just for that reason alone.

Criteria for successful completion can include reaching a certain point in the task or screen flow, a maximum number of errors or wrong turns (for information-finding tasks), and whether you will consider the task "complete" if the participant reaches the appropriate end point but makes mistakes along the way.

Timing or Other Benchmarks

You may want to use time as a criterion for success or as a benchmark. If you do set benchmarks that are based on timing, it's recommended you do this very thoughtfully and under just the right circumstances. For example, time-on-task is a good measure for validation/summative tests, but it is rarely appropriate for early exploratory or formative tests. It is inadvisable to measure time-on-task if you're also asking participants to think aloud, because doing so typically slows task performance. For more about benchmark timings, see the Benchmark Timings sidebar. If you don't want to use time as a benchmark, you could use error rates; for example, completing a task with no errors of any kind.

ABOUT BENCHMARK TIMINGS THAT ESTABLISH THE MAXIMUM TIME LIMITS FOR PERFORMING

If appropriate, establish *benchmarks* that represent either the average or maximum time to perform the task. Benchmarks help to evaluate participant performance during a test. While they are not absolutely necessary, they can help you to monitor and evaluate the results of a test session more precisely, because successful participant performance is a reflection of both correct behavior and timely completion.

For example, if a participant takes 5 minutes to correctly enter his or her name and address on an email system, the design is obviously flawed from almost anyone's standards, and you need to know that. During the test, you need to track when a participant is outside the boundaries of some designated maximum time. You may choose to intervene at that point, or let the participant continue and note on your data collection form that he or she "maxed out." You will certainly have to stop the participant eventually, if he or she cannot complete the task correctly and to continue to collect data on other areas of the product.

It is important to determine and arrive at fair and reasonable benchmarks. There are a number of ways to do this, but before describing them, it should be emphasized that they need not be deadly accurate. In fact, if you are conducting iterative, ongoing testing, you will be revising the benchmarks from test to test as you learn more about realistic time frames for task completion. Sources of benchmark times include:

◆ Any original case studies, interviews, or customer visits you may have performed or been privy to. You should not only note what tasks the end users perform but also how long they typically take. Obviously, not only is task definition essential for testing, but it should also be an integral part of the design process. (Better late than never if you are the first to ascertain the tasks that your end users will perform.)

◆ Any usability objectives that were included as part of the product or functional specification. Typically, the usability objectives include targets for time to complete functions or tasks.

◆ Any usability data from previous tests that were performed.

◆ Polling in-house end users who fit the user profile in one's own company. Simply asking them how long it takes them to perform common tasks will get you started.

Because time benchmarks are subjective, they may be controversial. Product developers may rightfully feel that the benchmarks should be longer than the test moderator provides. To anticipate this potential controversy before the test begins, it pays to give developers the benefit of the doubt by erring on the side of overly generous benchmarks.

(continued)

ABOUT BENCHMARK TIMINGS THAT ESTABLISH THE MAXIMUM TIME LIMITS FOR PERFORMING *(continued)*

Jeff established benchmarks for one test for an organization with no previous usability testing experience. The text was for a hardware product that would be tested with documentation. Jeff had three engineers provide estimates of the maximum time that they felt a user would need to correctly perform each task on the test. He also had three technical writers on the project give the estimates because their perspective on the end user was different. He then averaged all estimates, and, to give everyone the benefit of the doubt, he multiplied the average for each task by a constant of 2.5 to come up with the maximum time for a participant to complete the task. This constant was rather arbitrary and quite generous. Jeff simply wanted everyone to feel that the participants were given ample time before the task was classified as "incomplete." The generosity was due to Jeff's confidence given his familiarity with the product design and its potential flaws as well as participants exposing the problematic areas, even with the generous time allotments.

As it turned out, some of the tasks took up to three times longer than even these generous benchmarks, which really drove home the point about difficulties. Experience has taught the authors that poor product design will make itself known eventually.

Measuring time on tasks is not always the best, most accurate measure of task success. If you are asking participants to think out loud, doing so takes time and unnaturally lengthens the duration. Instead, you may want to count only errors against the success criteria or completion criteria along with numbers and types of prompting.

Tips for Developing the Task List

While this may seem straightforward, it is a very subtle process. The trick is to *indirectly* expose usability flaws by having the participants perform tasks that use the parts of the product in question. What you are really testing is the *relationship* of your product to the end user. From the end user's viewpoint, your product and its associated documentation are a means to an end, either used to solve a problem or provide a service.

The tasks that you develop for the test need to reflect this relationship and, as much as possible, allow the test to expose the points at which the product becomes a hindrance rather than a help for performing a task. Let's look at a simple example of a task to satisfy a test objective and, in so doing, review some possible pitfalls.

Example Task: Navigation Tab on a Web Site

Suppose that one of your test objectives is to test how easy it is to understand a label for a tab that appears on an image-sharing web site that amateur and professional photographers use. The test objective is written as, "Establish whether users can understand the meaning of the XYZ label." There are six tabs with text labels on the web site, but the XYZ label is the problematic one. It's called Organize.

On the current version of the web site, users expect to use the feature to change the order in which their images appear on the viewing pages, but this feature is for organizing images into categories.

If you simply take the objective at face value ("Establish whether users can understand the meaning of the XYZ label."), you might decide to have a task that has the test moderator:

Show the participants the XYZ label and have them explain its meaning to you.

In other words, the test moderator will get feedback about the label. This seems simple and direct, because the label is the offending aspect of the product. However, this is oversimplifying the situation. By performing a simple analysis, you ascertain that there are actually three discrete processes associated with correctly using the simple label.

1. Noticing the label
2. Reading the label
3. Processing the information and responding correctly

In addition, these three processes occur within the very specific context of using the web site to post images on the web:

- If you simply show the participants the label, you only address the second and third processes. You will not know if the participants even notice the label, which precedes the other behaviors. You will also negate the entire context. In the course of using the web site, the participants will perform a particular task(s) at the time when they are supposed to be reading the label, not having someone point out the label and ask them what they think. This "context" is critical because it dramatically affects their ability to process information.

- You also need to address how the location of the label on the web page affects things. If it resides among five other labels and other actions, you should see how the participants perform with those potential distractions in place.

Tasks

Participants start from one of three starting points: All participants will use www.H.com to book a hotel room (up to the point of entering a credit card number or just before completing the rewards reservation) in a major U.S. city that has multiple H properties. Within that task, participants will select a hotel and room based on a combination of price and amenities. Each group will start at a different point:

Group 1   Start at H.com

Group 2   Start at non-branded search from Google (example: premium San Francisco hotel 4 star hotel).

Group 3   Start from a branded search from Google (example: H Hotel Atlanta)

Let the participants start where they would normally start: Because you'll select participants for different combinations of characteristics, expect that different types of participants are motivated to do different things. Briefly interview the participant at the beginning of the session to get some impression of how the particular participant approaches booking travel arrangements–especially accommodations–and let them perform the task within their own context. This way, in addition to getting a feeling for the overall usability of www.H.com, you can also identify usage patterns that could be further investigated in follow-on research. Finally, you will also get a better understanding of the traveler's thought processes and how H.com fits into that traveler's life.

Figure 5-5 Task description for an exploratory usability test

Having analyzed label usage, context, and location, you know that merely asking the participants to explain the label's meaning does not really suffice. Instead, you have to provide a task during which they are expected to use the label, and ascertain whether they notice, read, and use the label correctly (see Figure 5-5). In fact, the label is actually secondary to the task of putting images into collections that it supports.

The actual task, then, that exposes the label's usability is:

Arrange images into collections.

Notice that the task description does not even mention the label.

The label usage is explored indirectly by the test moderator while the task is performed. The test moderator must note where the participants look and so forth, and then question them during the debriefing session.

Having arrived at the correct task to meet your objective, let's classify it according to the four parts of a task as we outlined in the previous section. The table below shows a description for each of the four parts of a testing task.

TASK COMPONENT	DESCRIPTION
Task	Arrange images into collections.
State	Web site with six navigation tabs leading to different sections of the site.
Successful completion criteria	Participant finds the Organize link and then groups preloaded pictures into sets.
Benchmark	Participant puts more than two pictures into one set with no "wrong turns."

Ways to Prioritize Tasks

Now that you have reviewed an example of developing a task, the next issue is ascertaining what tasks you need to include. Due to time constraints, very rarely do you actually test the full range of tasks that comprise an entire interface, documentation, or both together. (It is impractical to conduct test sessions that last for days at a time, unless you are willing to commit an inordinate amount of resources.) Instead, you typically face a situation of testing a representative sample of the product's functions.

When choosing this sample of tasks, it is important that you exercise as many of the most important aspects of the product as possible and address all test objectives. Filter or reduce your task list to something manageable, while ensuring that you capture as many of the usability deficiencies as possible. The following list outlines some common methods you can use that prioritize or pare down the task list without needless sacrifice.

- **Prioritize by frequency.**   Select those tasks that represent the most frequently performed tasks of your end user population. The most frequent tasks are the ones that the typical end user performs daily, possibly up to 75 to 80 percent of the time, when using the product. For example, if you were testing a word processing package, you would want to make sure that the end user could easily perform the following tasks before you concern yourself with the more esoteric tasks such as "how to hide a comment that does not print out."

  1. Open a file.
  2. Save a file.
  3. Edit a file
  4. Print a file.

Often, tests are filled with a series of obscure tasks that less than 5 percent of the end user population will ever find, never mind use. Why? Our theory is that the development team finds those "five percenters" the most interesting and challenging tasks to implement, because they are usually the leading edge of the product. Unfortunately, the typical end user does not share the developer's priority or enthusiasm for these obscure tasks.

If, after applying the "75 percent usage guideline," there is still time to test more tasks, include tasks that at least 25 percent of your end user population perform regularly. Only when you are sure that the frequent tasks are covered should you include the less frequently performed tasks.

▪ **Prioritize by criticality.**   Critical tasks are those that, if performed incorrectly or missed, have serious consequences either to the end user, to the product, or to the reputation of the company; for example, when the tasks result in a support line call, cause loss of data, or cause damage to the product or bodily harm to the user. In short, you want to make sure that you catch those tasks that result in the most pain and potentially bad publicity.

▪ **Prioritize by vulnerability.**   Vulnerability in this case means those tasks that you suspect, even before testing, will be hard to perform or that have known design flaws. Often, the development team will have a good handle on this and, when asked, will voice concern for a new feature, process, interface style, section of a document, and so on. If so, include tasks in the test that address these major areas.

Sometimes, developers pretend, in the name of "being unbiased," that all functions work equally well (or poorly), and that none are particularly problematic. Whether for a well-intended or a less noble reason, they do not want known problems exposed during the test. Consequently, tasks that are obviously hard to perform and that represent whole components, web pages, or sections of a document are left out of the test and prove to be albatrosses much later when there is no time to fix them. To avoid that, use *your* critical judgment about which tasks/features are not quite worked out, are new or never-before-tested features, or have been difficult for in-house personnel to perform. If you are unsure, a human factors specialist can help determine the vulnerable aspects of the product by performing an evaluation. (An expert evaluation can also help you to tighten your test objectives in general.)

▪ **Prioritize by readiness.**   If you are testing very late in the development cycle, you may simply have to go with functions that are ready to be tested or forgo testing entirely. While this is not ideal, it is sometimes your only choice. You will not always have the luxury of waiting for every last component, screen, and user manual section to be completed. *Remember, it is always better to test something than nothing.*

Describe the Test Environment, Equipment, and Logistics

This section of the test plan describes the environment you will attempt to simulate during the test and the equipment that the participants will require. For example, you might want to simulate a sales office for a product that insurance agents use. Or, perhaps chemists use your product in an environmental laboratory. Or, suppose that you simply want to test the product in a very noisy, somewhat crowded office where phones are constantly ringing. Whatever the typical operating environment, try your best to simulate actual conditions. Not only does this help the participants to take on the role of actual end users, but it also means the test results will be a better predictor of the product's performance in the place where it is normally used.

The equipment described here only includes the equipment that participants will use. Examples of equipment are phones, computers, printers, and so forth. It is not necessary to describe data collection equipment or cameras you will be using to monitor the test. Figure 5-6 shows one example.

Explain What the Moderator Will Do

This section helps to clarify what you as a test moderator will be doing, and it is especially important when there will be observers of the test who are unfamiliar with the testing process. (See the example in Figure 5-7.) Specify when the test moderator will do something out of the ordinary that may lead to confusion. For example, sometimes it is unclear why and under what circumstances the test moderator is probing and intervening. This is especially

---

Test environment

We'll use a controlled setting to conduct the sessions. The study will take place at Acme Research in Fresno, California. There will be a testing room with a one-way mirror to an observation room.

Participants will use a Windows PC and Internet Explorer 6.0 with a high-speed connected to the Internet. The PC that the participant uses will also have Morae Recorder installed on it and a webcam attached. The webcam will capture the participant's face; the Morae software will record what's happening on the screen (and can collect other data). I will bring a digital voice recorder to the sessions to create a set of audio recordings for backup.

Figure 5-6 Test environment description of location and setup

---

Moderator role

> I will sit in the room with the participant while conducting the session. I will introduce the
> session, conduct a short background interview, and then introduce tasks as appropriate.
> Because this study is somewhat exploratory, I may ask unscripted follow-up questions to
> clarity the participants' behavior and expectations. I will also take detailed notes and
> record the participants' behavior and comments.

Figure 5-7 Moderator role description

true when the test moderator may be role-playing or intentionally playing devil's advocate with an overly acquiescent participant.

List the Data You Will Collect

This section of the test plan provides an overview of the types of measures you will collect during the test, both performance and preference data. Performance data, representing measures of participant behavior, includes error rates, number of accesses of the help by task, time to perform a task, and so on. Preference data, representing measures of participant opinion or thought process, includes participant rankings, answers to questions, and so forth. The data collected should be based on your research questions. Sometimes these measures will have already been alluded to in a previous section of the test plan, such as the methodology section. You can use both performance and preference measures either quantitatively or qualitatively, depending on the test objectives. See Figure 5-8 for example measures for a test of a hotel reservations web site.

Listing the evaluation measures you will use enables any interested parties to scan the test plan to make sure that they will be getting the type of data they expect from the test.

The following is a sample of the types of measures you might collect during a typical test.

Sample Performance Measures

- Number and percentage of tasks completed correctly with and without prompts or assistance
- Number and type of prompts given
- Number and percentage of tasks completed incorrectly
- Count of all incorrect selections (errors)
- Count of errors of omission
- Count of incorrect menu choices
- Count of incorrect icons selected

Measures

To answer these questions:

- How easily and successfully do travelers get started with making a reservation on the site?
- Does the starting point make any difference in whether travelers are successful in reaching their goal on www.H.com? If so, what are the differences?
- What paths do travelers take to completing a booking?
- How well does the site support the paths and goals of the travelers? That is, how closely does the organization and flow of the site match travelers' expectations?
- What obstacles do travelers encounter on the way to completing a booking?
- What questions do travelers ask as they work through their reservation?
- How do travelers feel about how long it takes them to complete an online booking, both in the perceived amount of time and the number of steps?

I will collect both performance and preference data during the test sessions.

Performance:

- Errors of omission
- Errors of comission
- Number of tasks completed with and without assistance—I will track two levels of prompting when participants need assistance.

  None   Participant completed a task without prompting.

  Try again   Participant completed a task when asked, "Can you think of any other place to look?"

Preference:

- Appropriateness of site's functions to users' tasks
- Perceived amount of time and number of steps
- Ease of use overall
- Usefulness of terms and labeling

Figure 5-8 Sample measures for a test of a hotel reservation web site

- Count of calls to the help desk
- Count of user manual accesses
- Count of visits to the index
- Count of visits to the table of contents
- Count of "negative comments or mannerisms"
- Time required to access information in the manual
- Time required to access information in online help
- Time needed to recover from error(s)
- Time spent reading a specific section of a manual
- Time spent talking to help desk
- Time to complete each task

Qualitative Data

- Think aloud verbal protocol
- Quotable quotes: (for example)
  - "I loved it — when can I get one?"
  - "You guys have done it again — you're *still* not listening to customers."
  - "Wow, I'm very, very impressed."
  - "Can I please leave now — keep my money and the product."

Sample Preference Measures

Ratings and rationale concerning:

- Usefulness of the product
- How well product matched expectations
- Appropriateness of product functions to user's tasks
- Ease of use overall
- Ease of learning overall
- Ease of setup and installation
- Ease of accessibility
- Usefulness of the index, table of contents, help, graphics, and so on
- Help desk replies to inquiries
- Ease of reading text on the screen

Preference and rationale for:

- One prototype vs. another prototype
- This product vs. a competitor's product
- This product's conceptual model vs. the old model

Describe How the Results Will Be Reported

This section provides a summary of the main sections of your test report and the way in which you intend to communicate the results to the development team. For the report contents section, simply list the sections that will appear in your test report, as shown in the example in Figure 5-9.

For the presentation section, describe how you will communicate results to the development team both prior to and following the report. For example, you might hold an informal meeting with those on the critical path of the project just after the test is completed and prior to analyzing all the data. Then,

---

Report contents

I will deliver a draft of the final report to my point of contact at www.H.com that:

- Briefly summarizes the background of the study, including the goals, methodology, logistics, and participant characteristics

- Presents findings for the original questions to investigate

- Gives quantitative results and discusses specifics as appropriate to the question and the data

- Provides visuals of pages of www.H.com that are relevant to specific questions where they will help reviewers understand what we are talking about

- Discusses the implications of the results

- Provides recommendations

- Suggests follow-on research

H will review the draft and comment on it. I'll incorporate agreed changes and then present a summary of the findings in a meeting at H's headquarters

Figure 5-9 Description of what will be in the report

following completion of all analyses and the test report, you might follow that with a formal presentation to the entire project team, as well as other interested parties, management, and so forth.

Sample Test Plan

If we roll up the parts of the plan that we have included as samples above, the test plan deliverable comes to about 10 pages. To see the full plan, go to the web site that accompanies this book (www.wiley.com/go/usabilitytesting). The product being tested is a hotel room reservations system on a web site. There, you can view more examples of test plans, as well as download templates for test plans and other related deliverables in the file Ch05 Hdotcom_test_plan.doc.

Set Up a Testing Environment

For many of those contemplating the implementation of a usability testing program, the discipline has become synonymous with a high-powered, well-appointed, well-equipped, expensive laboratory. For some organizations, the usability lab (and by that we mean the physical plant) has become more prominent and more important than the testing process itself. Some organizations, in their zeal to impress customers and competitors alike with their commitment to usability, have created awe-inspiring palaces of high-tech wizardry *prior to laying the foundation for an ongoing testing program.* Not realizing that instituting a program of user-centered design requires a significant shift in the culture of the organization, these organizations have put the proverbial cart before the horse, in their attempt to create instant programs, rather than building programs over time.

This approach to usability testing is rather superficial and short-sighted, and has a high risk of failure. It approaches user-centered design as a fad to be embraced rather than as a program that requires effort, commitment, and time in order to have lasting effects on the organization and its products. It isn't uncommon for newly built, sophisticated usability laboratories to become the world's most elaborate storage rooms. Having succumbed to the misperception that equates the laboratory with the process itself, these organizations have discovered only too late that usability testing is much more than a collection of cameras and recorders. Rather, a commitment to user-centered design and usability must be embedded in the very philosophy and underpinning of the organization itself in order to guarantee success.

In that vein, if you have been charged with developing a usability testing program and have been funded to build an elaborate testing lab as the *initial* step, resist the temptation to accept the offer. Unless there is an agreed strategy in place to conduct numerous controlled usability tests, a lab still may not be the best place to conduct them. Rather, start small and build the organization from the ground up instead of from the top down.

The point is, you need *not* have an elaborate, expensive lab to achieve your goals. In fact, starting small forces you to focus on all the other factors that make for a successful program such as building relationships with business partners and ensuring that whoever is planning and conducting user-centered design activities has basic knowledge of methods and techniques.

Decide on a Location and Space

In the early days of usability testing, the main assumption was that nearly all usability tests were highly structured and quite formal. In addition, most usability testing was done on products used in offices. Technology has expanded greatly in the last 15 years and so has the application of usability testing. As we have learned through our own experiences, not all testing *should* be done in a lab setting, and sometimes doing testing in a lab simply is not practical. The location of the test sessions is intricately linked with the design of the study and who the users are. There are other considerations as well, as we discuss in the next section.

The discussion in the rest of this chapter assumes that you will want people to observe the sessions who are not employed in moderating the test. Consider carefully from what location you want the observers to observe. You, as the moderator, get to decide. Are you comfortable having observers in the room with you? (Remember, you'll have to train them on how to be in the session.) How do you feel about observers possibly talking among themselves while observing from outside the testing room?

Also, especially for beginner moderators, we recommend that you concentrate on moderating and get some one else to take notes or log data.

In a Lab or at the User's Site?

Determine the appropriate location of usability tests by considering these factors:

- Your test design and measures
  - Is the test exploratory/formative or validating/summative?
  - Must you sit next to the participant because you will collect qualitative data, need to prompt or give hints, or manage the product being tested?

- Or, do you need to observe from outside the testing room because the participant should have no interaction with you (or awareness of you) while performing tasks?

- Logistics

  - Is there space available at your work place, such as an extra office or conference room?

  - Is the location accessible to participants? For example, for older adults, you'll want to have accessible parking, elevators if the testing room is on a floor other than the ground floor, and level surfaces for navigating from the front door to the testing room.

  - How important is it that the study's sponsor be anonymous? If participants should not know who is sponsoring the research because it may bias their responses, it may be better to hold sessions in a location other than your company's offices.

  - Are there aspects of the testing setup (perhaps because of your product) that could only be created in a lab setting? For example, the product is a prototype that isn't portable, a piece of equipment that is difficult to move, or the combination of equipment is novel or specific.

  - Is there special equipment needed for collecting data that would only work in a lab setting? For example, are you collecting eye-tracking data?

- Public relations within your company

  - Are you using this test to demonstrate some idea or practice to people internally?

  - Will you have observers? How many? What positions do they hold in the company? Why are they observing?

  - What will give observers the best experience — being in the room with participants or observing from another location? *If this is your first test, we strongly urge you to locate the observers outside the room where you are testing* because you'll have enough to deal with just getting through sessions with participants.

- Availability of participants

  - Is it essential for participants to be in a lab setting? Why? What might you miss or gain by having the sessions in a lab versus where people normally do the tasks you want to observe?

  - How easy is it for participants to leave their daily routines to take part in your study? For example, Dana had one client whose customers ran small businesses and who typically were the only people in their "offices." Dana's client had decided to have two-hour in-lab sessions during regular work days with these sole proprietors so that her client's management could easily observe. However, getting participants to come in to a lab proved extremely difficult because they would effectively have to shut down their business operations not only for the duration of the sessions but also for the travel time to and from the sessions, which was considerable. The normal incentive of a little cash just wasn't enough to bring in appropriate participants. (There's more on participant incentives and compensation in Chapter 7.)

One more option may be to conduct *remote* usability test sessions. We talk about this in Chapter 13.

Test in Multiple Geographic Locations?

You may feel some pressure from your marketing or market research partners within your company to conduct usability testing in multiple locations. There is a romantic quality to traveling to different markets to conduct tests, and anyone who has traveled knows that people are different in different regions of the world. But do the people in different places find different usability problems from the people who are close by your offices?

The answer is: Occasionally. Some research shows that testing in multiple locations will reveal many of the same problems. As much as 80 percent of usability problems may be the same across locations. But the other 20 percent may be location or context specific and that can make being on location well worthwhile.

So, just as you take into account other factors that make people different from one another, such as age or education level, you probably should look at location as well. Needs of users may be different from city to city (San Franciscans generally don't need snow tires for their cars; drivers in Boston are much more likely to use them). Terminology may be different from region to region ("purse" or "pocketbook"? "pop" or "soda"?). Motivations and experiences will be different, too, possibly from floor to floor inside a corporation (the mail room versus "mahogany row"). These things and others make up what we'll call the user's "context."

When considering whether to test in multiple locations or in a location outside your immediate area, start by thinking about the user's context (as well as budget and time availability). If the context of one type of users is significantly different from the context of another type of users in a way that will impact your product, you should try to go into those different contexts to test. The context might be geographical (for example, weather-driven buying decisions in the south versus the north) or hierarchical (for example, administrative assistants versus directors of a company) or both (or something else).

Consider testing in locations other than the one you might normally test in when:

■ The location is dominated by one type of business or culture (Microsoft in Seattle; government workers in the Washington, DC area; very high concentrations of Arab Americans in Dearborn, Michigan).

■ The experiences, exposure, or attitudes of local people is different from the target audience.

■ Locals won't use the product you're testing.

What about international users? They *are* vastly different from each other. Tokyo is very different from San Francisco or Bonn or Beijing. In this case, you're encouraged if at all possible to test in the appropriate countries, defined as a country where your product anticipates a significant market (keeping in mind the guidelines above for international locations, as well). Of course, this presupposes that your budget can absorb the cost. In the absence of testing on location internationally, you can get some useful data by:

■ Remote usability testing, that is, by listening to people on the phone while they use your product. If the product is software or a web site, you can easily set up the session to see what is happening on the participant's computer screen as well.

■ Including participants in your study who are recently arrived foreign nationals. Often you can find participants who have been in your country a few weeks or months through temporary or placement agencies.

  Though they are in your country — and may have different attitudes and motivations from people who stayed in their home country — they won't have assimilated yet, so you can gain insights because of the lingering bits of context and culture that they have carried with them to their new location.

If you can't go to other countries because of budget or other constraints, there are other ways to get some data about what makes people from different countries different. Try remote testing, as described above, or look at competitive products or designs that may be regional or location specific. Consider working through the salespeople or other customer-facing groups at your company, such as call centers, especially if the call center keeps a database of issues searchable by geography.

In a nutshell then, with the exception of international markets, testing in multiple geographic locations must be carefully considered before making the additional investment. Most often, it's driven by superficial factors such as an opportunity to visit mom in Peoria or as a travel perk for a hard-working development or marketing team. (We have to admit that neither author has vehemently resisted our clients' the decision by our clients to test in exotic locations, regardless of scientific relevance.)

The 80 percent rule, which states that most usability problems are the same across locations, means that most of the time, if you only test locally, that's just fine. So, if you do not have budget to conduct testing in more than one location, you can feel reasonably confident about only testing locally or in one location. You can then look at other creative ways to get feedback about location differences.

Arranging Sessions at a User's Site

Taking your usability test on the road requires some special planning because the logistics are not trivial. The steps to planning are shown in Figure 6-1. If you are doing testing in the user's workplace, you must get permission of the management there to do the testing (as well as for installing anything on their systems, if that is necessary). Once you do that, you may be able to get help with recruiting participants from the manager who gave you permission. Exercise caution with this approach, however, keeping in mind that the manager probably will be biased in her selections. There may be company policies about whether participants can take part in a test during the regular workday and whether they can accept honoraria, incentives, or compensation for the time they spend with you.

Next, you must get permission from the participant, make an appointment, and ensure that the participant understands the purpose and format for the session. You should have a short conversation with the participant by phone before you visit the person to confirm the appointment, explain the study, allay any fears she might have, and answer any questions. Be sure to tell the participant generally what you will be doing during the session, whether there will be others with you, and whatever else you might need at the participant's location to make the session worthwhile for both you and the participant. Remember that you are a stranger entering this person's personal space, whether in a workplace or a home. For that reason, you should be organized

---

When testing at the participant's workspace: Planning the sessions

- Get permission from management (if appropriate) and the participant
- Make appointments with the participants
- Confirm appointments by phone and letter or email
- Send instructions and non-disclosure forms ahead, if at all possible
- Get addresses, get directions, and if needed, get information about parking
- If you're testing software or a web site from a laptop that you are supplying, remember to install it and any data capturing software ahead of time
- If you will have an assistant accompany you, assign him or her specific responsibilities, such as setting up the video and audio equipment, notetaking, etc.

Figure 6-1 Planning a session at a participant's workspace

When testing at the participant's workspace: What to take with you

- Scripts, forms, and questionnaires
- Business cards
- Identification
- Audio recorder, recording media, batteries, power cords
- Video recorder, recording media, batteries, power cords
- Tripod
- Extension cord
- Pens and some hard surface to write on such as a clip board
- Prototype, laptop, or link to what is being tested
- At least one observer/note taker, especially if you're going into someone's home

Figure 6-2 What to take with you to a participant's workspace

and pack everything you need and have it with you. Figure 6-2 provides a list of the essentials.

When you arrive at the place where you will observe the participant using the product you're testing, introduce anyone who is with you, ask to be shown to the place where the participant would normally use what is being tested, and quickly get set up to conduct the session and collect data.

If you are going to test software or a web site at a participant's site, you may want to do it from a laptop that you control. This way, you can load the software or web site just the way you would like to test it, and it will be ready to go as soon as everyone settles into their places for the session. Figure 6-3 gives some tips to consider when doing testing in the field.

When testing at the participant's workspace: In-session tips

- Position yourself so you can see what the participant is doing without being in the participant's main field of vision.
- Focus the video camera over the participant's shoulder onto the object being tested, making the angle wide enough to capture the participant's hands (or however they interact with the product).
- Position the main observer/note taker behind you and the participant, if possible.
- Consider not taking notes yourself. Either assign an observer to take notes or write down your notes and impressions after the session (or both). If you do decide to take notes during the session, expert field researchers strongly recommend that you not take notes by typing into a computer as some participants may feel intimidated.
- If you're doing multiple sessions in one day, leave as much of your equipment put together between appointments as possible. Leave the camera on the tripod and the power cord plugged in. This will make setting up when you get to the location that much quicker.
- Build in a cue in the session introduction script to remind yourself to start the recordings or assign this to the person accompanying you to the tests.
- Be respectful of the person's workspace or home.
- Arrive and leave on time.
- When the session is done, check to make sure you have collected all of your equipment and belongings.
- In addition to any honorarium given to the participant before you leave, send a personal thank-you note by regular post.

Figure 6-3 In-session tips

Minimalist Portable Test Lab

The portable lab setup has no room or rooms designated for testing. Rather, the testing equipment, such as cameras and PCs, is carted around to different available locations. This is a very cost-effective way to begin a usability testing program if management has neither the inclination nor space to dedicate a permanent location for holding the tests. Eventually, some of the same equipment and data gathering software can be utilized when a permanent "home" is acquired.

In this setup, you load software (such as Camtasia or Morae from TechSmith) on a laptop that will capture a video image of what is happening on the computer screen during the session. We find that capturing this video data is easy to do and can be very useful. You may also want to focus the video on the participant's hands or face. In this case, you would need a separate way to record the video, such as a webcam or a small video camera that is mounted on a tripod. See the next sidebar for a checklist for usability testing on site.

Advantages

- **You get to see the user's context.** The setting should reflect where real work is done with the product, complete with realistic environmental issues such as space, light, noise, interruptions, and so on.
- **It makes it easier typically for participants to take part.**
- **This is a very cost-effective solution** because no costs are incurred for a physical location.
- **Because the equipment is portable, you can bring the test to the field**, either renting space near existing customers, such as a hotel conference room or a company sales office or going to people's homes.
- **The PC and cameras need not be dedicated to the portable usability lab.** They could be part of your normal working desktop arrangement.

Disadvantages

- **Planning and logistics can be complex compared to doing all the testing in one place.**
- **Field sessions can take more time** for the moderator and observers because you have to find your way to the participant's location, find parking, conduct the session, and either travel on to the next session or back to the office.
- **There may be limited space for observers.**

- **There may be uncomfortable (pets, traffic) or inconvenient (lack of space, no surfaces to work from) environmental aspects.** These factors can take away from the efficiency of the test or that simply don't offer any particular illumination on the performance of tasks.

- **Not having a permanent space means having to settle for whatever space is available.** This can lend a tentative air to the discipline of testing altogether.

- **If you will be doing a lot of testing, moving around delicate equipment can shorten the lifespan of that equipment.** In addition, you should retest the equipment before each test to ensure that it works.

- **There is the possibility that on-site issues could confuse or complicate your study or introduce artifacts that you'll have to handle carefully in your data analysis.**

Setting up a Permanent or Fixed Test Lab

Here we describe different testing setups/environments for office settings. Each setup has advantages and disadvantages, and each lends itself to a particular style or philosophy of testing, as well as to the degree of testing sophistication. Because this is a book for "beginners," we will recommend what we feel is the setup that provides the best value (e.g., objectives vs. cost) for a start-up testing enterprise.

Simple Single-Room Setup

The simple single-room setup, shown in Figure 6-4, is the most basic type of testing setup, both in terms of resources and the amount of space required. It represents the minimum environment required for testing that can accommodate observers, essentially a quiet secluded room. Within the room, the test moderator is located a few feet from the participant at about a 45-degree angle. As you can see from Figure 6-1, the idea is for the test moderator to be close but *not too close*. It is important to remain within the peripheral vision of the participant, so that the participant can sense where you are at all times, but not so close that your presence is distracting or anxiety-provoking.

The main concern with this type of positioning is that the test moderator might inadvertently bias the participant through subtle (or not so subtle) nonverbal cues. However, if such biasing can be minimized, there are real advantages to being close to the participant, and for very interactive testing, such as exploratory testing, this degree of intimacy is required.

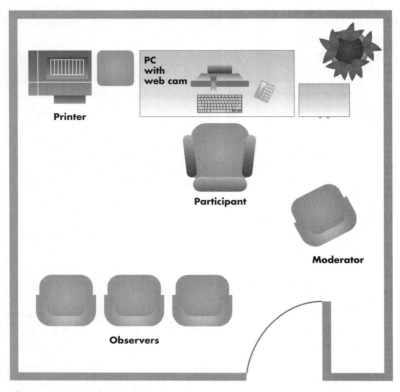

Figure 6-4 Simple single-room setup

We are assuming that you will use a small room. Some practitioners use large rooms with this setup however, so as to accommodate large numbers of observers. See the section "Large Single-Room Setup" later in this chapter concerning this setup.

Advantages

- **The test moderator has an excellent sense of what is going on with the participant.** Not only can you read the typical verbal cues, but you have a much better sense of the participant's nonverbal cues and mannerisms, such as a slight frown or a raising of the eyebrows. You can see exactly what the participant is doing down to small mannerisms and subtle changes in body language.

- **During early phase exploratory tests (as we described in Chapter 3), where much interaction is desired to interrogate the participant during the test, this position accentuates a sense of teamwork.** At this early stage of the product lifecycle, the participant is almost a partner who is helping to design the product or documentation. In fact, during an exploratory test, you and the participant are right next to each other.

■ **For difficult tests, where the participant has to struggle with the material, it enables you to encourage and overcome the participant's self-consciousness.** The participant does not feel nearly as alone or "on the hot seat," as he or she would feel without you present in the test room. It is also more natural on the part of the participant to think aloud when the test moderator is in the test room.

■ **Observers may be invited by the test moderator to ask follow up questions or to write their questions down and pass them to the moderator for later asking.**

Disadvantages

■ **The test moderator's behavior can affect the behavior of the participant.** If you are not mindful of your speech, mannerisms, and so on, you will inadvertently and subtly react to what the participant is doing. Even if you do not make any outward remarks, the participant may pick up a sigh or a shift in your posture in response to what he or she is doing. That in turn can cause the participant to veer off from the direction in which he or she was going or look to another page. It is especially crucial to avoid making notes when it appears the participant has finished a task. This can cue the participant that he or she has finished a task successfully even if the participant is not sure. Likewise, your writing or typing may suggest to the participant that he has done something incorrectly. Even if this is true, you do not want to telegraph that.

■ **There is very limited space for observers.** Obviously, the number of observers who can view the session is dictated by the size of the room. If the room is really small, you probably would want to exclude observers entirely or include only one. It is never a good idea to crowd many observers around a single participant, as it can be very intimidating. Also, it is much harder for you as the test moderator to control the behavior of observers when they are so close to the proceedings. See Chapter 8 for guidelines for observers.

If you would like to have many observers — 5 to 30 — see the section "Large Single-Room Setup."

Modified Single-Room Setup

This setup (Figure 6-5) enables you to use a room large enough to position yourself at a workstation behind or to the side of the participant without

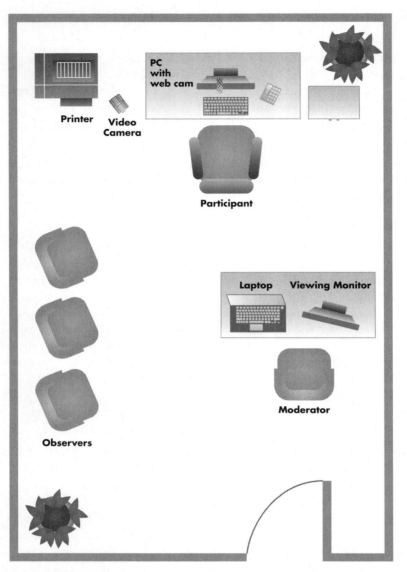

Figure 6-5 Modified single-room setup

impinging on the participant's "space." Positioned at a desk outside of the line of sight of the participant, you are free to use a software data collection program running on a desktop computer. You view the proceedings on the participant's screen via a second computer monitor on your desk. You view the participant's face on the second viewing monitor on the moderator's desk. As with the previous setup, the accommodation of additional observers is dictated by the size of the room.

This is not our favorite setup, but if you are a moderator with a little experience and you are working alone without a note taker, this arrangement can be quite workable.

Advantages

- **The test moderator is more free to move about, take notes, use data logging software while the test is going on, and yet is still within visual proximity of the participant.** Being somewhat removed from the participant, you need not be as concerned about controlling body language, mannerisms, and so forth. In addition, you may use a computer without distracting the participant.

- **The participant does not have a complete sense of isolation, because the participant is still in the room with the test moderator.**

- **This setup is also more likely to encourage the participant to think aloud, than if left alone in the test room.**

Disadvantages

- **Loss of proximity to the participant limits what the test moderator can see directly of the proceedings.** It is possible to miss subtle behaviors. It is crucial to have a good angle via the video camera on what the participant is seeing and doing, because you may be blocked from seeing directly.

- **Because the test moderator is not within the participant's peripheral vision, if the test moderator is directly behind the participant and within 10 feet or so, the test moderator could make the participant feel very uneasy and overly self-conscious.** The guideline here is to remember when you are behind the participant but within ten feet, you must stay within the participant's peripheral vision. Farther back than approximately ten feet should not cause any discomfort to the participant.

- **As with the simple single-room setup, there is limited space for observers.**

- **If the participant can hear you typing, he or she may feel intimidated or may assume that he or she is doing things wrong that you are recording.**

Large Single-Room Setup

Similar to the setup found in the section "Simple Single-Room Setup," the moderator and participant are situated near each other (see Figure 6-6). In this case, though, by using a much larger room — such as a training room — you can invite many more observers to each session. (Some usability practitioners

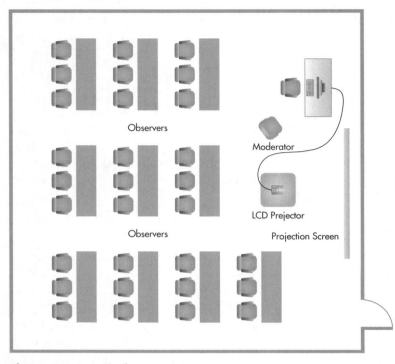

Figure 6-6 Large single-room setup

routinely have up to 30 observers per session.) Here, the participant and moderator are in front of the room. Both wear microphones so that the observers can hear without strain. The image of the participant's screen is projected onto the wall above the participant or above the observers, who could even be facing *away* from the participant.

Advantages

- All the advantages of the simple single-room setup also apply to this one.
- It accommodates a large number of observers.
- Because so many observers can attend, debriefings between or after sessions can be more useful than when a smaller number attend.
- You may not have to record sessions because everyone who wants to observe can.
- With present, engaged observers, you can gather notes and insights from them more easily.

Disadvantages

- It takes training and practice to manage a large number of observers.

- The moderator must be steadfast in enforcing proper behavior of observers to prevent them from biasing the test, which can be distracting to the moderator.

- This setup requires additional equipment: microphones and a projector.

- The observers probably will not be able to see the participant's subtle behaviors or facial expressions.

Electronic Observation Room Setup

The electronic observation room setup (see Figure 6-7) enables the observers to be physically separated from the testing activities. From a separate observation room, they can watch but are not set up to communicate directly with the test moderator.

The signal from the video camera(s) as well as the screen image, if the test involves software, web sites, or web-based applications, are both directed to video monitor(s) in the observation room. The room could be in a completely different part of the building or adjacent to the testing area.

When the testing area is adjacent to the observation room, you typically use speaker phones dialed into each other to provide observers with audio for the session.

Communication between the test moderator and observers can occur face to face or via notes during breaks or at the end of sessions, or by instant messaging (if you are taking notes on a computer) during sessions. If you use Morae from TechSmith and all of your observers are on the same local area network (LAN) as the testing machine, observers can use one module of Morae to see and hear a feed from the testing room from wherever they are. Likewise, you can set up WebEx, NetMeeting, or GoToMeeting under which to run the participant's session so that others outside the immediate area can "observe" remotely.

Advantages

- **All the advantages of the simple single-room setup also apply to this setup.**

- **Observers get to view the test as much as they like without having to worry about interfering.** They are free to come and go as they please without distracting anyone. This is especially crucial for very lengthy tests, where observers may be interested only in certain portions or certain types of participants. More important, they are able to talk among themselves, discussing test observations.

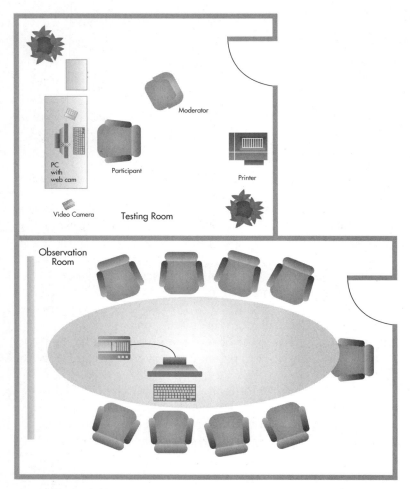

Figure 6-7 Electronic observation room setup

Disadvantages

- As with the simple single-room setup, the test moderator's behavior can adversely affect the test.

- Unless you have a permanent setup, you will need to tie up two conference rooms or office spaces for up to a week.

Classic Testing Laboratory Setup

This setup (see Figure 6-8) consists of one room designated as the testing room and a second room designated as an observation and control room. The only individual inside the testing room is the participant. All other test personnel, including the test moderator, observers, camera operator, and so forth are stationed inside the control room viewing the proceedings through a one-way mirror. All communication between the test moderator and participant occurs

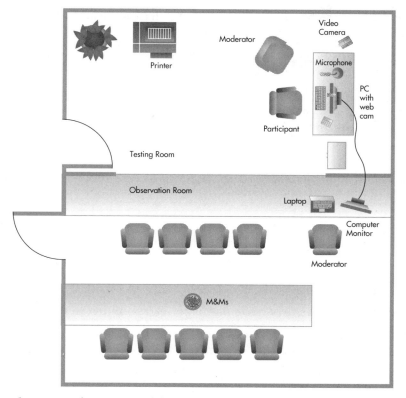

Figure 6-8 Classic testing laboratory setup

through an intercom and speaker arrangement, and, in the more elaborate laboratories, the test is extensively monitored with multiple video cameras, audio tape recorders, data loggers, and other modern electronic equipment. However, as an alternative, depending on the type of test, the test moderator could also be in the test room with the participant.

This setup requires a large capital outlay and commitment to testing by management. However, if you are interested in trying out such a setup for a test that you are conducting, you may do so for a modest rental fee. Simply locate a lab facility (there are many throughout the country; www.Quirks.com has a directory of such facilities). Some facilities do none of their own research but only make the space and equipment available for a per diem rate. Research firms, market researchers, universities, and other corporations may have lab spaces that you can rent. Most come with a receptionist and other niceties. Many also offer participant recruiting.

Advantages

- **It allows unparalleled unobtrusive data collection.** Because the test moderator is not in the room, this eliminates almost entirely any possible biasing effects due to inadvertent nonverbal communication or mannerisms.

- **Being in a (nearly) soundproof room, the testing team and observers can easily communicate among themselves about the proceedings and discuss possible product improvements.**

- **This environment can accommodate many observers (typically 4 to 12) viewing the test at one time.**

Disadvantages

- **Depending on the skill of the testing staff, the control room setup can create a very impersonal environment.** This is sometimes referred to as the "guinea pig" syndrome, with the participant feeling overly self-conscious during the test. (This effect can be exacerbated by the type of intercom system used, some of which make the test moderator's instructions sound like the "voice of God.") This self-consciousness is worse for less sophisticated (in terms of exposure to high-tech equipment) participants who are insecure about their abilities. The test moderator may need to mitigate the effects of this setup by staying in the room with a less sophisticated participant.

- **Unless you have ideal camera placements, you may not be able to see exactly what the participant is viewing or experiencing.** For example, sometimes you may not be able to tell where in a document or on a screen a participant is looking unless there is a dedicated and well-placed camera (or you are employing eye-tracking equipment). To compensate, you may need to use a "thinking aloud" protocol, which may not fit in with your test design.

- **For exploratory tests, the control room setup may offer little advantage to moderating the test, because you will need to be next to the participant in any case.** However, for observers, it is still superior to the other types of setups.

- **Observers may begin redesigning while chatting in the observation room without considering all of the data and observations.**

Recommended Testing Environment: Minimalist Portable Lab

The setup in the section "Minimalist Portable Lab Setup" is the setup we recommend for organizations just beginning to test and for those with limited resources. It gives for the best tradeoff of test moderator access to the participants, accommodation of observers, and cost (because there is nothing in the way of physical plant required). While the setup doesn't specifically accommodate viewing of a test by observers, it is extremely flexible in that you can use it in any combination of room (or remote) configurations. Management will look favorably on such a situation, if it makes more efficient use of existing facilities.

Eventually, if your organization adopts a full-scale testing program, you will want to switch to a dedicated lab similar to the classic testing laboratory setup shown in Figure 6-8.

Gather and Check Equipment, Artifacts, and Tools

No matter the location of the test, there are basic articles of equipment, tools and materials that you will need to gather and check before you can do your dry run or pilot session.

Basic Equipment, Tools, and Props

In addition, there may be items that are particular to a test that you must ensure are properly prepared. The following table gives a list of basic equipment, forms, and note-taking tools as well as artifacts and props.

Basic equipment	PC or laptop Recording software Web or video camera
Forms and note-taking tools	Recording waivers Nondisclosure forms (if appropriate) Consent forms Questionnaires Summary of participant characteristics Session script Scenarios for participant Instructions for observers Session schedules Receipt forms for honorarium
Artifacts, props, and so on	Prototype or what you are testing Account numbers User IDs and passwords Bogus data or other items to make the session realistic (for example, a cell phone with messages, a camera with images to download)

Gathering Biometric Data

At the writing of this edition, equipment traditionally used in other types of experiments to gather data from participants about how their bodies respond to stimuli is being incorporated in some types of usability testing. Eye-tracking is very popular with companies concerned with where to place advertisements on their web pages. Heart rates, blood oxygen levels, and other measures are interesting to your business partners in advertising or sales.

This equipment is still fairly expensive, and the output is difficult to interpret. As market and user research continue to evolve, we expect that the prices for equipment will come down and researchers will better understand when and why to collect this biometric data and what is meaningful and useful about it.

Identify Co-Researchers, Assistants, and Observers

You may be the lone person working on usability testing, at least at first, but that does not mean you should do everything by yourself. Ask for help, get others involved by giving them specific jobs during the test sessions.

Data Gatherer/Note Taker

A data gatherer takes notes or classifies the expected critical activities and events of a test into coded categories. For example, if the participant is expected to access four screens during a test, each screen could be categorized with a different letter: A, B, C, or D. During the test, when the participant accesses a particular screen, page or module, the data gatherer need only record a letter for that action. At the same time, the data gatherer could also note the time in order to cross-reference with the video or audio recording, unless he or she is using data logging software that is synchronized with the video recording.

Before the test, the person who designs the test and the data gatherer develop appropriate data gathering tools or devices. You can use simple Word files for entering long-hand notes that include pick lists that anticipate issues or cover specific data you want to collect. Or you can set up more elaborate data gathering tools in Excel, a database program, or some other logging application.

If you are recording sessions using Morae or other similar tools, you can configure the software to collect some types of data for you automatically.

Timekeeper

Timekeepers are responsible for (you guessed it) keeping track of the beginning, ending, and elapsed time of test activities. Typically, the timing of each task will be recorded separately. This can be done in real time as the test proceeds or after the fact by reviewing each video recording and noting the times; however, this is more time-consuming. We recommend that the test moderator *not* be the one who tracks the timings as it is very labor intensive and distracts one from capturing the *what* and *why* of the participant's activities.

Product/Technical Expert(s)

This is one or more individuals who know the technical aspects of the product being tested. Their role is to ensure that the product does not malfunction during the test. For example, if a system crashes and jeopardizes the test, someone needs to be available to restore it or provide a working backup. This is crucial if you are testing at an early stage of development when the product is temperamental and "buggy." If the prototype or product you are testing is unstable, you should have at least one product expert available at every test session to troubleshoot. If there is a group of people on the development team who can take on this role, it makes sense to coordinate their time so at least one is always present.

Additional Testing Roles

Additional testing roles will depend on the nature of the test. One or more people might be needed to simulate different roles during the test, as part of the test design. You might need someone to staff a hotline in order to simulate "help" calls during the test. Or, you might need someone to send a text message to a cell phone or to mimic a repair person sent out by the company.

Test Observers

A test observer is not particularly a testing role per se. Rather, it refers to anyone else who attends a test, whether members of the development team, members of other projects, managers, or even members of other companies who are developing products that interact with yours. While not strictly a testing role, observation of the test by a variety of people helps the product and the organization immensely. The product benefits because the people responsible for product development get direct feedback from representative users. In addition, testing often brings a positive change in perspective toward user-centered design, which can help the development of future products. All development team members should be encouraged to attend as many test sessions as possible.

Find and Select Participants

The selection and acquisition of participants whose background and abilities are representative of your product's intended user is a crucial element of the testing process. After all, your test results will only be valid if the people who participate are typical users of the product, or as close to that criterion as possible. If you test with the "wrong" people, it does not matter how much effort you put into the rest of the test preparation. Your results will be questionable and of limited value.

Selecting participants involves identifying and describing the relevant behavior, skills, and knowledge of the person(s) who will use your product. This description is known as the *user profile* of the target audience and should have been developed in the early stages of the product development. Then, once that has been determined, you must ascertain the most effective way to acquire people from this target audience to serve as participants within your constraints of time, money, resources, and so on.

Characterize Users

Now your first thought might be that the information describing the user profile should already exist and be written down somewhere within your organization, because the design and makeup of any product is *supposed to be* predicated on knowing the end user. While this is so in theory, experience shows that this information is rarely collected systematically or written down. Or, if it is written down, it does not quite make it to the desks of the design team, the people who really need it. Or, if it makes it to the desks of the design team, they either pay it little mind or have a distorted version of the information.

To test this premise in your own organization, go around and ask three or four different staff members in the product team to describe users of the product they are working on. Most likely, you will receive three or four very plausible, but very different, descriptions of the end user. Or, you will get a vague answer such as "small business owners" or "accountants." This simply means you will have to dig further to find the correct, more detailed information that will enable you to bring in a reasonable group of the right end users.

It is just this lack of a clear delineation of the characteristics of the end user that contributes to usability deficiencies of products in the first place. Because product team members do not know or do not agree on the characteristics of the end user, it is difficult for them to develop a consistent, well-designed product that meets the end user's needs. Testing just happens to be one of the first activities that makes this lack of a clear end user characterization so painfully obvious.

Let's begin by discussing how to document the user profile of the target audience — a description of the behaviors, expertise levels, knowledge, demographic information, and other relevant factors required of the people who will be using your product. The profile should reflect behaviors and expertise that are related to the product you are testing.

Visualize the Test Participant

The specific characteristics that make up the user profile will of course depend on your product and the tasks you want participants to perform in the test. Tie the main objective of your test to the user profile. Start by visualizing and describing the person you want to be in the testing room with you. This is a simple narrative sentence or short paragraph, such as this:

> *We want to find out where in the process of booking a room at one of our hotels travelers meet obstacles to completing reservations* [the test objective]. *The user of our web site reservation system travels at least a few times a year and stays in a hotel each time. He or she typically books his or her own travel online, especially leisure travel. He or she may belong to hotel rewards programs.*

While this is rather general, you can probably conjure up the image of someone who might fit this description. That's exactly the idea: See a person rather than a list of qualifications. Now, on to expanding your understanding of the target audience and documenting it.

Differentiate between Purchaser and End User

When determining the user profile, make sure to differentiate between the purchaser or buyer of the product and the actual end user. Sometimes the user profile is slanted toward the person who makes the buying decision but who knows very little about the problems that the end users face. You probably would not want to bring in "purchasers" to test the product; that will give you a very slanted view of how the product is performing.

Another potential pitfall is the fact that the end user of the product and the end user of the documentation may differ. This is especially true for large systems being developed for internal end users, where only one or two people, such as the system administrator, will receive documentation. The rest of the end users will be left to their own devices or will have to ask specifically for the documentation.

Look for Information about Users

We assume that there is no established user profile (a written set of character-istics) or set of profiles in place as you begin to think about usability testing. So, where shall you look for information to develop a detailed user profile? Let's discuss some of the potential sources of this type of information in your organization. Once you and your team agree on a profile or two or three, then you can determine who among those should be included as participants in the usability test. The following sections list some typical places and people from whom to ascertain the user profile. Keep in mind that the format or content of the information you get may not make an obvious user profile. You may have to apply some analysis and critical thinking to establish those characteristics that make up realistic human traits and behavior.

If you can, interview these sources yourself rather than through a third party, so that you can probe and elicit the type of information you need. If they do not have the information you require, you may be forced to acquire that information directly from the end user, via surveys and phone calls. In fact, a clear depiction and understanding of the user is so crucial that even if you have that information, you may *still* want to verify it with phone calls or visits to user workplaces or by conducting a quick survey.

Requirements and Specification Documents

There are several documents created in the early stages of product develop-ment that may be useful in beginning to generate a user profile: the functional specification, business requirements document, design specification, or use cases.

- The functional specification or product requirements document is the blueprint for the product. It describes the product's intended function-ality, as well as the tasks that the end user will perform. Most functional specifications include a comprehensive description of the intended user population (if an internal product) or market (if an external product) for the product, which is the basis for your user profile.

- If all you find in the functional specification is specifications for functionality, you may find market segment information in a business requirements document (often referred to as a BRD). The BRD outlines the business case for the product or its planned upgrade, including information about whom the product is targeting and why.

- A design specification typically describes the system architecture for supporting a software product or web site but may include end-user characteristics as part of the assumptions and dependencies it covers.

- Use cases typically include information about end users as "actors" — someone who interacts with part of the proposed system. The actor wants to achieve some goal, so you may learn useful things about tasks that the team envisions users doing.

Structured Analyses or Marketing Studies

Developers, technical writers, or human factors specialists may have already completed task analyses or similar analyses prior to any design work. These usually include the skill and knowledge set required to use the product effectively. In larger corporations, there is almost sure to have been a marketing study conducted for each unique product, which has a similar breakdown.

Product Manager (R&D)

If you are unable to get your hands on specific documents, analyses, or reports, there are certain individuals who should be able to help determine the user profile. Among them is the product manager who should have his or her finger on the pulse of the marketplace and should have a clear understanding of the end users for whom the product is intended. The product manager may also have access to reports and surveys that describe the user profile in detail or she may be able to describe example customers whom she has met.

Product Manager (Marketing)

Marketing may have done some in-depth analyses that have not yet been distributed to the design team. These could be the results of surveys or focus groups similar to the ones to which the product manager has access. Very often all the information you need is contained in reports of this type but in a form that is not all that accessible. (This is why it often goes unused. The design team has more than enough to do without reading through a long report.) You may have to distill much of the information into a more concise form.

If you do end up condensing this information, make it available to the development team for its design work, as well as using it for setting up the usability tests. Having a simple one-page narrative depiction (like the sample persona in Figure 7-3) of the end user on the desk of every designer and developer would be a boon to product development.

Competitive Benchmarking and Analysis Group

Some organizations assign a group (or an individual) to do extensive benchmarking of their own and competitor's products. Consequently, they will have a good handle on not only who is using their product but who is using their competitor's products as well. This can be a wonderful source of information for establishing the user profile.

Define the Criteria for Each User Group

When classifying a group of users (and therefore, participants for your usability test), it is important to be crystal clear about the meaning of such terms as "novice," "expert," and so forth. Often these terms are bandied about so indiscriminately that they are useless. In actuality, unless you define these categories you almost assuredly are *not* speaking of the same thing. Novice can mean many things to many different people, and it is important that you take responsibility for translating buzzwords into operational definitions. Therefore, when talking to the people who supply you with information about the end user, beware of words such as "novice" and "expert" unless you define them.

An operational definition should quantify a user's experience in terms of some objective reference point such as complexity of typical tasks and the frequency with which a specific task is performed.

Define Expertise

It is tempting to use time and frequencies as a measure of expertise. While these are measures of experience, they do not always describe expertise. For example, in one study Dana ran, she looked for people with a range of experience using the web. The original screening criteria looked at the average amount of time spent on the web over a week and how long the participant had been using the web overall. Though Dana expected that someone who had been using the web for a few years for 60 hours per week would be an expert web user, this was not the case. One notable participant did nothing on the web but play four specific games, getting to each from shortcut icons set up for her by her grandson. She didn't know how to use a web browser at all.

Dana changed the operational definition of "novice" and "expert" for that usability test to include knowledge of using a web browser and evidence of the person doing a range of complex tasks on the web. This matrix of expertise (shown in Figure 7-1) also avoided the possible mismatch of expectations when participants are asked to rate their own expertise.

It's more accurate to use criteria that are measurable, objective "facts" rather than subjective self-classifications on the part of potential end users. A self-classification has the end user rate his or her own abilities and skill level, which is more subject to misinterpretation and wide variance.

For example, when attempting to classify a group of end users as "novice," before using them in a usability test, do not simply accept their own rating of themselves as "novice," "expert," and so on. Instead, find out by using a method something like the matrix in Figure 7-1. Although it still relies on participants reporting what they remember doing, at least it does gather more objective data about what they have done. This latter method has the advantage of using criteria on which everyone can readily agree. The team can determine a "score" for how each combination of tasks and frequencies defines different levels of expertise. For example, someone who marked all the tasks in the "Every week" row would likely be an expert user of the Internet. Likewise, someone who marked all of the tasks in the "Never" row probably would not qualify for most usability tests of web sites (depending on the objectives and research questions). People marking boxes between those extremes then become defined as "novice" or "intermediate," again,

When	Research health information such as conditions, treatments, or drugs at websites	Take part in online auctions	Play games alone or with others on websites	Pay bills through a web site	Totals
Never (0)					(number of Xs * 0)
Once per month (1)					(number of Xs * 1)
Once per week (2)					(number of Xs * 2)
Daily (3)					(number of Xs * 3)
Several times a day (4)					(number of Xs * 4)
					(total Xs * point value in each row)

Figure 7-1 Sample matrix for defining web expertise

depending on the objectives of the test. With self-rating, however, you run the risk of each end user having different interpretations of what is meant by such terms as novice or expert. You are dependent on the user's self-image to guide the classification.

Specify Requirements and Classifiers for Selection

Having visualized whom you want to be your test participant, gathered data from internal sources about the target audience, and defined criteria for the groups, now try to think in terms of *requirements* and *classifiers* as you flesh out a user profile. Requirements describe what participants must come into the session knowing already. Classifiers help you put study participants into categories (or groups) that may explain some effects you see in the test.

To make the concept of a user profile or user characterization more concrete, you can take the traveler profile a bit further than the original visualization. In this test, a participant must:

- **Stay at a hotel a few times a year:**   We want people who would normally stay in a hotel rather than with friends or family or at a hostel, or rather than a vacation home or time-share.

- **Book some travel and accommodations online:**   Because this is an online reservation system, we want people who are familiar and comfortable with doing searches and credit card transactions on the web.

These are requirements. There's a temptation to get more specific. What kinds of hotels do they stay in? How long are their stays? Which web sites do they use to make reservations through? But none of that really matters for selecting participants for this test. You can find out those interesting things later from a background questionnaire or in the session. Doing so may give you some context for analyzing the data from the test, but knowing these things ahead of time will not help you know why participants performed the way they did with your reservation system. It may help to be more specific in the timeliness of the requirements — that is, participants should have done these things recently.

For a company's hypothetical online hotel reservation system, there are many possible audiences for the web site: business travelers, leisure travelers (who could be the same people as the business travelers), administrative assistants who book travel for others, spouses of travelers, hotel employees, rewards program members, meeting or event planners, and so on. To keep this test (and our example) simple, let's say that you want to concentrate on two user groups to see if there are differences in how successful they are with the reservations system: people who are members of your rewards program and people who are not. These are classifiers.

This breakdown has implications for the test design and implications for finding participants. You know that most users of the web site reservations system are rewards members. Should you then make sure that most of the participants are rewards members? It depends on the business requirements and the goals of the test. Is it the goal of the test to make the site easier to use for rewards members or for all users? Do you want to compare error rates or other measures between the two types of users? People who are rewards members may indeed use the site more frequently than non-members, giving them many more opportunities to learn its quirks and to invent their own workarounds for any hindrances. These people could reveal interesting findings that may suggest to the design team things they could do to improve the interface. But if one of the business goals is to attract more people to the site — people who are not rewards members — certainly you want a significant number of non-members to take part in your test.

Document the User Profile

You have gathered information about target users from various parts of your company. Then you interpreted that information to develop requirements and classifiers for the usability test. Having a written profile of the target audience (either supplied to you or formed by your own research) should help you, the designers, and the developers throughout the development of the product. Such a snapshot is not only beneficial for designing a usability test but also helps the team to visualize the person for whom they are designing the product, another benefit of doing this type of analysis. We use the term *person* in the singular, simply because developers are more likely to have one person in mind when they are designing, rather than many different types of people. Unfortunately, the person they visualize, in lieu of real data, is often himself or herself, even though the developers may not even remotely reflect an actual end user. So, an accurate picture of the user can be a real boon to the design process because it helps to keep the designers and developers on track. Figure 7-2 shows a demographic profile for the hotel reservation system web site. This is the type of data you may get from marketing, research and development, or product managers. Figure 7-3 shows an example narrative persona for an archetypical user of the site. Someone in human factors, technical communication, or interface design or even marketing may have created something like it. The user profile you develop may end up being a combination of these and other types of information. If you are using personas, you should develop one for each distinct user group that typifies an aggregate of several representative individuals.

Demographic Characteristic	% of Target
Rewards membership	
platinum & elite members	50%
silver & gold members	20%
non–members	30%
Travel frequency	
infrequently: 1–5 trips per year	25%
moderately often: 6–12 trips per year	40%
very often: 13 or more trips per year	35%
Types of travel	
mostly business	75%
mostly leisure	25%
Age	
21–30	25%
31–40	25%
41–50	25%
51–60	25%
Gender	
female	45%
male	55%

Figure 7-2 Example demographic profile for target market of a hotel reservation web site

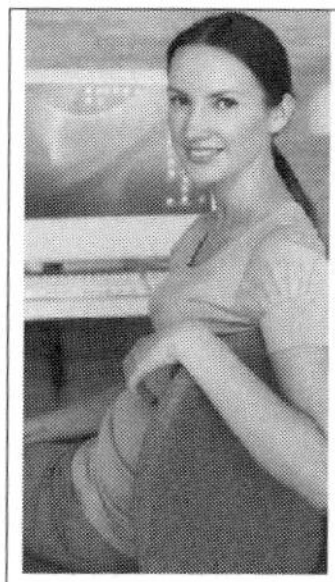

Business–Trip Beth

- Beth is a middle-level manager in a large company. She's about 45 years old and married.
- She goes on several business trips per year. Two or three are to professional conferences, three or four more are large business meetings, a few more are client site visits.
- Her hotel must have Internet access. It must be close to the site of the meeting she's going to. Free breakfast is nice. She wants to be able to work out while she's on the road, too, so she looks for a pool or a fitness center.
- She looks for a positive but predictable experience at her hotel, so consistency of service across properties from city to city is important.
- Beth doesn't care so much about the price of the hotel because her company is paying—instead the hotel should be comfortable, convenient, and close to where she's going.

Figure 7-3 Example of a brief persona for one audience in the target market of a hotel reservation web site

Divide the User Profile into Distinct Categories

The user profile describes the range of skills, behaviors, and experience that make up the entire universe of target end users. Every end user should fall somewhere within that spectrum. However, you are not interested in individuals alone. Instead, you should identify entire groups of end users who share many of the same characteristics on the user profile. These groups, sometimes identified by similar occupations or job titles but often as roles (for example, "frequent traveler," "club member," "voter," or even "patient," "parent," "vendor," or "client"), will use the product and its support materials in different ways and for different purposes. This is also where your classifiers come in. Use those to help you group users into categories.

It is important that you understand the user profile for each target audience. For example, the hotel reservations web site previously mentioned is intended for both rewards members and travelers who are not rewards members (our classifiers); each group may use the site differently. If you were testing that web site, you would want to select some members and some non-members. The proportion depends on the priorities of the business and the objectives and goals for the study. You don't have to try to match the proportions in the target market segments.

Or, suppose you were responsible for testing a banking system that both tellers and "back office" staff members will use. You will want to have some tellers who will use the system for performing daily customer transactions. You will also want to have some "back office" staff members who will use the system to generate reports and conduct different analyses. The tasks of the two groups are different.

Each group will have similar characteristics when compared to other members of their group, although with varying levels of expertise. With each group, make sure that you are representing these varying expertise levels, if any. For example, test some novice tellers, some experienced tellers, some novice "back office" staff, and some expert "back office" staff. Suggestions for how many of each type to include are discussed later in this chapter.

In the hotel reservations web site example, rewards members are likely to be very experienced with the site and non-members are likely to have less experience with the site. But you want both groups of users to cover a range of levels of previous experience with the site. Or you may assume that participants' overall travel booking experience is more important than their direct experience with your site. In that case, you might want to classify the participants based on the frequency with which they book accommodations in the course of a year, or whether most of their travel is leisure or business-related, again depending on the objective and goals of the test. To represent these different skill levels, you may want to use a matrix test design, discussed in the next section.

Consider a Matrix Test Design

Because you want to see a range of behavior and performance within your small group of participants, consider a matrix design for the test that balances different variables or classifiers in such a way that no particular user group or *cell* of the matrix is left out.

Take the banking example. These days you can assume that having some computer experience is a requirement for getting a job either at the teller wicket or in the back office, so that's probably not a useful way of classifying these participants. What could determine levels of expertise in the two roles that would be important to your test? Possibly a combination of time on the job and types of responsibility may describe an "expert" teller from a "novice" one or an "expert" back office clerk from a "novice" one. You could look at the factors you use to determine expertise as *domain knowledge* (for example, what the participant knows about being a teller) or *tools knowledge* (for example, the efficiency and effectiveness with which the participant uses the software or other technology required in her job). You'll want some of each and you'll have to create some type of operationalized definition for determining who falls into which cell.

Good test design means that you balance the mixtures of user groups in such a way that the major categories or cells are all represented. For the banking example, you might test 16 participants whose job and experience level look like the ones in the table below (assuming that you have clearly defined the criteria for "novice" and "expert"; see "Define Expertise," above).

USER GROUP	NOVICE	EXPERT
Teller	4	4
Back office clerk	4	4

Determine the Number of Participants to Test

The number of participants you decide to test depends on many factors, including:

- The degree of confidence in the results that you require
- The number of available resources to set up and conduct the test
- The availability of the type of participants you require
- The duration of the test session

Ultimately, you have to balance your need for acquiring participants with these (and probably other) practical constraints of time and resources. If you require statistically valid results, you will need to test enough participants to conduct the appropriate analyses and generalize to your specific target population, as well as to rigorously control for potentially biasing conditions and factors.

If, however, you are simply attempting to expose as many usability problems as possible in the shortest amount of time, then test at least four to five participants of each user or audience cell. Research indicates that testing four to five participants of each type or cell will expose the vast majority of usability problems. However, we add that we are a bit uncomfortable testing only four participants, and we try to test at least eight participants if possible. While you may expose most of the usability problems with four participants, there is still a good chance you may overlook a problem that could have severe ramifications.

An important consideration is whether you will conduct more than one test during the product development life cycle. If you are going to conduct multiple tests, then you can feel more confident testing fewer participants in each test. For example, if you conduct three tests with five participants each, you end up testing fifteen people. If you will be conducting a single test, however, then you will be better served by having more participants for that lone test.

If you use a matrix design, try to test at least four participants per user group (one cell of the matrix equals a user group). If you cannot fill all cells with four participants, then consider biasing toward the users who are like most users in your target population. In the banking example, if you suspect that most end users would be novices, make sure that most of your participants fit that category.

Write the Screening Questionnaire

The screening questionnaire is the means for qualifying and selecting participants to participate in the test. Its content is typically obtained from the characteristics, requirements, and classifiers that you included in the user profile and test plan. The questionnaire is usually presented over the phone, although you can also give it to potential participants by email or in a web-based questionnaire. If you will be using a colleague, an outside consultant, or an agency to help you recruit participants, the screening questionnaire is your primary way of describing the people you need in an unambiguous format. While some agencies will develop their own screeners based on information you provide, *you must review their questionnaires before they begin using them*, to ensure that your instructions have been understood.

A screening questionnaire can be extremely simple or quite involved, depending on the variability and background of the potential participants of the product. Either way, developing the screening questionnaire exposes any uncertainties and lack of clarity in one's own understanding of the end users. It forces you to express the background of your participants in precise, measurable terms.

The following sections give some simple guidelines for developing a screening questionnaire to be administered over the telephone. The assumption is that you have assigned someone else to acquire participants. If you do the recruiting yourself, we encourage you to use the questionnaire more as a checklist for directing a more conversational interview with participants. We will walk through the steps for developing a screener below:

- Review the profile to understand users' backgrounds.
- Identify specific selection criteria.
- Formulate screening questions.
- Organize the questions in a specific order.
- Develop a format for easy flow through the questionnaire.
- Test the questionnaire and revise it.
- Consider creating an "answer sheet."

Review the Profile to Understand Users' Backgrounds

Doing usability testing is just one of the reasons you develop the user profile. However, the user profile should prove a useful tool for visualizing the person you want to be in the testing room so you can articulate the requirements and classifiers and use those to form screening questions. If you don't have a user profile that documents the characteristics of the target users you want to have in the usability test, go back to the beginning of this chapter to "Characterize Users."

Identify Specific Selection Criteria

Focus on and pull out those characteristics that are unique to your product and not just general categories of the population. For example, experience using a cell phone and a camera may qualify as a requirement for a product that combines the two. But, because the product will be used by all age groups, you need not screen for a particular age group to include in your test sample. Later, as you are acquiring participants, you can simply make sure that you get a mix of different ages.

To follow the example for the hotel reservations web site, your objective is to learn what differences there are in how different types of travelers make hotel reservations. The team decides it wants to see whether there are differences between rewards members and travelers who are not members of the rewards program. To select participants, then, some criteria are:

- Are they members of our hotel rewards program? We want some of each, split into equal sized groups, if possible.

- Are they members of *any* rewards program? For participants who are not members of our program, do they ever belong to rewards programs? For this test, we want one group of people who do not join rewards programs.

Can you see where you might end up with questions to ask potential participants from this?

For the banking example, let's focus on just the back office folks for now. The objective of the test is to learn whether users who are new to the back office can use the new system as efficiently and effectively as those who have extensive knowledge of the particular operations of this back office. Is it possible that the new system could cut down on training time? To select participants to help you find this out, you will need workers who have been in their jobs for a long time (whatever you and your team determine is an appropriate amount of time), but also some who have been through little or no training. So, some selection criteria might be:

- New hires who may have been through company orientation and had some introduction to their new jobs but who have not started to be trained on operations procedures yet.

- Some workers who have been through formal training and an observation (sometimes called "probation") period but are still fairly new to the job.

- Super-workers who have mastered the operations procedures as well as the systems used to perform them. (You may need to develop a test to determine mastery, or may rely on the evaluation of supervisors.)

We will discuss the kinds of questions you might ask to screen participants in these studies in the next section.

Formulate Screening Questions

Once you have isolated the different factors for which you are screening, you need to formulate questions to ascertain whether a person has that expertise and other characteristics defined for the test. Use the same approach you would use for creating any sort of questionnaire, especially if you will be handing your screener over to someone else to do the recruiting and scheduling. We present a number of question formats in Chapter 8. Besides those question formats, you will have to operationalize a definition of expertise. Determine levels of expertise by creating a way of checking proficiency (what we call a *criterion test*) such as an actual quiz or a matrix similar to the one we show in Figure 7-1. Because people are often reluctant to divulge exact personal details, if you must gather personal information, such as age or salary, frame your questions in ranges. For example, instead of asking, "What is your annual household income?" ask instead:

"Into what category does your annual household income fall?"

_____$20,000–$45,000   _____$46,000–$55,000

_____$56,000–$75,000   _____$76,0000–$100,000

You might ask respondents for the test of the hotel reservations web site to list all of the rewards programs they belong to: "Tell me about rewards memberships. Is that something you do? What memberships do you have?" If people have trouble remembering, you might suggest they take out their wallet to flip through membership cards.

The case of the bank employees is slightly different. You can find out how long workers have been in their jobs from the human resources department or from the group supervisor. If you want to include workers who have mastered particular tasks or operations procedures, you may also be able to find that out from a supervisor. To be sure, you could ask candidates to tell you about their jobs, what their specialties are, what they like and don't like doing and why (you may want people who don't like doing the task you will be testing, to see if the new system improves their attitudes about it), and when the last time was that someone asked them for help on the task or procedure (perhaps an indication of expertise). Or, you could develop an assessment test.

Organize the Questions in a Specific Order

It makes sense to place those questions that are most likely to disqualify a person first on a questionnaire, while being mindful of basic telephone etiquette. For example, if you are testing a graphic design product designed for seasoned end users with knowledge of color theory, you would not want to ask 20 very general questions only to find out in question 21 that the person you are speaking with does not know saturation from hue. You should establish that background early in the call to limit the phone time. On the other hand, that is not the type of high-level question you can ask first either. You need to work your way into it.

For the hotel reservations web site, you might want to eliminate candidates who don't book their own hotel rooms at all, so you would ask a question such as: "For your last three (or five; pick a number) trips, who made the arrangements?"

Develop a Format for Easy Flow through the Questionnaire

Allow the caller to branch from one question to the next without thinking too much about the answers. This is especially important if you use an outside agency and the callers do not have an in-depth understanding of your product.

Figure 7-4 shows an example of a screening questionnaire that was developed for the usability test of an accounting package for small businesses. This questionnaire could be administered by phone or with slight adjustments by email. Note how the questions are intended to screen for a user who does his or her own bookkeeping on a PC, and who has experience using other office-related software. In administering a questionnaire like the sample one, the caller should not offer the choices listed below the questions, but simply mark them based on the respondent's answers. Likewise, if

---

1. How long have you been involved in your business (that is, how long since you founded, bought, or joined it)?

    [ ] Less than 3 months   **[Terminate]**
    [ ] 3–6 months   [Continue]
    [ ] 6–12 months   [Continue]
    [ ] 1–2 years   [Continue]
    [ ] 2 years or more   [Continue]

    [**Recruiter:** Recruit a mix.]

2. Who in your company does the bookkeeping and accounting?

    [ ] Someone hired to do it/an employee   **[Terminate]**
    [ ] My partner   **[Terminate]**
    [ ] Me   [Continue]
    [ ] I do some, someone elsedoes the rest [Continue]
    [ ] My accountant/bookkeeper   [Continue]

3. Do you use a PC with Windows or a Macintosh computer at work?

    [ ] Mac   **[Terminate]**
    [ ] Windows   [Continue]
    [ ] Don't use a computer at all **[Terminate]**

    [**Recruiter:** Must us a Windows–based PC at work.]

4. Which of the following do you currently use day–to–day as you do business? (Check all that apply.)

    [ ] Microsoft Word
    [ ] Corel WordPerfect or WordPerfect Office
    [ ] Microsoft Outlook/Outlook Express (email)
    [ ] Eudora (email)
    [ ] Microsoft Excel (spreadsheets)
    [ ] Quattro Pro (spreadsheets)

    [**Recruiter:** Participant must use at *least two of the **Microsoft*** products.]

5. Which of these activities do you complete for your business at least some of the time? (Check all that apply.)

    [ ] Track expenses
    [ ] Bill customers
    [ ] Track payments from customers
    [ ] Pay bills
    [ ] Track employee time
    [ ] Track accounts receivable
    [ ] Generate financial reports like Profit & Loss statements or Balance Sheets
    [ ] Check account balances

    [**Recruiter:** Accept only candidates who do at least three of the activities at least some of the time.]

Figure 7-4 Sample screening questionnaire

the questionnaire is to be administered by email, only the questions should appear without the possible answers. Note also that the questions focus on behaviors, not demographics. Figure 7-5 shows data collected by using the sample screener. (For an expanded sample of questionnaires and spreadsheets for recruiting and screening, go to the web site that accompanies this book: www.wiley.com/usabilitytesting.com.)

Test the Questionnaire on Colleagues and Revise It

(Yes, you are right. This *is* a usability test of the screener!) If it is a phone questionnaire, use the phone. You would be surprised, but it makes a difference. If it is an email or web-based questionnaire, test it that way. Observe as a colleague tries it out by answering the questions to see what types of answers you get. If they are not what you are expecting, you must revise the questions, so it is clear that future respondents will understand what you want to find out and so you will be able to determine easily whether they qualify for the study.

Regardless of whom you use to help you acquire participants, control the process as much as possible by being as specific as possible about your needs, anticipating miscommunications, and writing down the exact words you want the procurers to use. It is your study, they are *your* results, and the whole affair is seriously compromised when the wrong people show up.

Consider Creating an "Answer Sheet"

If your questionnaire format does not make answers obvious, develop an "answer sheet" separately or right on the questionnaire that provides the replies that qualify a participant and how many of each category you need. This can be as simple as a table or spreadsheet. We like a spreadsheet such as the one in Figure 7-5 better because you can later filter and sort the data you have gathered. (For an expanded sample of such a spreadsheet, go to the web site that accompanies this book: www.wiley.com/usabilitytesting.com.)

Find Sources of Participants

Okay. So far so good. You have analyzed the user profile for your product, received confirmation that indeed you understand who the end user is, and have developed a list or matrix of the people within your user profile who you would like to test with a description of their characteristics. The next step is to recruit the people who fit this description to participate in your test.

Now let's discuss some of the sources from which you can acquire participants. The following sections discuss the most common ones. Some sources

Q1 How Long in Business?	Q2 Bookeeper	Q3 Computer	Q4 Software	Q5 Business activity
more than 2 yrs	me	PC	Word Outlook	track expenses bill customers track payments pay bills track acct time gen rpts check acct bal
1–2 yrs	me	PC	Word Eudora Excel	track expenses pay bills track acct time check acct bal
3–6 mos	me	PC	Word Outlook Excel	track expenses bill customers track payments pay bills track emp time track acct time check acct bal
more than 2 yrs	me	PC	Word Outlook Excel	track expenses bill customers track payments pay bills track emp time track acct time check acct bal
more than 2 yrs	me	PC	Word Eudora Excel	track expenses bill customers track payments pay bills track acct time gen rpts check acct bal
3–6months	me	PC	Word Outlook Excel	track expenses bill customers track payments pay bills track emp time track acct time gen rpts check acct bal

Figure 7-5 Data collected from screened participants, displayed in a spreadsheet

require creativity and tenacity to exploit to the best advantage. Some sources generate large numbers of responses but don't always net quality responses. We have listed our ideas for sources in order of how much work or expense each takes for the test moderator or recruiter, from least work and expense to most expense and time.

Internal Participants

Our general assumption is that you are conducting usability tests of products that will be released to consumers outside your company. Being at the top of the list of sources makes internal participants the easiest and cheapest participants, but not necessarily the best. Internal participants are those participants who fit the criteria of the rest of your user profile with one exception: They also happen to work for the company that is manufacturing or developing the product. Many usability tests are conducted using internal participants exclusively. This can be problematic because, by virtue of their affiliation, these participants are "different" from typical end users. They are part of the corporate culture, and they have inside information that others do not have. They also have a vested interest in seeing that the product is successful.

Does this mean that you should never use internal personnel as participants? No, not at all. It simply means that you should probably not use them as your *primary* participants. There are many ways, however, that you can use internal participants to good advantage. A few of these are:

- **To test the test.**   When you are in the early stages of coming up with your test and want to pilot it, internal participants are a valuable resource. Your focus should *not* be in gathering usability information during the pilot test. Instead, use the test to make sure that your materials are clear and understandable, that the test design is sound, that you have not forgotten any important tasks, and that your hardware, software, and documentation are in order and ready for testing.

- **To conduct early exploratory research.**   Internal participants make good exploratory participants as long as they are unfamiliar with the product and meet the target user profile. With early exploratory research, you are not as concerned with the subtle issues of later validation tests. Instead, you are more concerned with overarching problems of the product, such as the mental model, primary navigation techniques, organization of documentation, organization and navigation of an online help system, and so on. Internal participants can quickly help to determine whether you are on the right track, without the expense and time necessary to recruit outside participants.

- **To conduct "best case" testing.**   In "best case" testing, which is often employed at an early stage of development, you see how someone who is very experienced and more familiar with the culture (i.e., a ringer) uses the product. The idea is that if this best case user has trouble, you have *serious* design problems. In some cases, the internal participant will be more critical than the external participant, more willing to point out problems and not hold back. If the product passes the best case scenario, you should quickly follow with a less experienced end user to verify the soundness of the design. If it does not "pass" the best case scenario, do not bother with further testing. Instead, head back to the drawing board for further development work before testing again.

Of course, in some cases the internal participant is the end user. By all means, in that case, use them exclusively for your test. For example, in the banking system example, the banking system may have been developed internally for internal use. The end users are certainly internal to the company.

Finding internal participants may be as straightforward as searching your company directory on the intranet and firing off an email to someone who seems to be in an appropriate position to see if he or she indeed meets the selection criteria. Otherwise, your company's human resources department may be able to direct you to qualified end users in your own organization. For example, if you are working on a product that requires a certain expertise and you cannot use people who are working on the project directly, the human resources (HR) department or the company intranet can direct you to people within the company who would tend to have the appropriate experience. You then could call them up yourself, do the screening, and make all the arrangements for using them as participants.

By the way, if you decide to use outside agencies to recruit test participants, the human resources department may want to coordinate that. HR may have already set up relationships with these companies through other people doing research studies in your company of whom you may not be aware.

Qualified Friends and Family

All of us know people who may be qualified to participate in a study. This is especially true of products that are used by the population at large and for whom the characteristic audience is very broad-based. You might have friends or family who share all the characteristics of your internal end users with the exception that they do not work for your company, which is a real advantage.

If you do end up using friends and family in your study, make sure that your relationship does not affect your professionalism. When testing, do everything exactly as you normally would, including reading the orientation script, being sure not to talk about the study until after it is completed, and not being overly chummy during the test.

Web Site Sign-Up

If you are planning to do extensive testing, you will probably want to develop a database of qualified candidates for your product so that you can move quickly when it is time for a test.

Setting up a web form and a database to gather and store information about potential participants may take some nontrivial setup time, but once it is set up, you can sit back and watch the panel of possible participants grow. Many large companies include links on their web sites that invite people to "opt-in" to their participant databases. The forms collect basic demographic and behavioral data generally related to the company's product line in the online form. By doing this sort of thing, when a study comes up, you can do a simple search of your database for key characteristics to narrow the list of likely candidates, whom you can then screen more specifically for the test you're about to do.

There are several advantages to this approach. One is that the people who sign up at your web site are definitely motivated to take part in improving the products they use. They probably have some idea about what you might be doing, that is, they are probably familiar with marketing focus groups, at least. Because they have joined your list of their own free will, you are free to contact them about taking part in your research. One caution is that your sample may be skewed toward people who are particular fans of your company, or who habitually sign up for surveys, focus groups, and other types of paid research.

Update the database after each test, showing the date of the last test. The advantage of this approach is that you are always ready with a list of potential participants who represent the market breakdown for your product on short notice.

NOTE Please note that depending on your needs and how frequently you conduct tests, it may require a full-time administrator to manage the database and manage the participant contact prior to the test.

Existing Customers from In-House Lists

An excellent source of participant candidates is your own company's list of existing customers. If there is no formal list, explore other sources such as warranty card returns, various promotions to which customers have responded, or mailing lists. When contacting such customers, it is imperative, given that you are representing your company, that you make clear that there are no strings attached and there is no hidden agenda. That is, their participation is not a marketing strategy intended to eke out more sales but simply a means to gather information about future products and improve them accordingly. You should say this in writing in the recruiting email, mentioning that this research is *not tied in any way* to a sales promotion.

Customer lists are a great source of participants who are experienced. If you are running a study with both experienced end users and those who have never used your product, then use the customer lists as a means of gathering the experienced people.

NOTE One note about using customer lists: Check with whoever owns the customer list to determine whether it is acceptable company policy to use the customer list this way. Some companies decline to allow usability or other researchers inside the company to use customer lists as a way to contact customer-participants because the customers have not specifically agreed to be contacted for this type of activity. In some cases, customers have opted in or agreed to be solicited to participate in such activities.

Existing Customers through Sales Representatives

In larger companies the sales team may have access to the customers you would like to use for testing. However, they may not be particularly keen to give you direct access to their customers. And, because the sales reps already have relationships with customers around the country, they may have a different agenda than you do. In their zest to appear "in the know" to their customers about future products, they may say too much about the test. Or, they may simply be unaware of the usability testing process and the need for "average" as well as excellent performers.

Be specific about the types of people you need, as well as the importance of being vague about the subject matter of the test. In one test that Jeff helped design that used existing customers and for which the sales reps served as the recruiters, one participant had obviously been primed by a sales rep. For his "test" of a new release of an existing product, he had diligently *studied the entire* 300-*page user guide of the current product the night before*. It seems that he took the notion of a usability "test" a mite too far. The key to counteracting these tendencies is to communicate clearly to your recruiters (the sales reps). That way you can nip these problems in the bud.

User Groups or Clubs, Churches, or Other Community Groups

Many companies sponsor product user groups who meet at conventions annually and hold other events locally or online throughout the year. Your company may do this for its products or services. There are also many enthusiasts' clubs that might be tapped as sources for participants for usability tests. (Be mindful of particular biases here because participants will have an avid interest in giving you feedback about something they have joined a group to engage in more deeply.)

You might also check for web sites devoted to particular interests, disciplines, or products to find sources for participants. There you may be able to contact members directly or post a call for participants on forums or message boards, for example, if the rules allow you to do so.

Typically, these groups are composed of people who range anywhere from novice to the most expert users. What makes them an especially valuable resource is the fact that you may be able to contact everyone in the group at once by contacting the head of the group directly or the planner of the group's meetings. You can then ascertain when the next meeting is and prepare a solicitation to be distributed at that meeting. Have all the people who are interested contact you directly as soon as possible after that meeting. The entire process could be conducted via email.

Also investigate church groups and civic or community groups such as neighborhood associations or merchants' associations. In these small subcultures, people are very likely to know the occupation of other group members and what their technology interests or aptitudes are. Although people in these groups are often very receptive to involvement in studies, you might offer extra incentives, such as a small donation to the church or group for each person from the group who is selected for the study in addition to the individual participant's honorarium. There may be biasing effects from using people in groups or clubs, because many will be affluent enough (and probably well-educated) to have free time to be actively involved.

Societies and Associations

Professional societies and associations can be a good source of participants who do particular jobs or are in specific professions. If you or someone in your company is a member of an appropriate association, you may be able to put out a casual call for participants through listservs or email distribution lists. The groups may also have forums, blogs, or other technology-mediated social networking available that you could put out a discrete message or posting on. This may not be appropriate in some groups, though, so do check on the etiquette for making your approach. You may instead have to purchase a list from the association. You can usually do this by contacting its main office, paying a fee, and being sent a list electronically. The association will probably put restrictions on what you can use the list for.

If you want to include people with disabilities in your test, contacting organizations such as the American Foundation for the Blind, Lighthouse International, Disabled American Veterans, and National Council for Support of Disability Issues, or the American Disability Association can get you started. For more on testing for accessibility, see Chapter 13

Referrals from Personal Networks, Coworkers, and Other Participants

For some user groups, the best way to find participants is through personal contacts. This is especially true for finding participants on either end of the age scale. For example, parents are usually reluctant to put their children in unknown situations with strangers. Likewise, many older adults are less likely to be found in online sources and are skeptical about strangers phoning them to take part in user research. Some older adults can feel quite vulnerable and will be very leery of sales scams. So, if you want to have consumers in your test who are under age 17 or over age 65, the best way is to ask your friends, family, and coworkers to put the word out and to make introductions so you may then contact these prospective participants without scaring them off.

Unless you must keep it secret that the test is happening at all, we have found that putting the word out among our professional and personal networks will often turn up a source of participants or individuals who fit the user profile.

You may want to use people in your test who have taken part in other activities for the company. If this is not your first test, you may want to invite participants from the earlier tests back or contact them to get referrals to other people they know who might be suitable for your next test.

You might even have a form that your participants complete at the end of each test where you ask them if they'd be willing to participate in future tests. On the same form, you can ask for referrals (phone numbers and/or email addresses) of friends and others who might be willing to participate in a similar study.

Craigslist

A web site called Craigslist (`www.craigslist.org`) is an online classifieds listing that includes posts for everything that newspaper classifieds used to contain and more. The site has listings in every state in the United States, every province in Canada, a couple dozen international cities, and 50 or 60 countries outside of North America.

Putting a listing to solicit participants in the ETC section of the Jobs part of the site for the target location can be extremely fruitful; for example, see `http://sfbay.craigslist.org/etc`. (Craigslist charges a small fee for job-related postings in some cities.) Dana has received hundreds of email responses within hours of a posting going up on the site.

This has both great advantages and disadvantages. We recommend putting enough qualifying questions in the posting to prevent people who aren't qualified from responding, or so you can easily see who does and doesn't qualify as you make your first pass through the responses. After that, you must be ruthless in weeding people out. (For example, Dana has eliminated people from the pool if they don't answer all of the qualifying questions or if they give vague answers to questions about occupation such as "consultant" or "engineer." She also eliminates people if their response was inaccurate or incorrect in referring to the activity for which they were signing up, such as calling a usability study a focus group.) The quickest way to start going through the responses is to set up filters in your email inbox to sort them for you automatically.

Alternatively, you can include a link in your post to an online survey. Dana has used tools such as SurveyMonkey (`www.SurveyMonkey.com`) to gather responses to qualifying questions and then followed up with phone screening interviews. The phone interviews usually include one open-ended key question that would expose the respondent as a fake if answered incorrectly. This might be a question specific to a product or a domain or topic that you are not expert in but that you could get the answer for from a subject matter expert in your company. For example, what chemistry a DNA scientist prefers for preparing samples.

This convenience sample is definitely skewed. The people who respond to Craigslist ads for paid research and usability tests are usually subscribers to the site. This means that they are the type of people who frequent online bulletin boards looking for this type of activity. While most are fine and well-intentioned people (who make very good test participants), some are not.

If you use Craigslist repeatedly for tests, you'll find that some people who respond to your posts are semi-professional usability testers. (In some tests, you may want that.) Some are what we call "cheaters and repeaters." It is entirely possible that normal people who have rich and active lives could have many different interests and experiences that could legitimately qualify them for all types of user research. However, the *cheaters* actually make up new identities or profiles for themselves so they can get into studies (even to the extent of making up fake student or other ID cards). *Repeaters* are people who respond to every posting whether they're qualified or not. You'll want to keep track of these people over your next tests or research projects. If you know that others in your company have done research with users, you may want to get them to review your list of participants before the final confirmations are completed to see if there are any people on the list who may have negative reputations. Some recruiting and market research firms coordinate efforts on "cheater and repeater" lists, notifying one another if they encounter an offender so all can keep a clean respondent panel.

College Campuses

College students are always looking for extra cash and are delighted to help out by participating in usability tests. If college students are part of your user profile, by all means set up relationships with local colleges. (College campuses can also be a rich source of international participants.) One way to acquire students at colleges is to work directly with the college's outreach department, which seeks out relationships with local businesses. In their desire to establish these relationships, these outreach departments will often bend over backward to help you acquire what you need. In the case where there is no department providing that service, you will need to find a way to contact the students directly. Several ways are through:

- Job boards or web sites
- Events listings
- Bulletin boards

- Advertising in the college newspaper
- Word of mouth among college acquaintances
- Contacting the head of the psychology department (psychology departments are constantly conducting experiments using the student population as participants.)

You may need permission to post your needs on bulletin boards (analog or digital), and you may have to pay a fee to post to a web site or event listing.

Because it is so easy to acquire college students and because they love the extra cash, you run the risk of overusing this population. As with any other group, college students have their own specific characteristics, which may bias your study if you use them exclusively. For example, college students are probably more willing to try new things than the general population, and they are less apt to purchase products in their more precarious financial state. Therefore, use them judiciously and not as your sole source of participants, unless they are the sole targeted user.

If you specifically want college students, you may have to test on or near campus if there is a great distance between campus and your workplace because many college students may not have their own cars.

Market Research Firms or Recruiting Specialists

Market research firms recruit people for their client's marketing studies. A few firms specialize in recruiting participants for usability studies as well. Consequently, they will know exactly what you are talking about when you tell them that you need particular end users for a research study. Some market research firms may not understand usability testing per se, but bringing in computer users, scientists, doctors, lawyers, chemists, general consumers, and so on, for the purpose of gathering opinions and preferences is their business. The larger ones can get any type of person you ask for, for a price.

Almost all major cities now have at least one market research firm. Because they network with each other in order to conduct studies around the country and internationally, once you find a good one, you can usually find another agency in a different city if you need to. With so much communication being done electronically, a recruiting specialist based in one city can easily recruit participants in other places. These firms therefore are the vehicle to use when it is important that you conduct usability testing in different geographical locations. They can also help with some of the other types of research tasks, such as surveys and focus groups.

There is much less of a concern of a professional firm biasing the participant and saying the wrong thing than there is with other sources. However, it is critical that you provide a clear, concise screening questionnaire because the marketing firm still will not understand your product or possibly much about the person that you are looking for. So, be precise, clear in your communication, and specific in your screening questions.

Market research firms can also supply the facility for conducting the usability test. They typically are set up with focus group observation rooms complete with microphones, digital video/audio output, video conferencing, and one-way mirrors. This is definitely the way to go when it is important that you conduct an anonymous study of your product (e.g., the company who made the product is not mentioned) and cannot have participants come to your own location.

Expect to pay a premium for acquiring participants from these firms, especially if you need people quickly. They may ask anywhere from $125 to $300 and up per person, depending on the difficulty of obtaining the person and the amount of contact required. This does not include the actual compensation that you pay to the participant. However, once again, if you use the firm on a regular basis, you can negotiate the price down considerably.

Typically, the firm will want to over recruit by 20 percent in order to ensure that you get the right number of people. If you say you need 10 end users, the firm typically will want to line up 12 people and have 2 of them act as substitutes if another person cancels or is a "no-show." (The lingo is "recruit 12 for 10.")

We recommend that you request a daily spreadsheet summarizing the criteria of the potential participants for your review and acceptance before confirming the participant's participation. This way, you can ensure that any tradeoffs that must be made are the right ones from your point of view and that you are getting the desired mix of participants and characteristics.

Employment Agencies

Employment agencies can be a good source of some types of participants. There are temporary and employment agencies for almost every position in the work force, from file clerk to programmers to system analysts.

If you would like to conduct international usability tests but are unable to travel to other countries, employment agencies might be able to assist you in finding people who have been in your country for a very short time and have not completely assimilated yet. While having them in your study is not the same as testing in their home country, you can get some useful data by using foreign nationals from the target country. (For a discussion about whether geography matters, see the section "Testing in Multiple Geographic Locations" in Chapter 6.)

Pricing varies by location in the country and of course, by the skill level of the person you require. Expect to pay for end users at an hourly rate, which includes the agency fee and the person acquired. You may have to pay for a minimum of time, usually 4 hours. Once you establish a relationship with an agency and use them on an ongoing basis, you can negotiate both the hourly rate and the minimum time required for people.

Because agencies are used to placing people in jobs, some training may be necessary to help the person or agency you are working with to understand what you need. Be clear about what you are doing and what your needs are. Do not expect the agency to understand the discipline of usability testing. Having explained usability testing to a number of different agencies, we have had mixed results. We try to keep it very simple. Simplicity and brevity are also important, so that the agency cannot inadvertently describe the testing procedure to potential candidates. In short, tell agencies only as much as they need to know to acquire the right participants and no more.

In addition to the screening questionnaire that you give the agencies to use, give them a written description of the exact way in which you would like your study described to potential candidates. Ask them to read your description verbatim. Keep it simple, keep it short, and, if necessary, keep it vague, such as, "We're conducting research." Personally, we do not even like to use terms such as "We'll be looking at ease of use." We prefer to fill in the participant about the exact nature of the research once he or she arrives.

One last point. It may be necessary (and advantageous) for you to go through your own human resources department in working with temporary agencies. Some companies prohibit their employees from contacting agencies directly. If that is the case, spend some time to educate the HR person who will work the agencies on all the potential pitfalls mentioned previously.

Newspaper Advertisements

If you have plenty of lead time and want to specifically recruit people who are less technology savvy, advertise in your local newspaper either in a display ad area or the classified ad section for "participants needed for research study." (Response rates are likely to be higher for display ads than for classifieds.) You might also try online versions of the same newspaper; some newspapers offer special rates for advertising in both the print and online editions.

In the advertisement, be vague. (Let's be precise about what we mean by vague. Just refer to market research or product testing without providing precise details about what the person will be doing.) Only state the qualifications necessary and the approximate amount of money you are willing to pay for qualified participants. You can have interested candidates either communicate to a web site address or respond by phone.

Responding by phone is much more labor-intensive on your part, especially if you get many more interested people than you have slots for, but it is faster if you are working against a deadline. If you can, use a phone line with an explanatory message on voice mail or a standard answering machine. That way you can return calls at your leisure.

Including a link in the ad to a web site with an online questionnaire not only allows you greater control over the process but also controls the number of responses. Either way, people have to be quite motivated to take part because they have one extra step to go through to respond to the ad. Make it clear in your ad that people must qualify to participate. Of course, this assumes that your participants are computer and Internet users.

Screen and Select Participants

As we have mentioned a couple of times, you'll need to put together some type of process to determine whether the candidates you have qualify for the study. This *usually* takes the form of a document that contains a table of qualifications (see the sections "Define the Criteria for Each User Group," and "Choose the Number of Participants to Test," earlier in this chapter) and a set of multiple choice questions (see the previous section "Write the Screening Questionnaire"). The table lists requirements and classifiers along with a range of the number of participants you would like to possess these attributes. The multiple choice questions operationalize the selection/elimination process. The document, typically called a *screener*, includes scripted language for starting a phone interview process, getting through the questions, scheduling the participant (if qualified), and closing the interview.

Screening Considerations

We highly recommend that the interviewer not read off the answer choices but instead simply check off the choice that is closest to the respondent's answer. A screener is an excellent tool to use if you have never recruited participants before or if you plan to use an agency to do recruiting.

Use the Questionnaire or Open-Ended Interview Questions?

We have found that the quality of participants and the "show rate" is higher if you recruit in an apparently more casual and personable way, using a screener as a checklist during a more conversational interview. Here you can ask open-ended questions to get the respondents to volunteer information about themselves that will reveal whether they qualify. There are several advantages to this approach. First, you build rapport with the candidate. The rapport results in a stronger feeling of responsibility and commitment in the participants. They are more likely to show up for the session and be on time. Second, it is less likely that the candidate will give an answer just because he or she thinks it is the correct one to get into the study. Third, you can ask follow-up questions that may expand or clarify something important to the study. Finally, you can make better on-the-fly adjustments to your selection criteria. This doesn't mean that you're biasing the sample, but instead it helps you incorporate things you learn as you interview respondents and make intelligent tradeoffs if some requirement or other becomes difficult to meet.

For example, Dana worked on a study of a web site for registered voters. She wanted people from both rural and urban places (a classifier), but the study took place at harvest time. Many of the people in rural places would only be available after sundown (and a very, very hard day) or if it rained. If Dana had used only a scripted questionnaire, she might not have found out *why* people weren't available. But in a casual conversation, she found out why and what the options were for getting these types of participants. A typical script would simply have collected data about a possible participant, such as occupation: "What is your occupation?" and availability: "We have these appointments available. Which one would you like . . . ?" Only to have the person say "farmer" and "none." Instead, a conversational approach engaged the study candidate. For example, a dialog might go thus:

> Recruiter: "Tell me about what you do for a living."
> Possible participant: "I'm a farmer. I grow wheat."
> Recruiter: "How's the crop this year?"
> Participant: "It's a good year. We're harvesting right now. I just came in from the fields."
> Recruiter: "How long will the harvest go on?"
> Participant: "About another week."
> Recruiter: "Ah. We were hoping to complete our study this week. Would you be interested in participating during an evening? Or maybe after your harvest is over? I will see if we can extend for a couple of days."

Complete the Screener Always, or Only When Fully Qualified?

There are two schools of thought about whether to go through a screening questionnaire completely with every respondent even if they don't meet all of the selection criteria. One school recommends stopping the questioning as soon as someone hits a "reject" or "terminate" answer. In other words, the potential participant's answer to a question is outside of the targeted characteristic for your user profile. This can help you talk to many more possible respondents in a short time without spending the time talking to people who don't qualify. The other school recommends going through the entire set of questions regardless of whether the respondent meets one or more elimination criteria. This approach has its plusses, mainly that you have alternates available in case you do end up adjusting the selection criteria. You can consider them "maybes" in case you run short of participants. Or there may be some who might be acceptable as pilot participants or back-up participants in case of cancellations.

Conduct Screening Interviews

Now that you have the questionnaire developed (see the section "Write the Screening Questionnaire," earlier in this chapter), here are some guidelines for administering it over the phone or having someone do it for you. The guidelines work for email communication, too.

Inform the Potential Participant Who You Are

If the usability test is being run as an anonymous one (the name of the sponsoring company remaining confidential), then of course the research firm or person calling should mention this fact and give the reasons for anonymity. For example, "Hi, my name is Sandy. I'm calling from a research firm called UsabilityWorks." If the study is anonymous, add something like this: "Because my client is a household name, I can't tell you the sponsor of the research. You will learn it at the end of your session, if you are selected for the study," if that is indeed the case.

Explain Why You are Calling and How You Got the Contact Information

Briefly explain the nature of the research. For example:

Michael Reel at the Franklin County Clerk's Office suggested I contact you about a research study I am working on. I am working with him and the Office of the Secretary of State to evaluate how usable a new web site is for registered voters.

To do this, my colleague Dana would like to observe you using the web site and then ask you a couple of questions. We're doing individual 30-minute sessions all day on Tuesday, August 28. Does this sound like something you might be interested in?

By all means, be sure to mention that the session requires the participant to be recorded, because you want participants to raise any objections to being recorded now, and not when they arrive for testing. Ask the potential participant if he or she is interested in hearing more, and, if so, explain how long (worst case) it will take you to ask all the questions on the screening questionnaire. (If it is a really long questionnaire, fudge a little bit about how long it will take. Many professionals simply say that it depends on the answers, which is true, we suppose.) If the person is not interested, then express your thanks, mention how much fun he or she will be missing, and, if appropriate, ask for recommendations of other interested parties.

Go through the Questions in the Questionnaire

Based on your test plan's user profile and the questions you have formulated for the screener, question the person about his or her qualifications, such as computer experience, job responsibilities, and equipment used.

> **NOTE** If you are using an outside agency, have the agency first try the questionnaire on you as if you were a potential participant. See how the person who calls you responds to different and/or ambiguous answers to the same question. It is your money and your study. Make sure that the agency does it right.

If possible, use the questionnaire as a checklist for managing a more conversational interview, turning the questions into open-ended queries so as to get the respondents to volunteer information about themselves. This way, the respondent is less likely to be able to guess the "right" answers to get into the test, and you may learn additional things that could be useful to know.

As You Eliminate or Accept People, Mark Them Off on Your List

There is nothing more embarrassing than calling the same person and getting them out of the shower two days in a row. Gather responses to the questions either on copies of the screener or in a spreadsheet like the one in Figure 7-5, and use it to maintain the data you gather throughout the recruiting and screening process. (For an expanded sample of such a spreadsheet, go to the web site that accompanies this book: www.wiley.com/usabilitytesting.com.)

Include a Few Least Competent Users in Every Testing Sample

We have found that we learn an extraordinary amount by including one or more least competent users (LCUs) among participants, *even if they do not make up a significant percentage of the eventual end users.* An LCU is defined as an end user who represents the least skilled person who could potentially use your product. In the example of the user profile for the chemical engineering market, the LCU is a person with no computer experience, who has never used even a word processor, who is a high-school graduate, and so on. The LCU need not fall at the bottom of *all* the scales, but the LCU should be at the bottom of the majority of them. Why include LCUs even if the user profile is projected at mostly expert users? Simply this: If your least expert group can successfully use the product, if *they* can muddle their way through the usability test, then you can assume that most other groups will also be able to use the product. Of course, there are exceptions to every rule, but by and large, we have found the LCUs to be excellent indicators of a product's overall ease of learning.

On the other hand, if the LCUs cannot get through the test, that is *not* necessarily an indictment. It does, however, reveal clues on how to fix fundamental problems of intuitiveness, orientation, or organization through redesign, more or better information in the instructions, and so forth. In addition, during early product development and exploratory tests, you learn much about the end user's mental models through the eyes of the LCU, before the LCU has been "polluted" by previous experiences with similar products. If your product is targeted toward new audiences, the LCU test can obviously help predict problems for those folks.

Beware of Inadvertently Testing Only the "Best" People

Very often when acquiring participants, and especially when you do not have primary control of participant selection, you will be sent only the very "best" people by your contact or recruiter. By "best," we mean that regardless of the category of end user, whether it is novice, expert, or whatever, you are sent the cream of the crop, the high achievers. Your first reaction to this might be very positive, but on close inspection, it is easy to see the potential problem here. The "best" end users typically possess the skills to plow through even the most hard-to-use products and perform admirably. Consequently, the product "tests out" much better than it should, and provides a false sense of confidence to the design and marketing team. Later, after release, when average and poor performers use the product, many of the design flaws that exist, but did not come out during the test, are exposed.

This situation is especially apt to occur when you are acquiring participants under the following conditions:

- When you will be testing end users from within your own company, usually from a department with which you are not familiar.

- When you are acquiring people directly from an established customer and participation is seen as an enviable perk. In this case, the manager responsible for providing people sends participants to your company as a reward for a job well done at their company. Invariably, these are their best performers.

- When you are acquiring people from an established customer through your own sales force. In this case, similar to the previous one, there is also a hidden agenda. Your sales rep very often has strong relationships that he or she would like to further by using the testing as a perk. These relationships are often with the best performers and most influential people in your customer's organization. You never see the average or poor performers.

We mention these situations as warnings because "best" people are hard to predict. We have learned this the hard way, having had people show up as participants who were so accomplished that they should have been *designing* the product, never mind using it. Such users were able to foresee and work around the most troublesome areas, almost as if they knew they were there. These participants also downplayed whatever problems they encountered, although they were critical ones. They can also be the *most* critical. One or at most two of these people during a test is reasonable, but if you see three or four, it plays havoc with your test results.

What makes the situation even worse is when the development team attending the test does not agree that these people are "ringers." The team is more than happy to bask in the glow of receiving unexpected but excellent results. Now, if you could just get all "ringers" to buy the product in sufficient numbers, everyone would be happy.

Expect to Make Tradeoffs

Because to some extent your participant characteristics are a projection of who you and the team are hoping the participants should be, you may find that the pool of respondents you have to select from meet some of the requirements you want, but not all. This is when it is useful to have interviewed participants conversationally rather than by going through the multiple choice questionnaire by rote. The conversational screening allows you to ask follow-up questions that could help you decide whether a respondent is close enough to the visualized profile to give you valid data. If you or your agency use the straight questionnaire and are finding that it is difficult to schedule enough suitable participants, you and your agency should review where the respondents are not meeting the requirements and adjust accordingly. The agency may have learned something useful that will help you eventually secure an adequate number of participants and so could go back to already interviewed respondents to ask follow-up questions. These last minute trade offs are not uncommon, and as long as you document them and account for any biases they may have introduced, it is fine to make them.

Schedule and Confirm Participants

As you interview participants to see whether they meet the selection criteria, we recommend that you collect their top three available dates and times as well but not make any immediate commitments. This gives you greater flexibility in moving participants around on your personal scheduling Ouija board before finalizing the session schedule and mix of participants.

When you have the availability information, you can also set priorities among the pool of participants. If there are people in the pool whom you definitely want to be in the study, but they have limited or special times available, schedule them first and then schedule other people with more flexible schedules around them. Availability may be tied to the incentive offered. If you're having difficulty finding and scheduling qualified participants, you may need to increase the amount that participants will be compensated for their time, or flex your session schedule to nonworking hours.

Once you have decided who should be in which sessions, send an email (or, if email is not available, phone or send a letter if there is time) to the participant with the information about the appointment time, date, and location. Include any special instructions (such as where visitor parking is or requirements for checking in at reception), along with a reminder about the amount and conditions for getting the incentive. In your follow-up communication, ask participants to acknowledge that they have received it by replying to you.

Then confirm, confirm, and confirm again. The day before the participant is scheduled, do another reminder with the same information that was in the scheduling communication. On the afternoon or evening before the participant's session, phone him or her. Try very hard to get the person rather than leaving a message; this increases the chances that the person will show up and do it on time.

THE RECRUITING PROCESS IN A NUTSHELL

Give yourself a solid two weeks to do recruiting and scheduling once the screening criteria are identified. Here's a basic outline and timeline for the process.

1. **Identify participant characteristics and mix.**   Week 1

2. **Identify sources for participants.**

3. **Write the screening questionnaire (screener)**

4. **Test the screener.**

5. **Find participants.**   Week 2–3

     ◆ **Create listings, ads, or invitations — include at least basic select/reject criteria such as availability.**

     ◆ **Post or send out listings and invitations.**

     ◆ **Receive responses.**

     ◆ **Filter and sort responses to narrow down to more appropriate candidates.**

6. **Refine screener further, revise selection criteria if necessary.**

7. **Select from responses.**

8. **Send out more questions or ask follow-up questions if needed.**

9. **Check the sample of respondents against mix matrix.**   Week 3

10. **Select candidates, review the mix.**

11. **Contact selected candidates with appointment dates and times.**

12. **Confirm with participants, send session information including directions and forms.**

Compensate Participants

It is customary to compensate those who serve as participants, although it need not always be monetary compensation. Participants acquired "off the street" or via an agency for a study where your company has been kept anonymous should all receive monetary compensation and possibly a small token of appreciation such as a pen or a T-shirt. Expect to pay the going rate on the open market for the skill level you are requesting. If your product will be used by administrative personnel, expect to compensate them by paying the hourly rate for administrative assistants. If you will be testing lawyers or doctors or other professionals, you may need to pay close to the hourly rate for that profession. If you will simply be testing with typical "consumers," with no specific profession required, expect to pay an honorarium of about $50 per hour, depending on location (participants on the coasts or in large cities may be more expensive than people in smaller cities or rural places in the middle of the country). Participants are always happy to accept cash; checks or gift checks will also do, but try to make sure participants get the check at the end of the session rather than by mail later. You may need to test in the evening or on weekends if your user profile indicates end users who are not available during the regular work day. If money is no object, however, you can get people to come in whenever you like.

Your company may require participants to sign receipts showing that they have received a check or cash in exchange for their participation. Check with your accounting and/or legal department to determine what your company requires.

Participants sent from one of your company's large clients, however, should be compensated differently depending on the relationship of your two companies. If their participation is part of an ongoing research relationship where they benefit from being privy to your company's future product line as much as you benefit from their input, then a token gift alone might suffice.

Even in the case where you have an ongoing research relationship with your customer, if participants must be imported to your location your company should offer to foot all the expenses such as travel and meals associated with having the person participate. If no strong relationship exists, you could provide anything from a small honorarium to paying the person's salary for the time he or she participated. Some other compensation choices are: free or discounted products from your company's sales catalog, gift certificates, or a simple memento, such as a T-shirt or calculator.

While you should always provide something of value in appreciation for participation, it is of the utmost importance that you do not imply in any way that compensation is tied to the person's performance. Participants simply get paid for showing up and giving it their best, and that's it. Even joking about this with the person is not a good idea, as it plants a seed in the person's mind that he or she needs to be "positive," which may prevent the person from being critical.

Some workplaces, unions, or professions don't allow people to take incentives, honoraria, or gifts. If someone wants to take part in your study but declines the incentive, find another way to thank them for their participation.

Protect Participants' Privacy and Personal Information

If you collect personal information about participants, you have a responsibility to protect that information and keep it private. For example, if you must collect information such as participants' Social Security number because your accounting department asks for it, ensure that it is only used for that purpose. Don't include it in materials distributed to others, such as a schedule of sessions or the final report. Do tell participants why you are collecting the personal information and what you are going to do with it. You should also tell them how long you are going to keep it.

Keep the identities of your participants anonymous. During the sessions, try to minimize how much you say their names, especially if the session is being recorded (and even more if the recordings will go into highlights videos that will be seen widely in your company). Try to strike a balance between being personable during the time participants are with you and protecting their privacy later.

Don't use names to label recordings or files. You will need to put names on session schedules to ensure that the right people show up and that they match the selection criteria. However, you should never use names — not even just first names — in reports. Refer to the participants by some other identifier, such as U1, U2, etc. (for user one, user two, etc.) or P1, P2, and so on (for participant one, participant two, etc.).

Absolutely do not share video or audio recordings of participants for any reason other than the reasons that participants agreed to. You should have participants sign recording permissions that spell out that you are using the recordings only for data analysis and internal reports. Once the sessions are complete, store the recordings securely, either on media that can be locked away or digitally protected with passwords.

CHAPTER 8

Prepare Test Materials

One of the more labor-intensive activities required to conduct a usability test is developing the test materials that will be used to communicate with the participants, collect the data, and satisfy legal requirements. It is important to develop all required test materials well in advance of the time you need them. Apart from the obvious benefit of not having to scurry around at the last minute, developing materials early on helps to explicitly structure and organize the test. In fact, if you have difficulty developing one particular type of test material, this can be a sign that there are flaws in your test objectives and test design.

While the specific content of the materials will vary from test to test, the general categories required will hardly vary at all. This chapter contains a list of the most common materials you need to develop a test, as well as examples of the various types of test materials. As you develop them, think of these materials as aids to the testing process. Once they are developed, their natural flow will guide the test for you. Be sure to leave enough time to include the materials in your pilot test. The test materials reviewed in this chapter are as follows:

- Orientation script
- Background questionnaire
- Data collection instruments
- Nondisclosure agreement and recording consent form
- Pre-test questionnaire
- Task scenarios

- Post-test questionnaire
- Debriefing topics guide

All the parts can be rolled up into what we sometimes call a *session script* or a *session checklist*. You don't have to do all of the materials for every test. Create materials that support the goals of your test and that will deliver the data needed to answer your research questions. For example, for small usability tests you can typically get what you need about participants from the screener, then interview participants briefly at the beginning of sessions — so there are no background or pre-test questionnaires. There usually is no training required for participants to take part, and enough preference data comes out organically during the session that having a post-test questionnaire is overkill or there is no need to compare impressions between the beginning and end of sessions. Let your research questions and test design dictate the combination of the items you need to make your test work.

In this chapter, we also cover considerations for preparing yourself to test a prototype or an incomplete product. There is a special section on common question formats, as well. Although the information about question formats follows the discussion about the post-test questionnaire, you can use these formats for any of the questionnaires included in your usability test design.

Guidelines for Observers

Observers can be important to your test for a variety of reasons, not the least of which is being able to use their notes later. You should encourage people to observe testing sessions regardless of whether you have a laboratory setup or are using a less formal arrangement.

Whether your observers will be in the room with you and the participant or in a separate observation area from the test participant, it is always a good idea to give observers some direction, because this may be an unusual activity for them. You should at least develop a list of pointers about what to do and not do while observing. You may want to include hints about what to look for and how to get the most out of being present. Consider conducting a short briefing meeting before you start conducting sessions to train observers about the method you are using and to run down your guidelines for observing.

Typically, guidelines for observers ask them to show up on time and stay for the entire session. The guidelines also usually include notes about body language and making noise, taking notes, and what types of questions to ask when they are invited to do so. Figure 8-1 assumes that observers will be in the room with the participant, but most of the rules apply even if the observers watch from a separate room, especially if the room is not sound proof.

Guidelines for observers

Running a successful usability test requires observers to adhere to strict guidelines so participants feel comfortable and willing to share information. To make sure your presence as an observer does not cause discomfort to participants or otherwise affect the quality of the data we collect, please observe the following rules:

Arrive before the Session Is Scheduled to Start. It is important for you to be present when the participants arrive so you can choose your seat and get settled and ready to begin taking notes. Participants may interpret your lateness as disregard for what they have to say, and a stranger entering the room is distracting and disruptive.

You Must Stay for the Duration. We would like participants to forget that anyone else is in the room. Having people constantly coming in and going out is very distracting. Therefore, once we start the session, it is imperative that you stay until the session is complete. If you cannot stay for the duration of the session, please do not come at all.

Turn off Your cell Phone or Leave It at Your Desk. If you bring your computer, turn off email and instant messaging. It's a short session. Please be fully present and ready to pay attention to the moderator and the participant.

No Laughing, Grunting, Aha-ing, or Distracting Body Language. Participants may think you are laughing at them. Please do your best to keep as quiet as possible. It is important that observers do not make facial expressions or utter comments during the session. Space has been inserted on the script for you to take notes. Please turn the pages of the script quietly.

Ask Open-Ended Questions about what happened in the session when invited by the moderator to do so. Don't offer design or feature alternatives. Avoid asking about preferences or opinions.

Keep the Participant's Identity Confidential. We have promised the participants that their identity will be kept confidential. Please help us maintain this confidentiality.

Figure 8-1 Sample guidelines for observers

Orientation Script

The orientation script (also known as the introduction script) is a communications tool meant to be read verbatim to participants. It describes what will happen during a test session, sets the tone for that session in the minds of the participants, and is intended to put them at ease. It achieves this by informing the participants of what they will be doing, and reinforcing the fact that the product, not the participant, is being tested. Remember that participants often have only the vaguest idea of what they will be doing, possibly having been presented with only some ambiguous reference to "participation in market research" or the like. For a particularly nervous participant, introducing the session this way can provide reassurance that he or she is actually the "right" person in the "right" place.

The script may be read to the participants in the testing area or in a "waiting or meeting area" prior to moving to the testing space. Our own preference is to read it just before beginning testing activities, which occur in the main testing area.

When developing an orientation script, there are three major guidelines to remember.

Keep the Tone of the Script Professional, but Friendly

It should *not* be chummy or overly familiar as if the participants were your buddies. For example, in the food service industry, the waiter who asks for your name and continues to use it ad nauseam during the meal comes to mind as an instance of this lack of professionalism in the guise of improved service.

Keep the Speech Short

Unless you have an extremely complex test, limit the orientation script to a few paragraphs. Anything longer than that will not be retained by the participants in any case. Any instructions beyond two pages probably means that you are including actual test materials, such as task scenarios, as part of your script. We show two examples in Figure 8-2 and 8-3. Figure 8-2 shows a script you might use for a simple, exploratory test. Figure 8-3 has very specific instructions for a benchmark comparison test.

Session Introduction

"Thank you for agreeing to take part in our research study. My name is Dana, and this is Russell. May I have your signed consent form, please? Thanks. [*If they haven't brought a signed one with them, give one to them now and have them review and sign.*]

"During the rest of the session, I'll be working from a script to ensure that my instructions to everyone who participates in the study are the same.

"I'm here to learn about how voters use a new web site.

"During the session, I will ask you to use the web site to do a variety of things and will observe you while you do them. As you do these things, please try to do whatever you would normally do.

"Please try to think out loud while you're working. Just tell me whatever is going through your mind. Please know that we're not testing you, and there is no such thing as a wrong answer. Your doing this helps us understand what works or doesn't work about the site.

"By the way, I'm an independent researcher who had nothing to do with the design of the site you're about to try out. So please be honest in your feedback—I need to know exactly what you think, not what you think I want to hear. Russell is here from the secretary of state's office to learn and take notes.

"The whole session will take about 30 minutes.

"Do you have any questions before we begin? [*Answer any questions.*]"

Figure 8-2 Sample orientation script for a basic test

Introducing the Study

Before the test session begins, participants will complete a short background questionnaire (see page 1) along with the nondisclosure agreement and video release form. We'll spend a minute exchanging pleasantries. Then I'll give them an overview of our activities together.

Start time: _____

Thank you for agreeing to participate in our usability study today. During our session, I'll be using this script to ensure that, as far as possible, my instructions to everyone who participates are the same.

Our objective today is to observe you using two software programs designed for small business bookkeeping and accounting. During the session, you'll be working on your own while I observe you from another room.

I'll be taking notes and we're recording the session. All of the equipment in the room is to make sure that my notes are accurate.

In this session, we'll have you do typical tasks, to learn how these programs work for people like you. Please keep in mind that we're not testing you—it's you who are helping us evaluate the software.

Here's how the session will work:

- On the table in front of you, face down, are cards with some bookkeeping tasks I want you to do.
- You'll do the tasks one at a time, first on one software program and then the other. Please don't look ahead at the other tasks and don't skip any tasks.
- I'll direct you from the other room about what to do and when to do it.
- When directed, pick up the appropriate task sheet and read the task aloud. When you are ready to start, say "I'm ready to start."
- Start working on the task only once I have said, "Please begin." I'll start recording time as soon as you touch the keyboard or the mouse—so don't touch either one until you're ready to start the task.
- When you have completed the task, say aloud, "I'm done." Place your hands in your lap to signal that you're finished and waiting for the next task. [*Moderator: Make sure the camera is at a wide angle on the user so you can see this behavior.*]
- After each task, you'll answer a couple questions about your experience doing the task on that software.
- At the end of the session, you'll answer one more questionnaire.

Do you have any questions before we begin?

Figure 8-3 Sample orientation script for a benchmark comparison test

Plan to Read the Script to Each Participant Verbatim

Do not attempt to memorize the script, paraphrase it, or simply "wing it" from session to session. Here is why this is so important:

- You want to present the exact same information to each participant so that all the participants are exposed to identical conditions prior to the test. By paraphrasing the script, you may change what you say in very subtle ways.

> **NOTE** If you feel self-conscious reading the script or feel that it sets an overly formal tone, simply tell the participant why you are reading it. For example, "I'm going to read this script to you now so that I provide the exact instructions to you that I provide to everybody else, and so that I do not forget anything of importance."

- People are easily influenced by past events. Imagine that you have just tested the first four participants and are about to test the fifth one. Three of the first four have performed miserably. Not only did they have great difficulty with the product, but they hated using it. You may be feeling down and discouraged, and are unknowingly about to project your feeling of frustration to the fifth participant by the manner in which you introduce the session. However, reading the script forces you to use the same language, which in turn makes it easier to control the nonverbal aspects of your communication, such as your mannerisms, expressions, and voice modulation. In short, it is harder to express your own frustration when you read the script.

- More than one test moderator may be conducting the test over a period of time. If that is so, there is a need to minimize the differences in the test moderators as much as possible. At the very least, reading the script controls the initial information that is communicated to the participants.

- Those members of the development team not present at the sessions will want to know precisely what was said to the participants. Showing the script to interested parties who were unable to attend the usability test accomplishes this objective. It also communicates professionalism and rigorousness on your part.

- You may forget an important point. There are so many details involved with moderating a test, why make it hard on yourself? Use the script and cross "what to say" off your list of things to remember and worry about.

Write the Orientation Script Out

Now that you know the important reasons for creating a script, you need to actually create one. The following sections list the typical contents of an orientation/introduction script. However, do *not* feel that you need to include every category in your own script. If you do, you might end up writing an essay.

Make Introductions

Introduce yourself, of course, and anyone else whom the participant is likely to encounter during the usability test. You need not go into great detail about people's backgrounds; just a passing reference to the function of each person is fine. For example, you might say, "That person over there will be managing the recordings," or "That person over there will be keeping track of time to ensure that I let you go on time." *Never* volunteer the fact that any person associated with the test or observing in the same room has worked on the product that the participants will be testing. Of course, if a participant asks (hardly anyone ever does), then by all means tell the participant the truth, but do not *volunteer* that information. The reason for this is simple; you want the participants to feel absolutely unencumbered about providing any negative feedback. Associating real people with the product only makes it that much more difficult for participants to be honest.

As test moderator, include yourself in this "non-association" guideline if you are affiliated with the product. (Ideally, you will not be affiliated with the product.) Explain your role as the person who will be moderating the test, observing, and taking notes. If you are not affiliated with the product, then play up the fact that you are a neutral observer. If you will be moderating the usability test in the test room, then explain exactly what you will be doing during the test.

Offer Refreshments

Being offered refreshments will help the participants to relax and feel at home. They are more apt to indulge if you already have a cup of coffee, soda, or water in your hand. "Breaking bread" together is a wonderful ice breaker. Do not downplay the fact that your participants may be nervous. It is very common and you need to address it.

Explain Why the Participant Is Here

You may think that they already know this information, but you would be amazed at what external recruiters tell participants about what they will be doing in the sessions. Provide enough detail and context about the product for them to perform the tasks. Do not feel you need to provide product history, number of participants being tested, and so forth. Express appreciation for their willingness to participate and how much their input helps produce a better product, *regardless of how they perform*. In no way, shape, or form should the performance of the participants be tied to their compensation for participating, even as a joke. You can be sure that the thought has crossed their mind. No need to reinforce it.

Describe the Testing Setup

Point out and describe the equipment. Let the participants know whether they will be staying where they are, moving to another room, and so on. Locate the restrooms. Let them know if:

- People are watching from behind a one-way mirror or from another room via cameras. Do not get cute here and say "Oh that old thing. It's just so we can see all sides of the equipment."
- The session is being recorded. It is *never* a good idea to lie to participants about being observed or recorded in order *not* to make them nervous. First of all, it is not ethical. Second, once the test starts, almost all participants forget their concerns about being watched and recorded, depending on the testing environment.

Explain What Is Expected of the Participant

Describe how the usability test will proceed without providing every last detail. Broach the subject of nondisclosure, if you have not already done so, and how that will be handled. Encourage them to perform as they normally would (e.g., same speed and attention to detail, given the fact that it is an artificial situation). Encourage the participants to ask questions and to take breaks if they need to.

Avoid any reference whatsoever to your expectations of their behavior or performance. Remain absolutely neutral in terms of their expected performance.

For example, do *not* say any of the following in order to make participants less nervous:

- "Most people find this extremely easy."
- "We brought you in for an extremely simple test."
- "I'm sure you'll have no difficulty with this product, so don't be nervous."

While well intentioned, these are exactly the *wrong* things to say. By making those references, you have essentially put the participants on the defensive if things *do* get difficult. At the slightest hint of adversity, they may begin to hurry and try harder in order to fulfill your expectations. After all, if it is simple and they are having a hard time, then by definition they must be slow. No one likes to think of himself or herself that way.

Assure the Participant That He or She Is Not Being Tested

This is probably the most familiar adage of testing, and you should certainly say this. However, do not hold out hope that they will necessarily believe you just because you say it. This slogan has become the "it's for your own good" slogan of our youth. It is often repeated but never believed. Only the manner in which the test is conducted, the way in which you react to the person's behavior, and the behavior of the observers will cause the truth of this adage to sink in. Your manner, body language, and voice modulation during difficulties all communicate much more than just the words. In sum, do not be surprised if at the first sign of difficulty, you hear the participant mutter that familiar refrain, "Oh, I'm an idiot. That wasn't the program's fault," or "I just need more time to learn how to use it."

Explain Any Unusual Requirements

Demonstrate and practice how these special situations work and reassure the participant that you will be available to remind him or her how to do it, if need be.

Mention That It Is Okay to Ask Questions at Any Time

Of course, explain that you may not answer those questions in order to simulate the situation of their being alone and having to rely on their own resources and materials at hand. Make that aspect of your role very clear. You are not there to solve problems participants encounter.

Ask for Any Questions

Before you begin, be absolutely sure that the participants understood your instructions. Due to being nervous and/or poor acoustics in the room, the participants may not have fully heard or understood your instructions. If you are not sure, ask them to parrot back a particular point by inquiring, for example, "Do you remember how to use the thinking aloud protocol?"

Refer to Any Forms That Need to Be Completed and Pass Them Out

This includes background questionnaires, pre-test questionnaires, permissions, and so on.

Figures 8-2 and 8-3 show examples of orientation scripts for different types of tests.

Background Questionnaire

The background questionnaire provides historical information about the participants that will help you to understand their behavior and performance during a test. It is composed of questions that reveal the participant's experience, attitudes, and preferences in all areas that might affect how they perform. For example, if you are testing a database management system (DBMS), it will be helpful to know if the participants have used a DBMS before, and, if so, which one(s) and for how long. While you will not know if that experience will affect their performance negatively or positively, you almost certainly know that it *will* affect their performance differently than a person without DBMS experience.

The background questionnaire is typically filled out just prior to the test. Sometimes, particularly if it is lengthy, you might mail it to the participant ahead of time.

The information you include in the background questionnaire is initially culled from the participant profile in your test plan. The background questionnaire is similar to a phone screener, although more detailed. The phone screen need only determine if a potential participant meets the selection requirements and can be classified in a user group. The background questionnaire, however, goes further by exploring previous training and experience. This more specific information can help explain a participant's behavior during the test. Perhaps the participant is choosing buttons or menu selections based on expectations formed from using a competitive product that no other participant used.

In addition to the previously stated reasons for acquiring the correct cross-section of participants and providing insight about each person's performance from a historical perspective, there are two more purposes for the background questionnaire. Both come into play on the day of the test, just prior to its beginning.

- **To confirm that the "right" people show up.**   It is amazing how often mix-ups occur when there are so many details to manage. If you did not make the phone calls or write the emails yourself to screen and select participants, it is important to verify that the people who show up actually possess the skills and knowledge you expected. It is not that unusual for agencies to misunderstand what you are doing and to send unqualified people. If you do get the wrong people showing up, you will need to decide on the spot whether to use them or release them. You will also need to communicate to the person or organization supplying your participants that they need to do a better job of qualifying the participants.

- **To provide a synopsis of each participant for the test moderator and for product team members who observe the test.**   If you anticipate that the usability tests will be observed by a design team or other interested parties, it is important that they know the background of each person while they observe the test. It is both confusing and misleading to observe a test without a sense of the skills, knowledge, and experience of the specific participant. There is no basis on which to judge how participants are doing or why they are performing as they are without this knowledge. To avoid this potential misunderstanding, make the data from the screening questionnaire and the background questionnaire available to the observers after the participant fills it out. The observers can reference it while the test proceeds.

Focus on Characteristics That May Influence Performance

Ascertain all background information that you feel may affect the performance of the participants. This could expand on the classifiers you specified in the screening process. Similarly, to develop screening questions when you are recruiting participants, form questions that focus on behaviors that you are interested in exploring. For example, in a study for an entertainment news web site, you might collect information about the last time the participant downloaded shows or movies from similar web sites. However, unlike screening, now you can ask more questions about participants that could set a context in which to analyze the performance data from the session. For example, for the test of the entertainment news web site, you could ask about other, similar interests or habits such as magazine purchases or what the last five shows or movies were that participants watched and in what venue.

Make the Questionnaire Easy to Fill Out and Compile

Design the questionnaire for the ease of both yourself (in analyzing the responses) and the participants (in having to remember their history), by avoiding open-ended questions. Have the participants check off boxes or circle answers. This will also minimize their time filling out the questionnaire (important if they will be filling it out the day of the test) and will decrease the number of unintelligible answers. You may want to automate the questionnaire by using a survey tool or other online form maker.

Test the Questionnaire

Try the questionnaire out on someone who fits the user profile or even on a colleague. It is amazing how easy it is for ambiguity to sneak in. Pilot testing the background questionnaire is just as important as pilot testing the other materials for the test, such as the screening questions (see Chapter 7), and the session script (discussed later in this chapter).

Decide How to Administer the Questionnaire

If the background questionnaire is brief (a page or two), then let the participants fill it out just prior to the test. You might even conduct an interview at the beginning of the session once the video camera is rolling to collect the information, or ask them to expand their answers, which also allows you to establish a rapport with each of the participants. If the questionnaire is lengthy, consider sending it to the participants prior to the test. They can either bring it with them to the test or email it back as long as there is sufficient time before the test. However, have a copy available prior to the test in case the participant forgets to bring his or her copy to the test.

Figure 8-4 shows a sample background questionnaire associated with the test of a hotel reservations web site.

Background Questionnaire

1) On average over the last 3 years, how many trips did you take each year during which you stayed at least 2 nights?

        ___ 1–5 trips per year

        ___ 6–12 trips per year

        ___ 13 or more trips per year

2) What types of trips were they?

        ___ mostly business

        ___ mostly pleasure

        ___ about half and half business and pleasure

3) How do you book your trips?

  a) Do you do it yourself or does someone else make the arrangements?

        ___ myself

        ___ someone else

  b) How did you book your last trip?

        ___ online

        ___ on the phone or another method (not agent or assistant)

4) What type of hotels did you stay in for your last three trips? Please tell me the names of the hotels:

        1. _____

        2. _____

        3. _____

5) Are you a member of any hotel rewards programs? Which ones?

        _____

        _____

6) Have you used your Rewards points towards a hotel stay within the last year?

        ___ Yes

        ___ No

        ___ Used points for something besides a hotel room

7) What is your age?

        ___ 21–30

        ___ 31–40

        ___ 41–50

        ___ 51–60

8) What is your gender?

        ___ female

        ___ male

Figure 8-4 Sample background questionnaire

Data Collection Tools

Taking notes during the typical usability testing session can be incredibly difficult. If you are moderating the test and taking notes yourself, your attention *will* be divided between recording what you observe and observing what is happening now. We strongly encourage you to enlist someone else to take notes or record data if at all possible. If it isn't possible, you should give even greater consideration to designing the most efficient, effective data collection tools (keeping in mind that by "data collection tool" we mean anything from a basic Word document with space for notes to sophisticated tracking software).

The purpose of the data collection instruments is to expedite the collection of all data pertinent to the test objectives. The intent is to collect data during the test as simply, concisely, and reliably as possible. Having a good data collection tool will assist analysis and reporting as well.

There are many data measures from which to choose, and these should be tied back to the test objectives and research questions. Let us not get ahead of ourselves though. Before simply collecting data, you need to consider the following six basic questions:

- What data will address the problem statement(s) in your test plan?
- How will you collect the data?
- How will you record the data?
- How do you plan to reduce and analyze the data?
- How and to whom will you report the data?
- What resources are available to help with the entire process?

The answers to these questions will drive the development of the instruments, tools, and even the number of people required to collect the data. Data collection should never just be a hunting expedition, where you collect information first, and worry about what to do with it later. This holds true even for the most preliminary type of exploratory testing. If you take that approach, you run the risk of matching the data to hoped-for results.

Also, an imprecise shotgun approach typically results in an unwieldy amount of data to reduce and analyze, and tends to confuse more than enlighten. The type of data you collect should be as clear in your mind as possible before the test and should be tied directly to the questions and issues you are trying to resolve.

For simplicity's sake, data collected during a test falls into two major categories:

- **Performance data:** This consists of objective measures of *behavior*, such as error rates, time, and counts of observed behavior elements. This type of data comes from observation of either the live test or review of the video recording after the test has been completed. The number of errors made on the way to completing a task is an example of a performance measure.

▪ **Preference data:**   Preference data consists of the more subjective data that measures a participant's *feelings or opinions* of the product. This data is typically collected via written, oral, or even online questionnaires or through the debriefing session after the test. A rating scale that measures how a participant feels about the product is an example of a preference measure.

Both performance and preference data can be analyzed quantitatively or qualitatively. For example, on the performance side, you can analyze errors quantitatively simply by counting the number of errors made on a task. You can also analyze errors qualitatively to expose places where the user does not understand the product's conceptual model.

On the preference side, a quantitative measure would be the number of unsolicited negative comments a participant makes. Or, qualitatively, you can analyze each negative comment to discover what aspect of the product's design the comment refers to.

In terms of the product development lifecycle, exploratory (or formative) tests usually favor qualitative research, because of the emphasis on the user's understanding of high-level concepts. Validation (or summative) tests favor quantitative research, because of the emphasis on adherence to standards or measuring against benchmarks.

Following are examples of performance data.

Counts and rates	Number of errors
	Percentage of tasks completed successfully
	Number and type of hints or prompts needed to complete task
	Number of omitted steps or procedures
	Scores on a comprehension test
Time durations	Time to complete a task
	Time to recover from an error
	Time to achieve a criterion level of competence
	Training time to achieve benchmark performance
	Time spent reading vs. working

Following are examples of preference data.

Participant comments and opinions	Preference of Version A vs. Version B in a competitive or comparative study
	Suggestions for improving the product
	Number of *negative* references to the product
	Rationales for performance (what the participant says about why he or she did what he or she did)
	Ratings or rankings of the product

Following is a systematic strategy for developing the collection tools that takes into consideration the six critical questions discussed previously.

Review the Research Question(s) Outlined in Your Test Plan

If after reviewing these, you have a difficult time ascertaining what data to collect, *regard that as an important message*. More often than not, it means that you need to clarify the research question(s) to make them more specific. This may require reinterviewing the designers and developers and educating them as well.

Decide What Type of Information to Collect

Match the type of data you'll collect to a problem statement of the test plan. Figure 8-5 shows several matchups of problem statements with data collected.

Research Question	Data Collected
How easy is it to perform a specific task using a new hardware product?	Error rate among all participants. Or Number of steps required to perform the task.
Do novice participants access the site map?	Number of unsolicited accesses of the site map before completing the task. And Explanations of what participants were looking for in the navigation categories that they did not find.
How accessible is information in the Contact Us section of the web site?	Time expired between searching for a specific piece of information and locating it on the correct page.
How effective is a tutorial in teaching a specific task?	Time expired between accessing the tutorial and successful completion of the task. Or Comparison of error rates of participants using and not using the tutorial.

Figure 8-5 Research Question/Data Collection Table

Please be aware that there are numerous ways to collect data that address these problem statements. The ones shown in Figure 8-5 are only examples.

If you are unsure where to begin, start simply. For a typical test, it is common to collect at least the following information for each participant observed:

- Whether each task was completed successfully
- Whether prompting or assistance was required
- Major problems/obstacles associated with each task
- Time required to perform each task
- Observations/comments concerning each participant's actions

Select a Data Collection Method

Once you are clear about the type of data you want to collect and how it will help you to achieve the test objectives, the next challenge is to develop the means for collecting that data. In terms of data collection instruments, you are limited only by your imagination, resources, and the time required to develop the instruments. Will you have help with the collection? Will you have help reducing and analyzing the data once it is collected? It makes no sense at all to design a data collection method that requires extensive analysis of 20 hours of video recordings if you only have 2 weeks after the test in which to provide a test report.

Envision yourself creating the test report and even making a presentation to members of the team. Visualize the type of findings you will want to report, if not the actual content. Then, given the amount of time and resources at your disposal, plan how you will get to that point once the test has ended. Your data collection effort should be bounded by that constraint, unless you realistically feel that you or someone else will be able to analyze the additional data later.

Fully Automated Data Loggers

Fully automated data loggers such as Morae, UserVue, The Observer, and Ovo Logger are tools for collecting data by using a computer, with little or no intervention required by the test moderator (once the data capture configuration is established) or the participant. The software keeps a record of mouse clicks or keystrokes (or both) made by a participant and when it occurred. It compiles this data for review after the test. Some loggers will not only count the number and type of keystrokes or mouse clicks, but will also show where in the product a participant was when trying to complete a specific task. Loggers can note which pages or screens were accessed and the total time spent on each, synchronized with digital video capture of what is happening on the screen at the time. Although loggers will collect this data for you, keep in mind that it can be time consuming to analyze keystroke and mouse click data. Consider carefully whether you actually need this data, and plan ahead for the additional time you will need to review and analyze it.

There are also tools for conducting automated or remote usability tests, such as Keynote or UserZoom. Typically, these are used for very large-scale usability tests where participants are not present in a lab but instead participate from wherever they feel like it. Interpreting the data from these tools is not always straightforward, especially with very large samples, and there are other ways to expose usability problems. Technology is not always the right *or single* solution for capturing usability data. Again, look at your test objectives and the questions you need to get answers to before investing money and time in such loggers or services.

Online Data Collection

Data collection by the test moderator can take the form of collection forms on a computer screen. The computer is used by the test moderator to record participant actions and to enter observations and comments directly into a file or database. Rather than noting the actions and events on a paper form, the test moderator enters events as they occur simply by choosing from predetermined choices on the screen. (Again, this could be as simple as a Word file with checklists embedded.) By simplifying the data entry down to the selection of a radio button or checkbox or code, the test moderator or observer can more easily keep up with a participant's performance during the test session. Whoever is collecting the data could also enter free-form text.

User-Generated Data Collection

Another form of data collection is one initiated by the participants themselves and is especially helpful to organizations with few internal resources. User-generated data collection can take one of two forms, either online or manual collection. In the online format, the participant accesses a data collection form on the same computer that is being used for the test. The form, usually a questionnaire or checklist, interrogates the participant about a task just completed. The participant can fetch the screen (more intrusive) or the software can display it automatically upon completion of a task or upon reaching a time benchmark (less intrusive). (One such tool is called the Usability Testing Environment (UTE) and is available at www.mindd.com for a substantial investment.) In the latter case, participants may even perceive that the data collection is a seamless part of their task. The questionnaire will typically cover such items as participant rankings for ease of use, preferences for one type of interface over another, frequency of using an index, and so on.

In the second format, manual collection, each participant fills out a written questionnaire after completing a specific task. Filling out the questionnaire represents a pause in the test, so the questionnaire needs to be structured to make it as unobtrusive as possible. In designing these questionnaires and checklists, one needs to be wary of the following two potential pitfalls:

- Wording the questions in a biased way
- Using terms unfamiliar to the participants

The user-generated/self-reporting technique naturally lends itself to the collection of comparative data (e.g., two different interfaces, two different manual styles, etc.) and to the type of test where subjective data (preference data) is the main focus.

Manual Data Collection

Manual data collection is performed by one or more human observers of the test either during or after the test, using customized paper data collection forms. This is the format you are most likely to use if you are just beginning to test. Data collected could be in the form of notes, observations, counts, or time durations. The forms employed can vary from the elaborate (custom-designed multi-page forms) to the simple (drafts of the screens or pages of the documentation being tested). The form can be used for collecting quantitative data, such as the number of times *documentation or help* was accessed, or qualitative data, such as specific comments made by a participant. It can also be used to collect interpretations by the observer of a participant's behavior. For example, you might note that a particular participant seems very confused while reading page 5. There are several examples of data collection forms to support manual data collection at the end of this section.

Other Data Collection Methods

As previously mentioned, data collection is limited only by your imagination. Several years ago, when Jeff and a colleague were conducting a test of some documentation, they came upon a simple way of determining what sections of the manual were being completely ignored. They glued together every page of the manual with a special glue that provided very slight resistance when a page was turned. The participants noticed nothing unusual during the test, attributing any stickiness of the pages to the fact that the book was new. At the end of the test, Jeff and his colleague had a foolproof method for establishing which sections of the manual were never used. Wherever the glue was still in place, they knew that a particular participant had never even glanced at that page, and they discovered whole sections that were still glued together. Jeff admits that this method resulted less from his zeal to break new ground in scientific methods than it did from simple laziness. Neither he nor his colleague wanted to focus on the pages that were avoided during the test, nor review hours of video recordings to establish what each participant was and was not reading.

When designing a data collection form that you and other observers will use, design for efficiency and ease of use. The idea is to anticipate the events that will happen during the test and to design the form or screen to limit the amount of data entry required as much as possible. Do *not* require a handwritten entry when a check-off box will suffice. By anticipating the type of data and the actions of the participants that you will be observing and noting, your form can significantly reduce the time required to collect data. This frees you to pay attention to the subtleties of the test and to probe each participant's behavior as needed.

Once you have minimized the amount of writing you will need to do during the test as much as possible, there are two methods still available for further reducing the amount of writing required by human observers:

■ One way is to write notes using shorthand or your own version of shorthand. Make sure that you have a translation of your shorthand available if someone else needs to read your notes.

■ The second method is to develop one- or two-letter codes or number codes to represent each critical event that might occur during the test. The test moderator jots the code down every time the critical behavior is witnessed. Figure 8-6 shows a simple shorthand coding scheme for data collection.

Customize your own codes to your specific needs. The coding schemes can get quite elaborate, so make sure that you can at least remember them without

Shorthand Code	Event
B	Begin task
E	End task
C	Click
S	Submit
P	Prompted by moderator
M	Exceeded time allotted
X	Incorrect action
CC	Completed correctly
?	Probe participant about this during debriefing
O	Observation by test moderator
T	Check the recording

Figure 8-6 Simple shorthand key

Participant #:	Date:	Time:
Task	**Issues**	**Observations, comments & notes**

Figure 8-7 Generic data collection form

Measures	Success Criteria
How easily does the voter know where the information is on the page?	They go to Voter Pamphlet section. They select from the pulldown. They read aloud the name of at least one race and the names of the candidates.
_____ No problem	Completed successfully?
_____ Wrong turns, but completed without assistance—how many?	____ Y ____ N
_____ Needed prompting	
_____ Needed specific instructions	
Where did the voter get stuck or confused?	
_____	
_____	
What surprised the voter? Was it good or bad?	
_____ No surprises	
_____ Surprised by:	
____ good?	
____ bad?	
How well did the voter understand the information they got from the system?	
____ No problem	
____ Had questions; what?	
____ Needed help	
____ Needed to be told specifically the meaning of the information they got	

Figure 8-8 Web page–based data collection form

having to look them up, as that defeats one purpose of having them. The other purpose is for quick evaluation of the data collection sheets during analysis. Make sure that the codes are easy to spot, especially if someone else will be helping you analyze the data.

If you will be using more than one observer to collect different types of data, consider using different data collection forms. One person's form might be specifically designed for noting times, while another's might be designed for capturing participant comments and observations.

The following figures give examples of two types of data collection instruments for manual collection. The first example, Figure 8-7, is a generic form that can be used for any type of product, be it hardware, software, web site, electronic device, or documentation.

Another example, Figure 8-8, is a collection form for monitoring the use of a web site for registered voters to find the name and contact information for their state legislators. In this case each task performed by the participant is represented on a single form with questions following.

Nondisclosures, Consent Forms, and Recording Waivers

Besides questionnaires to gather data from participants, there are a few forms you might consider including in your packet to get promises and permissions from participants: nondisclosure, recording permission, and informed consent:

- **Nondisclosure form.** The purpose of the nondisclosure agreement is to prevent the unauthorized disclosure of proprietary product information that participants may encounter during the test. This document is almost always required for those products developed for the external marketplace prior to release.

- **Recording permission.** The purpose of the recording consent form is to get written permission from the participants to record them during the usability test. Typically, this form also establishes how you may or may not use their image or voice. This permission should not be abused. Protect the confidentiality of your participants as much as possible by not showing or using their full name on the recording and by limiting the use of the recordings to those with a "need to know."

- **Informed consent form.** If you work for a public institution or agency, you may have to go through an internal review board (IRB) and then ask participants to sign a consent form that explains the study, describes the risks to the participant (or clearly says that there are none), and lists a person to contact with questions or issues.

Most likely you will want to have the legal department of your company review these documents to ensure that the language is correct and protects both your company and the participants. It is very important to inform the participants *before* they arrive that they will be required to avoid disclosing

Nondisclosure and Recording Consent

Thank you for participating in our product research program. Please be aware that information will be disclosed to you that XYZ Company does not wish to be disclosed outside of the company. Please do not reveal information that you may learn while participating in the study.

In addition, we will be recording your session to allow those XYZ staff members who cannot be present to observe your session and benefit from your feedback. Please read the statements below and sign where indicated. Thank you.

I agree that I will disclose no information to any person, firm, or corporation about the product research conducted by XYZ Company, or about the specifications, drawings, models or operations of any machine or devices encountered.

I understand that photographs and/or recordings will be made of my session. I grant XYZ Company permission to use these recordings for the purposes mentioned above, and waive my right to review or inspect the recordings prior to their dissemination and distribution.

_____   _____
Signature   Date

Figure 8-9 Sample of simple combined nondisclosure and recording consent form

what they learn, but more importantly that their image and/or voice will be recorded. While it is rare, some people will refuse to let you record them or will want to know precisely how your company will use their image.

If, in spite of precautions, you are faced with someone who refuses to be recorded and insists that he or she was never informed, you can either use them without recording them or release and compensate them.

Figure 8-9 shows a simple combined nondisclosure and recording consent form. Many organizations use much more elaborate ones than shown here. Should you decide to use this one verbatim, please ensure that your own legal department reviews it first.

Pre-Test Questionnaires and Interviews

Unlike the background questionnaire, which is also given before the test and which has a primarily informational purpose, the purpose of a pre-test questionnaire is to address specific test objectives, such as a participant's first impressions of a product (especially in an exploratory or formative test), to qualify the placement of participants into a specific group, or to establish their level of expertise. As such, the pre-test questionnaire is considered an integral part of the test design. It is worthwhile to discuss each of these purposes in detail.

Discover Attitudes and First Impressions

One purpose of a pre-test questionnaire or interview is to determine participant attitudes and first impressions about a product's ease of use prior to using it. That initial impression of a product can be a prime element of usability testing. For example:

- Does the product *look* easy to use?
- Does the participant understand the terminology?
- Is the product similar or very different from other products, or even from previous releases of the same product?

These initial impressions set the stage for the actual usage of the product, and it is often very helpful to understand the participant's feelings and expectations *before* that usage occurs. If a product *appears difficult* to use, then it already has an obstacle to overcome. Conversely, *if it appears simple* or *intuitive* to use, then it has an advantage, and an end user might expend more time trying the product before calling a hotline or abandoning it altogether. Therefore, gathering "pre-usage" information can help you to understand the participant's behavior later.

The test moderator might show the participant a screen, control panel, or the table of contents of a manual, and ask the participant to rank how easy the item in question will be to use. This first ranking will be based solely on first impression prior to performing any tasks. You might also ask the basis for the participant's ranking to understand the cause of any initial confusion or trepidation.

The research can also be expanded to explore how actual usage affected those initial impressions. This is accomplished by providing the exact same pre-test questionnaire after the usability test. (Guess what? This makes it a post-test questionnaire.) The intent is to investigate whether product usage increases or decreases rankings of initial impressions. If the rankings decrease, you know that the product's usage did not live up to its initial appearance. If the rankings increase, then you know that the participant's image of the product improves with usage — an excellent result indeed. This type of research can help one to understand just how much of an effect an intimidating or overly complex design is having on performance.

A variation of this theme goes beyond simply asking the participant to state his or her first impression of a product. You can also inquire about the participant's very specific understanding of those elements of a product that you expect to be self-evident without prior usage of the product. For example, the symbols or icons of the control panel on a printer should be self-evident to a novice user, as should the navigation labels of a web site. If not, it is very helpful to know that, and it is also helpful to see if a participant learns by using the product.

The research is identical to that stated previously. *Prior to any use of the product*, provide the participants with a knowledge-based test that asks them to define terms with which they are expected to be familiar. After the performance test portion of the usability test, have them fill out identical questionnaires to see if using the product increased, decreased, or had no effect on their understanding. Their performance can help drive the decision to retain or change terminology, always a political football at best.

Figure 8-10 shows an example of a terminology test used to determine the self-evidence of the terminology on a web site designed for people over the age of 50. A terminology questionnaire could be used for evaluating web site

Task 1: Thoughts and impressions of xyz.org home page

Participant #: _____

Imagine that you are on a web site for people who are age 50 or older. What would you expect to find if you clicked on each of the words below? Describe the term's meaning or intended usage as it would apply to the web site just described. If you don't know, please guess.

Join xyz	
Member Services and Discounts	
Computers and Technology	
Health and Wellness	
Learning	
Legislation and Elections	
Life Answers	
Money and Work	
Policy and Research	
Travel and Leisure	
Volunteering	
Community	

Figure 8-10 Example of a terminology questionnaire

navigation, commands or toolbar labels, screens, manuals, or other hardware products. Before having the participant fill out your pre-test questionnaire, let the participant view the product in question or let him or her fill out the questionnaire while looking at the product. This provides any context that would help to understand the terms. However, do not allow them to *try* the product.

Learn about Whether Participants Value the Product

Another purpose of a pre-test questionnaire or interview is to discover the opinions of the participants about the utility or value of the product prior to using it. This is different from the previous category in that here you are looking at the opinions of the participants about the value or utility of the product's raw functionality. While the former concern was a first impression of usability, here you simply want to know the inherent value of such a product *before even considering usability as a factor*. This is especially important research for cutting-edge products that are new to the marketplace or new to your target market. It is helpful to know if certain types of users harbor an inherent bias for or against a particular product or technology, and how using the product affects that bias.

For example, if you were testing a cell phone-based appointment calendar/organizer, you might want to know if your target audience initially harbors a fear or resistance to using such a product. Perhaps this group is composed of staunch users of manual or separate organizers and who have no desire to use one on their phones. You could ask them questions about the value of appointment calendars, and then ask them the same questions after they use the product. By giving similar or identical questionnaires to the participants before and after the usability test session, you can see if their opinions change for the better or the worse. This type of research is not only helpful in evaluating overall usability but also can provide valuable insights to your marketing team that can help to sell the product to different types of customers or offer it to different internal customers. In addition, it is always gratifying to see if your product can convert die-hard skeptics into customers.

The other very important issue here relates to the relative value of usability compared to other product factors. If you *just* consider the usability of performing relevant tasks and not the inherent value or desire to perform these tasks, you are doing yourself and the product a great disservice. You are missing an important piece of information if the question of usefulness is not examined. If end users value the benefits of a particular product, then they will put up with more problems than if their interest is minimal. Knowing this information can help you to prioritize your test results. Unfortunately, we have seen usability tests conducted in just this fashion; that is, with little attention paid to the inherent value of the particular product or technology. This usually happens when testing occurs late in the development cycle.

For example, as we are writing this edition there is a great trend to include social networking features in all types of web sites. ("Social networking" online is anything that would allow users of a web site to share information with one another, such as customer reviews of products or services, blogs, or wikis.) But on an intranet site for a financial services company, users may not value socializing electronically through the corporate equivalent of MySpace or Facebook with their coworkers. Including tools to support work might be more useful and appropriate.

Figure 8-11 shows an example of a questionnaire that explores the participant's opinions about the utility of a cell phone calendar prior to trying it.

Before you try out the product today, we want to understand the value you place on the idea. Please answer the questions below.

1. I think having a calendar function on my cell phone would be useful.

_____ Yes; how? _____
_____

_____ No; why not? _____
_____

2. I use these features on my phone: (*Please mark all that apply*)
_____ address book
_____ autodial
_____ alarm clock
_____ camera
_____ music feature
_____ text messaging
_____ other

3. Being able to synchronize appointments on the phone calendar with a calendar I could maintain on a web site would be useful to me. (*Circle one*)

Strongly agree	Agree	Neither agree nor disagree	Disagree	Strongly disagree

Why?
_____
_____
_____

4. I would pay for such a service.

_____ Yes; how much would you expect it to cost? _____

_____ No

5. In general, I enjoy using gadgets like cell phones and other high-tech products

Strongly agree	Agree	Neither agree nor disagree	Disagree	Strongly disagree

Figure 8-11 Example of a product value questionnaire

Qualify Participants for Inclusion into One Test Group or Another

The next two categories are entirely different reasons for the pre-test questionnaire, having to do with qualifying your participants. Suppose that your test design calls for both expert and novice participants along a certain dimension. Your screening questionnaire, given orally over the phone, may have initially placed potential participants into either expert or novice groups based on their answers to some general questions. Your background questionnaire collected information about their breadth of experience. Now suppose that you need to go the extra mile to more precisely establish a potential participant's background. A more detailed questionnaire given prior to the test can be used to ascertain the potential participant's experience level more accurately and to place him or her into the appropriate group. (Technically, what we are about to describe could be an add-on to the background questionnaire, even though the type of questions are different.)

For example, suppose that your test design calls for participants with varying levels of online investing expertise. A common means to establish a person's expertise is to simply have that person rate himself or herself, either by degree of expertise or by confidence level. Although this is better than guessing, it is not all that reliable. We have seen the most competent participants rate themselves as barely novice on a rating scale, and vice versa. There are two other ways to perform this rating that are more reliable.

The first way is to develop a chart, similar to the one shown in Figure 8-12, composed of the major functions of the product or application (or with behaviors that would be proxies for the types of tasks users will do with your product) with a place for the participants to estimate the frequency with which they perform those functions.

The participants simply check off a frequency of usage for each of the major functions of the product. Because you can assume that more frequent usage is associated with a higher degree of competence, you can assign the participants who have more frequent usage to the expert category.

The second way is a variation of the self-rating method, but with more precision and less subjectivity. Unlike the single overall ranking that is unreliable, this version asks participants to rate their expertise on a variety of functions. An example of this technique is shown in Figure 8-13.

The interesting feature of this technique is that it results in an overall score, for example 12, when all responses to all seven questions are tallied. Then, based on your understanding of the application, you provide arbitrary cutoff points in which novice, intermediate, and expert participants reside. In this case, novice participants are those who reside in the 0 to 10 range, intermediate participants reside in the 11 to 18 range, and expert participants reside in the

When	Research health information such as conditions, treatments, or drugs at web site	Take part in online auctions	Play games alone or with others on web site	Pay bills through a web site	Totals
Never (0)					(number of Xs * 0)
Once per month (1)					(number of Xs * 1)
Once per week (1)					(number of Xs * 2)
Daily (3)					(number of Xs * 3)
Several times a day (4)					(number of Xs * 4)
					(total Xs * point value in each row)

Figure 8-12 Sample user expertise questionnaire

Participant #:_____

Please rate your expertise on each of the following activities for using a spreadsheet:

Setting up a spreadsheet with multiple worksheets
Never done   Expert
0   1   2   3   4   5

Setting up and revising a formula
Never done   Expert
0   1   2   3   4   5

Sorting and filtering data
Never done   Expert
0   1   2   3   4   5

Creating charts
Never done   Expert
0   1   2   3   4   5

Setting up pivot tables
Never done   Expert
0   1   2   3   4   5

Figure 8-13 Sample user expertise questionnaire

19+ range. Both types of questionnaires attempt to quantify the rating rather than just having people assign labels to themselves.

Establish the Participant's Prerequisite Knowledge Prior to Using the Product

Suppose you had a product that was intended for end users who were mathematicians. Without this very specific critical knowledge, in this case mathematics, the end user will be unable to use your product effectively. To ascertain the person's knowledge in this area, give him or her a questionnaire (or in some cases an actual test) that establishes how knowledgeable he or she is. This is not at all unlike a screening questionnaire (see the screening questionnaire section in Chapter 7) or the criterion test used in conjunction with the development of prerequisite training materials (see the section "Optional Training Materials" presented later in this chapter). The only difference from the screening questionnaire is that you are not using this information to weed people out of your study. You are simply verifying the degree of their expertise in order to help evaluate their results. Very often the person will already have filled out a simpler version of this pre-test questionnaire as a screener because it was not possible to provide such an in-depth questionnaire beforehand.

The only difference from the criterion test used with prerequisite training is that you have no intention of training the person if he or she performed "poorly" on the questionnaire. If you discover that a particular person was really not qualified, you could choose to release that person or run the test differently.

Of course, there *is* one more reason for having your participants fill out this type of questionnaire, and it is a political reason — namely, to have the expertise of the participants as a matter of record in case a member of the development team challenges the test results by saying a participant was not qualified.

Prototypes or Products to Test

Of course, you must have something to test. Get your hands on it as early as possible, in whatever form it is in. It probably *won't* be a completed product, and that's fine. That is part of the point of testing early and often.

In fact, it may be that you are testing a very early prototype of some kind. Becoming familiar with the thing being tested before the first session — even the pilot session — is highly recommended. By using it the first time, you will have a much better idea what to expect when participants do try it out: where they might have difficulty, where they may ask questions, what isn't obvious on the first viewing. To conduct sessions, you must know just how functional the product is, so you can understand its limitations. For example, you may find yourself saying at various points, "As I mentioned, you are using a prototype today, which is not fully functional. In real life, what you just did would have worked." You need to know going into the session what those points are.

Use the prototype yourself as you develop the task scenarios. You may want to document the "correct" steps for completing the scenarios so you can check while the participant is working whether he is taking a wrong turn. Next, practice using the script while testing the task scenarios until you feel comfortable that you can track the expected steps for using the product to the task scenarios and the data you plan to collect. Finally, do a dry run with someone else as your participant.

Task Scenarios

Task scenarios are representations of actual work that the participants would conceivably perform using your product. Task scenarios are expanded versions of the original task list (previously developed as part of the test plan), adding context and the participant's rationale and motivation to perform those original tasks. In many cases, one task scenario will comprise several tasks from the task list grouped together because that is the way that people perform their work on the job.

Task scenarios for your test materials should describe:

- The result that the participant will strive to achieve
- Motives for performing the work
- Actual data and names rather than generalities
- The state of the system when a task is initiated
- Readouts of displays and printouts that the participants will see while performing the task

Task scenarios may be either distributed to or read to the participants. If written, use plain language that does not mirror language used in the product (which may prime or lead participants). You could develop the task scenarios at the same time as the task list, but doing it sequentially and in phases simplifies the process.

The following sections give five key guidelines for the development of task scenarios.

Provide Realistic Scenarios, Complete with Motivations to Perform

The motivations can be explicit or implicit. Use actual case studies, task analyses, customer phone calls, and customer visits as the basis for your scenarios. The closer that the scenarios represent reality, the more reliable the test results. In addition, the participants will find it easier to "stay in role" and overcome any latent hesitation and self-consciousness if the scenarios reflect familiar situations, with realistic reasons for performing the tasks. For example, rather than simply asking the participants to print a report from a payroll system, tell them briefly what the report is for and who it is for. The context of the scenarios will also help them to evaluate elements in your product's design that simply do not jibe with reality. (If the task scenarios result in participants commenting that they would never do that, you have a problem with the scenario or the product or both.)

Sequence the Task Scenarios in Order

Sequencing the task scenarios in the order they are most likely to be performed in helps to:

- Retain the illusion of authenticity.
- Guide the participants in approximately the same way they would learn on the job.
- Expose the snowballing effects of errors and misconceptions.

Taking the last point, for example, if a participant misnames a file in an early task, that is not all that serious. However, when in a later related task that same participant uses that file name as the basis for naming 20 subordinate files, the problem's ramifications become serious indeed, and may escalate to a higher priority when you view the overall results. This is just what you want to see happen in the lab.

If sequential order is not crucial to performance, then consider varying the order of presentation of scenarios to different participants. This approach, known as *counterbalancing*, enables you to avoid potential biasing effects, such as when a scenario that is always presented last benefits from a participant's experience with previous tasks. For an example of counterbalancing, see the "Within-Subjects Design" section presented in Chapter 5. Or, let participants determine the order of tasks. This way, you may gain insights about users' natural task sequences and priorities.

Match the Task Scenarios to the Experience of the Participants

Not all participants should exercise identical aspects of your product. Some system features, screens, and/or sections of a manual should never be accessed by a novice participant during the usability test because these features, screens, and/or sections of the manual are too advanced for a novice. For example, if you have a section in your manual on advanced features, you would not include task scenarios that accessed that section for first-time users. Conversely, more experienced participants may simply skip over basic features, screens, and/or sections of a manual. Therefore, if you will be utilizing participants of varying experience levels, make sure that the degree of difficulty of a scenario is congruent with the experience level of the participant.

Avoid Using Jargon and Cues

Avoid product jargon or cues that serve as giveaways of the correct results. Avoid wording that includes actual button names, menu items, and screen titles. It is crucial that you do *not* provide unintentional cues to the participants that they would not ordinarily experience outside of the testing environment.

For example, even asking a novice participant to *save a file* is a giveaway if there is a "Save" command on the product. It points the participant in the right direction. Instead, say something like "Ensure that the phone number of the person you just spoke with is retained in your phone." (We know this sounds ridiculous, and the participant may look at you funny and say "Do you want me to save the number?" If the participant does, just say yes, and realize that sometimes it is necessary to make a fool of yourself in the interest of science.) Of course, in very early exploratory testing, you may intentionally ask the participants to find a particular "Save" screen or command, but that is a different kettle of fish entirely.

Try to Provide a Substantial Amount of Work in Each Scenario

Do *not* guide the participants through the product piecemeal, unless your product is in such a primitive state that you must work that way. Rather, provide a goal, clearly stated in simple language, and let participants do the rest. For example, if you were testing a web site, an appropriate task would be:

"Using this web site, you want to send some books to your nephew for his birthday."

To accomplish this task, it is implied that the participants must either learn or exhibit the following skills:

- Search for and select books.
- Review the list of items being ordered.
- Enter the recipient's address.
- Specify the appropriate billing address.

Whether the participants can perform or figure out these intermediate steps in order to complete the goal of the scenario is precisely what you want to learn from the usability test. If you simply ask them to search for and select books and then fill out the addresses needed, you never see whether the participants can put it all together, as they must on the job. Your tasks should force the participants to exhibit their conceptual understanding of the product, and should expose *their* misunderstandings about how to use the product. A simplistic navigation of pages in a web site or document, or screens, or other hardware components is simply not a challenging test.

Remember, from the participant's viewpoint, the product *is always* considered a means to an end. The participant's central focus is the work and the procedures required to perform that work. The product being tested is incidental to that, not central. Not only is this an important principle for effective testing, it is also the basis for user-centered design per se.

Give Participants the Tasks to Do

Now that you have reviewed the five key guidelines for the development of task scenarios, you may be asking yourself whether you should read the task scenarios to the participants or simply hand them out for the participants to read. This question is valid and is accompanied by two schools of thought. One supports reading the scenarios to the participants, while the other supports distributing them and letting the participants read them. Following is some additional information to clarify this choice.

Reading Task Scenarios to the Participants

An advantage to reading the scenarios, especially if they are complex, is that you can interact with the participants and make sure they understand what to do. You certainly do not want to watch them flounder for 10 minutes or go completely down a wrong path simply because they misunderstood what to do. Reading the scenarios to the participants also enables you to control the pace of the usability test. This control is important if your test is very interactive, say during an exploratory test, and you will be probing the participants at the conclusion of each major scenario. You may want to read a scenario to the participant but then also give him or her a copy to refer to.

Letting the Participants Read Task Scenarios Themselves

Let the participants read the scenarios themselves if you are testing from another room or if you want to minimize contact with the participants, as you would during a validation test. Use your pilot test(s) to ensure that the scenarios are clear and unambiguous. Even with that safeguard, you still may want the participants to read the scenarios out loud and ask questions before beginning a task.

Decide if you want the participants to see only one scenario at a time. If there are many scenarios or if the scenarios are very complex, viewing them all at one time could be intimidating and distracting. Participants may try to get ahead of themselves even subconsciously, or they may perform in a different way if they know information from the current task is needed later. They may also look ahead in the documentation which could affect timing.

One way to control the flow of information and also help with timing a task is to have the participant access and read the tasks from a computer. A task clock begins to time the task as soon as the participant leaves the screen from which it is displayed. Upon completion, the participant accesses the same file, which shows the next task on the list. Or, you may ask the participant to check it off. That stops the clock on the first task. Using this method, you can set the program to display one scenario at a time, which effectively solves the problem of looking ahead.

Figures 8-14 and 8-15 show how a task list becomes a task scenario. Figure 8-14 shows the first seven tasks of the task list as it was developed for the product team. Figure 8-15 shows a task scenario for the participants.

Task Number	Description	Required to perform	Success criteria	Maximum time
1	Unpack the printer	• Unopened box • Quick setup guide	Printer removed from box and ready for next step	5 min
2	Connect the power cord	• Power cord • Quick setup guide • Printer	Power cord placed in its socket correctly	2 min
3	Choose the appropriate interface cable	• Four cables clearly marked • Quick setup guide • Table	Correct cable chosen from the four and participant indicates it is the correct one	2 min
4	Connect interface cable	• Interface cable • Quick setup guide • Printer • PC	One end of cable placed firmly in its seat in the prointer, the other end seated in the computer port	2 min
5	Install the printer cartridge	• Cartridge carton, • unopened • Materials in carton	Cartridge seated in its correct position aligned with blue guides	3 min
6	Load the paper	• Ream of paper • Printer paper tray • Quick setup guide	Paper placed correctly in paper tray, under the corner guides with spring-loaded bottom pressed down	3 min
7	Turn the printer on	• Printer with all connections, cartridge installed, paper loaded, etc. • Quick setup guide	Participant presses power button on	1 min

Figure 8-14 Example of a task list for setting up a printer out of the box

You have recently ordered a brand new printer, which has just been
delivered. Please set up the printer in the same manner as you normally
would at home. Signal me when you reach the point at which you feel ready to
print your first document. Any questions before we begin?

Figure 8-15 Sample task scenario for setting up a printer

Now in Figure 8-15 the tasks from the task list are subsumed under a
single task scenario designed for the participants to read during the test. The
scenario encompasses all seven tasks because these represent the first activities
for setting up a printer from the user's point of view. It provides a realistic
scenario to place the participant within a familiar context. Note that the choice
to use the documentation is left to the participant. Because of this, you may see
participants attempting to work on their own and then using the document.
Be aware that you may not see tasks occurring in the same order as shown
on your data collection form. Also be aware that with a different test design,
one whose objective was to establish the efficacy of the documentation once
it was accessed, you could have just as easily *insisted* that the participants use
the documentation.

Optional Training Materials

Prerequisite training refers to any training provided to participants prior to
the actual usability test that raises their skill level to some preestablished
criterion or allows them to be tested further along their learning curve. It could
range from a simple 10-minute description of the product to a comprehensive
two-day workshop. Following are several situations that warrant prerequisite
training and, as such, suggest when this type of training should be provided.

Ensure Minimum Expertise

In this situation, you want to make sure that the participants you are testing
possess some prescribed minimum level of expertise deemed necessary to use
the product effectively. The expertise in question could range from the ability
to use a web browser to expertise in accounting. In either case, a projected
end user of the product is expected to be proficient in some area, and you
want to make sure that each participant is qualified. For example, suppose
you are testing a photo retouching package that presupposes a certain level
of photography expertise. If your participants are unqualified, it will reflect
poorly and unfairly on the product, because the projected end user will have
more expertise. By checking each participant's expertise prior to the test and
providing some specific photography training in the cases where participants
fall short, you provide a fairer test of the product.

Or, in a common situation today, your product requires knowledge of how to use the features of a web browser, including setting up RSS (Really Simple Syndication) feeds. If you use a participant who has all the other appropriate characteristics of your user profile but who is a novice at using a web browser or a feed reader, you will spend the first part of your test watching the participant struggle to master the intricacies of using the browser or reader, and very little time on the behaviors that affect the product's success. Instead, why not provide prerequisite training on using the browser or reader and begin the usability test *after* the participant has shown proficiency.

Get a View of the User after Experiencing the Product

Here you want to evaluate usage of your product further along the participant's learning curve. Developers sometimes feel, and rightfully so, that the usability testing process is biased toward the testing of novices, and that they are unable to see experienced participants try out their products. Another way of stating the problem is that too often usability tests evaluate "ease of learning" (the ability to grasp the fundamental concepts and simple features of a product) and do not adequately evaluate "ease of use" (those behaviors that follow mastery of the early concepts and basic features). In other words, usability tests often measure how well a beginner uses the product, but not someone who is more likely to put the product through its paces. This is a legitimate criticism, because it is hard to refute the logic that a novice participant and one who has used the product for even a week will expose very different problems with a product and will use it quite differently.

One way to address this issue and at the same time make for a more comprehensive test is to test some participants who are further along the learning curve before beginning the usability test. However, if your product is new, participants with even a week of experience simply do not exist, and it is impractical to allow participants a week to get their bearings.

A solution to this dilemma is to artificially move the participants along the learning curve through intensive, structured, prerequisite training. The training should simulate a week (or two weeks, or a month if you prefer) of typical use. You accomplish this by first establishing the level of expertise for a week-old user (the skills and knowledge he or she would possess). Then you develop a data collection instrument to measure that expertise. Finally, you develop a training package that reaches those skills and knowledge. The training media could be self-paced, instructor led, online, or a combination.

For those participants who take the training, the usability test begins after they have achieved this criterion level of performance, that is, passed a proficiency test and met a minimum criterion of skill. If you approach the problem systematically, you probably can achieve criterion for a week-old user with two or three hours of training, practice, and questions. The important point is that you establish that the participants have met criterion before they are tested, so everyone begins from at least some minimum expertise.

As an added benefit, take advantage of these training sessions to study how the participants learn the product, almost as an informal exploratory session. But the "official" reason for the prerequisite training is to see how experienced participants perform on the product during the usability test.

You Want to Test Features for Advanced Users

Imagine that your product has a section devoted to advanced features strictly for experienced end users that you would like to test extensively.

~ OR ~

You have previously tested and established the usability of the simpler features of your product and do not want to retest those during your current test. This is similar to the last case, but instead of focusing on the experience of the participants, the focus is on a particular aspect of the product. The easiest way to explain is by example. The following are two examples of the preceding situation.

Example 1. Suppose that, because of time constraints, you want to start the test immediately with the advanced features of the product for some participants, but the simpler features or functions are a prerequisite for using the advanced features. You have not been able to locate or simply do not care to locate experienced end users of your product. Therefore, you provide prerequisite training that systematically teaches the simpler features, and begin the usability test immediately with the advanced features.

Example 2. Perhaps your software product consists of two sets of discrete functions. One set of functions is simple, familiar, and originates from a previous release of the product. You expect the end user to be able to use these right out of the box with little confusion, and previous testing has determined that documentation is not required. However, another set of functions is brand new and represents an advanced feature set. Everyone on the team agrees these features are not intuitive and require documentation to master. In this case, you are able to find experienced end users as participants, but want to make sure that they all share some minimum skill level.

The safest way to approach situations like these is to provide a criterion test (a proficiency check) to the experienced participants prior to the usability test that essentially qualifies them. If they pass the criterion test, they may immediately begin the usability test of the advanced features. If they do not pass the criterion test, then they first receive prerequisite training on *those features that they missed on the criterion test,* until they reach the criterion. Then they begin the usability test of advanced features.

This conservative approach ensures that you are testing apples and apples, and not apples and oranges. You operationally define what you mean by "experienced skills," check for the presence of those skills, and correct when necessary.

Use real examples and include a criterion test (e.g., "check yourself") at the end. If users did not "pass" the test, give them remediation until they are proficient. At that point, the actual usability can begin.

What Are the Benefits of Prerequisite Training?

Having discussed the purpose of prerequisite training, let's pause and discuss the advantages of this underused element of the usability test, because it offers some important benefits.

You Can Conduct a More Comprehensive, Challenging Usability Test

Because prerequisite training allows you to work with experienced end users (even if you cannot find any initially), you can exercise more sophisticated functionality of the product than you otherwise could when only testing beginners. For example, when testing a software interface, you can design tasks that require a grounding in the basics of navigation, error handling, and so on. Or, when testing documentation, you can observe participant behaviors *after* they have already understood the organization and layout of the document. You can watch people exercise the more subtle aspects of the design, which beginners do not normally use. Looking at it another way, you are testing ease of use more than ease of learning.

You Can Test Functionality That Might Otherwise Get Overlooked During a Test

Normally, during a usability test, there is not enough time to exercise the more advanced features, to see if they are intuitive or to see if the documentation's explanations are lucid enough to guide the participants successfully. With a test designed around prerequisite training, the tasks can begin with the more difficult and less obvious features. *This may be the only opportunity to see these functions utilized prior to release of the product.*

Remember, with this technique, you can witness behaviors that normally would not occur until after a week or two (or longer) of using the product. This is unusual and very advantageous. Rather than having someone call in a problem on the company hotline after product release, you get to see it occur in the lab. It also gives developers and technical writers the opportunity to work on functionality that ordinarily gets overlooked.

Developing the Training Forces You to Understand How Someone Learns to Use Your Product

A very real by-product of developing the prerequisite training is that it forces everyone on the development team to relate to how end users learn to use the product. Normally, the only people concerned with such information are the training developers and/or technical writers. In developing and observing the training, the product designers and developers often come to appreciate the level of a novice using the product, and the obstacles they face in learning the product.

Some Common Questions about Prerequisite Training

Q. In the case where you want to test the more advanced features of a product, is it not inherently biasing to teach participants how to use your product prior to a usability test?

A. Will anyone actually make errors during the test? These questions are often voiced as a concern. The answer to both is "yes," participants still make many errors, especially on complex products. Once the actual training is removed, *if the product is poorly designed and unintuitive to use*, participants stumble even on the tasks they have just learned. It seems that poor design always wins out. However, this technique probably will *not* work if your product is extremely simple, because participants can remember confusing points and inconsistencies. In that case, you may need to introduce a period of "forgetting" (a few days to a week) between the training and the testing to eliminate that tendency.

Also keep in mind that because the participants have received training in the basics, your test design should include more difficult, more challenging tasks than you normally would provide to novice users.

Q. Doesn't prerequisite training increase the total time required to run the test?

A. Yes, it does *and it also increases the overall expense of the test*. The downside of testing advanced participants is the time factor. You will need to build in time for your participants to take the training as well as the usability test. It is not unusual to spend an entire day or more with one participant for sophisticated products with complete documentation sets.

However, to mitigate that aspect, remember that the entire team, who may normally want to view the test, need not be there for the prerequisite training. In fact, the training could occur at an entirely different time. Nor must the test moderator be there, although it is better if the test moderator is present. If need be, someone else entirely can handle the prerequisite training. In that case, using the criterion test is doubly important to ensure consistency among training sessions that different trainers conduct.

Post-Test Questionnaire

The main purpose of the written post-test questionnaire(s) is to gather preference information from the participants in order to clarify and deepen your understanding of the product's strengths and weaknesses. The information you gather typically includes their opinions and feelings about the product's ease of use and ease of learning. Written questionnaires are used to collect general information across the entire population of participants. The same questions are asked of each individual in exactly the same way, and precision is extremely important.

Conversely, oral questions (discussed in Chapter 10 on debriefing participants and observers) can be adjusted for a single individual in order to better understand what happened during that *particular* session. Those questions are not standardized; there is a general subject but variation from session to session.

There are two major considerations when developing a questionnaire: Content and format:

- Content has to do with the subject matter about which you choose to inquire.
- Format has to do with the design and wording of each question and the arrangement of the overall questionnaire.

Developing an effective, unambiguous questionnaire takes time and effort. No matter how clearly you feel you have stated a question, someone is liable to misinterpret it. Do not think you can simply throw together a few questions just prior to the test. If you do not have time to develop the questionnaire properly, including several revisions and a pilot test, you are better off presenting the questions orally. With an oral format, you can interact with the participants and clear up ambiguities and misunderstandings on the spot. If you have never developed a questionnaire before, seek out some help from someone with more experience.

Now let us focus on guidelines for establishing the content of questionnaires. Later, we will cover the most common question formats and how they are used.

Use the Research Questions(s) from the Test Plan as the Basis for Your Content

Be concise and precise in what you choose to ask. Keep your questions to the point, and avoid digressing into abstract areas. A good test of the relevance of a question is to ask yourself how the answer will move you closer to a design decision. If it is unclear how the answer to a question will move you toward a design decision, you might want to strike the question or reword it. Especially if you will be debriefing and questioning each participant orally, it is not necessary to include every last item on paper. A 20-page questionnaire (yes, we have seen them that long) following a 2-hour test is no one's idea of a good time. Instead, make sure that the written questionnaire includes only those items that *each* participant needs to answer. These include:

- Major items directly related to a specific research question(s).

- Items related to specific trends or patterns among participants or those where you will be measuring statistical significance.

- Controversial items on which the design team has not been able to agree. (You will want a written record of those responses.)

Develop Questionnaires That Will Be Distributed Either during or after a Session

Depending on your test design, you may want the participants to fill out the questionnaire either during or immediately following the test session, or at both times. For longer test sessions (more than an hour), it often pays to separate the usability test into discrete phases comprising several tasks each and provide questionnaires to the participants after each is completed. This will help the participants to recall their reactions and feelings more easily because they will have just completed the tasks about which they are being questioned. Also varying the flow of the test during a long session can help to relieve boredom and fatigue.

Ask Questions Related to That Which You Cannot Directly Observe

Stick to questions that have to do with subjective preferences. Do *not* ask performance-related questions that can be more accurately answered through direct observation.

For example, if one of your test objectives is to evaluate how often the participants access the site map on a web site, you can best assess that by direct observation during the test. It is a waste of time and damages your credibility to ask participants to estimate the number of times they referenced the site map. The exception to this would be if you are unable to directly observe the test. In that case, though, you would still be better off having the participants note each time they accessed the site map during the test. Relying on their memory after the fact is not nearly as effective.

However, using the same example of the site map, what you *cannot* observe is:

- Whether the user thought the site map was well designed
- How the site map compares to others that they have used
- Whether it was organized the way they preferred

These are the types of issues that can only be implied and not definitively answered by observations, and they should form the basis of your questioning. One example of a questionnaire to gather data about how satisfied participants were with the product they used in the session is the SUS, or System Usability Scale. It is part of ISO standard 9241, where ISO defines "usability." Figure 8-16 shows a version of the SUS questionnaire customized for a usability test evaluating ballot designs.

For each statement, please put the letter in the box on that row that matches how you feel about the statement.

	Strongly Disagree				Strongly Agree
	1	2	3	4	5
I feel confident that I used this ballot correctly.					
I think that I would need to ask questions to know how to use this ballot.					
I think that most people would figure out how to use this ballot very quickly.					
Figuring out how to vote with this ballot was difficult.					
I think that this ballot was easy to use.					

Figure 8-16 System Usability Scale (SUS) customized for evaluating satisfaction of using ballot designs

Develop the Basic Areas and Topics You Want to Cover

The following table gives some suggested topics for post-test questionnaires.

GENERAL SOFTWARE SCREEN OR WEB PAGE ISSUES	Organization of screen matches real-world tasks? Amount of information adequate? Appropriate use of color? Similar information consistently placed? Problems with navigation? Problems with losing your place in the system? Computer jargon? Too much or too little information? Ease of reading?
GENERAL DOCUMENTATION ISSUES OR INFORMATION-RICH WEB SITES	**Accessibility:** Organization explicit and obvious? Directive and supportive information visually separated? More important information highlighted in some way? Index helpful? Necessary to read long passages to determine correct locations? Cross-referencing adequate? Both experienced and novice users accommodated? **Clarity:** Terminology confusing? Limited use of paragraphs? Adequate feedback after completing actions? Sentences appropriate length? Conversational tone appropriate? Adequate use of headings, lists, and tables to be skimmable? **Graphics:** Adequate use of examples? Illustrations or animations accurate? Text and illustrations integrated?

Organization:
Organized by user's job and tasks?
Adequate white space?
Consistent patterns and chunking of information?
Headings self-explanatory?
Consistent layout on a page of similar elements, such as notes, summaries and page numbers?

Technical Accuracy:
Task descriptions and procedures correct?
Examples provided technically accurate?

GENERAL HARDWARE CONTROL PANEL ISSUES

Terminology of buttons self-evident?
Placement of control panel appropriate?
Display messages easy to see?
Display messages in plain language?
Meaning of icons self-evident?
Consistency of operation for all controls?
Additional controls desired?

Design the Questions and Responses for Simplicity and Brevity

Minimize responses that require extensive writing, such as open-ended questions. Instead, use close-ended questions, such as checkboxes, scales, true-false statements, and short fill-ins. Close-ended questions eliminate any advantage participants with good writing skills might have over those participants with poor writing skills.

There are a variety of common types of formats of close-ended questions. See "Common Question Formats" later in this chapter for some tried-and-true formats (including examples of each) that you can use.

Use the Pilot Test to Refine the Questionnaire

Because it is difficult to produce an unambiguous and unbiased questionnaire (especially if you are very familiar with the subject matter), it is imperative that you conduct a pilot test of the questionnaire. The pilot questionnaire test, which should coincide with the pilot usability test, will give you a sense of whether or not the questions are eliciting the right information. Ask the participants specific questions about the questionnaire itself, such as "Were the questions confusing?" Also, look for biased questions and questions that "lead the witness" to the correct answer. Remember, it is very easy to inadvertently design questions that imply the answer you would like to see.

In addition to evaluating your questions, the pilot can also provide:

- Ideas for further questions
- Identification of questions that are superfluous
- A sense of how long it takes to fill out the questionnaire

Common Question Formats

You can use the following formats to develop questions for screeners, background questionnaires, and pre- and post-test questionnaires. (They work for surveys, too.) Some question formats will work in note taking or data gathering tools, as well.

Likert Scales

Likert scales are scales on which the participants register their agreement or disagreement with a statement. The judgments depicted in Figure 8-17 are quantified on a five-point scale.

Semantic Differentials

Semantic differentials are scales (usually seven point) on which the participants are asked to register the degree to which they favor one of two adjective pairs. You can use these scales to gather usability as well as aesthetic preferences.

Overall, I found the widget easy to use. (*Circle one*)

Strongly agree	Agree	Neither agree nor disagree	Disagree	Strongly disagree

Figure 8-17 Likert scale

Modern	3	2	1	0	1	2	3	Traditional
Simple	3	2	1	0	1	2	3	Complex
High tech	3	2	1	0	1	2	3	Low tech
Reliable	3	2	1	0	1	2	3	Unreliable
Easy to use	3	2	1	0	1	2	3	Complex to use
Familiar	3	2	1	0	1	2	3	Unfamiliar
Professional	3	2	1	0	1	2	3	Unprofessional
Safe	3	2	1	0	1	2	3	Unsafe
Durable	3	2	1	0	1	2	3	Fragile
Attractive	3	2	1	0	1	2	3	Unattractive
Interesting	3	2	1	0	1	2	3	Boring
Small	3	2	1	0	1	2	3	Large
High quality	3	2	1	0	1	2	3	Low quality
Expensive	3	2	1	0	1	2	3	Inexpensive

Figure 8-18 Semantic differentials

The judgments are quantified on a 1–7 scale, but you will notice that, in order to prevent any bias associated with higher vs. lower numbers, both ends of the scale read from 1–3, with 0 being a no-preference choice.

Using the rating scale shown in Figure 8-18, the participant would circle the number nearest the term that most closely matches his or her feelings about the product.

Fill-In Questions

Fill-in questions provide more latitude to the participants because they are free to say whatever they like rather than choosing from a predetermined list. Usually, you limit the amount of room for the answer with the provision that the participants can expand their answers during the debriefing session. Figure 8-19 shows an example of a fill-in question. Notice the limitation of three points and then on to the next question. This limitation forces the participants to prioritize their points and to place only the most important ones on paper.

Checkbox Questions

Checkbox questions allow the participants to choose from a preselected list of options as shown in Figure 8-20.

Branching Questions

Branching questions allow you to control the path of the participants through the questionnaire and address certain questions only to those whose experience

I found these three aspects of the web site particularly easy to use.

1._____
2._____
3._____

Figure 8-19 Fill-in question

Please check each of the features that you regularly use on your phone.

____ address book
____ autodial
____ alarm clock
____ text messaging
____ voice mail
____ camera
____ email
____ games

Figure 8-20 Checkbox questions

5. Are you a member of any hotel rewards programs?
_____ Yes (skip to question 7)
_____ No

6. Are you a member of any airline rewards programs?
_____ Yes
_____ No

7. If you answered "yes" to question 5: Which hotel rewards programs do you
belong to?
___ Marriott
___ Hyatt
___ Sheraton
___ Hilton
___ Holiday Inn
___ Westin
___ Starwood
___ Other

Figure 8-21 Branching questions

or preference warrants it. In the example shown in Figure 8-21, you are interested in seeing the value of a design change to the participants. In this case, for those who would rather use the software to configure the product, you would like to know just how much they are willing to spend.

Debriefing Guide

The purpose of the debriefing topics guide is to provide the structure from which to conduct the debriefing session. (For more on the topic of conducting debriefing sessions with participants and observers, see Chapter 10.) Unlike a questionnaire, which lists the specific questions that each participant will be asked, the debriefing topics guide lists the general topics that you want to discuss. It suggests a line of questioning, the exact nature of which depends on the circumstances during each test session. It is similar to a moderator's guide developed for a focus group in that not every topic is discussed. For example, you may ask a question about a section of the web site of only those participants that actually refer to that section during the test. If the participants do not refer to it, you do not ask that question or you may ask them why they did *not* reference it. Or, you may ask expert participants certain questions and novice participants other questions.

Keep in mind that, in addition to the guide, you will also be making notes during the test on the specific items that you need to probe during the debriefing session. So, there may be two sets of notes from which you are drawing the content of your debriefing session.

CHAPTER 9

Conduct the Test Sessions

Having completed the basic groundwork and preparation for your usability test, you are almost ready to begin testing. While there exists an almost endless variety of sophisticated and esoteric tests one might conduct (from a test comprising a single participant and lasting several days to a fully automated test with hundreds or perhaps thousands of participants), in this chapter we focus on the guidelines and activities for conducting the classic "one-on-one" test. This "typical" test consists of four to ten participants, each of whom is observed and questioned individually by a test moderator seated in the same room. This method will work for any of the four types of tests discussed in Chapter 3: exploratory, assessment, validation, or comparison. The main difference is the types of objectives pursued, that is, more conceptual for an exploratory test, and more behavior oriented for assessment and validation tests. The other major difference is the amount of interaction between participant and test moderator. The early exploratory tests will have much interaction. The later validation test will have much less interaction, because the objective is measurement against a standard.

For "first-time" testers, we recommend beginning with an assessment test as it is probably the most straightforward to conduct. In Chapter 13, we discuss several variations and enhancements to the basic testing technique that you can employ as you gain confidence.

In terms of *what* to test, we would like to raise an issue previously mentioned in Chapter 2, because it is so crucial. That is, the importance of testing the whole integrated product and not just separate components. Testing a component, such as documentation, separately, *without ever testing it with the rest of the product*, does nothing to ensure ultimate product usability. Rather it reinforces the lack of product integration. In short, you eventually would like to test all components together, with enough lead time to make revisions as required. However, that being said, there is absolutely nothing wrong with testing separate components as they are developed throughout the life cycle, *as long as you eventually test them all together*.

There is one exception to this rule. If you believe that the only way to begin any kind of testing program within your organization is to test a component separately as your only test, then by all means do so. However, you should explain to management the limited nature and value of those results.

Guidelines for Moderating Test Sessions

Before describing, via a series of checklists, the step-by-step testing activities of this stage, we would first like to cover the basic guidelines for moderating a test. These include guidelines on probing and assisting the participant, implementing a "thinking aloud" technique, and some general recommendations on how to work with study participants.

These guidelines are among the most important in this book for two reasons:

- This is the point in the testing process when you cannot only misunderstand what you are seeing, but you can very easily *affect* what is happening to the detriment of the participant or the product. Human perception is enormously affected by and predicated upon *preconception*. What we *think* we see is not necessarily what *is* happening. As proof of this phenomenon, after you moderate a test that is also being viewed by other observers, note the lack of agreement among yourselves about particular situations that were observed by all.

- These guidelines represent skills that are the hardest of all to teach via a book. As with any skill that has a strong flavor and grounding in interpersonal communication, moderating skills have a strong element of learning by doing and by practicing, rather than intellectual mastery. It takes many tests before one is really comfortable in moderating a test, and the best way to learn initially is to watch someone who knows how to do it.

Having now fulfilled our professional obligation to warn you to temper your expectations in mastering these skills and to proceed cautiously, let's discuss some of the basic guidelines for moderating a test.

Moderate the Session Impartially

Take the attitude that you have no vested interest in the results one way or the other. Present the product neutrally (this does not mean you need to be solemn), so that the participants cannot ascertain any preference on your part. Never indicate through your speech or mannerisms that you strongly approve or disapprove of any actions or comments offered by a particular participant.

React to "mistakes" or "wrong turns" in exactly the same way as you do to correct behavior. Never make participants feel stupid or inadequate (even inadvertently) by how you respond to their actions. If a participant is having problems, remember that it is the fault of the product. Period. Even if you say and do all the right things, participants will still blame themselves. If that happens, remind them of the value of their difficulties in understanding how the product actually works. Encourage them to freely explore areas without concern for "looking good."

Encourage participants to focus on their own experiences and to not be concerned with what other people of similar characteristics might hypothetically think or need. However, if a participant has insight about how some other category of end users might react to some portion of the product, hear him or her out. For example, if a manager has information about how his or her subordinates might fare during the test, by all means encourage that input. This can help you to refine later tests for the category of end users that was mentioned.

Be Aware of the Effects of Your Voice and Body Language

It is very easy to unintentionally influence someone by the way in which you react to that person's statements, both verbally and through body language. For example, moving closer to someone indicates acceptance of what that person is saying, moving farther away indicates rejection. Raising the pitch of your voice usually signals agreement, while lowering it communicates the opposite. To prevent these biasing effects, make a special effort to be mindful of your voice and body language. The best way to improve your awareness of how you are affecting a session is to review the tapes of your session, noting how and when you inadvertently provided cues to a participant. Do not be too hard on yourself. Even the most experienced test moderator slips up occasionally.

Treat Each New Participant as an Individual

While you know intellectually that each participant is unique, there is a very human tendency to be unduly affected by the performance and comments of the last person you observed. Make an effort to "clear the slate" psychologically prior to beginning a session. Remember to treat each participant as a completely new case, regardless of what previous results and sessions have shown. Try to simply collect behaviors without undue interpretation.

Leave time in the schedule for you as the moderator to take a break between sessions. If time is very tight, line up fewer participants rather than rushing many through in "assembly line" fashion. A seasoned moderator can handle four to six one-hour sessions in a day, depending on the complexity and demands of each session. Part of your data analyses will rely on your memories of participants and events. If you do too many sessions in a row, you stand to lose those helpful memories.

Remember, if you are testing five to ten participants, each participant represents a precious opportunity for your product. So favor quality over quantity, especially as it pertains to understanding cause and effect. If you do not understand why errors are being made, it is hard to come up with a solution.

If Appropriate, Use the "Thinking Aloud" Technique

The "thinking aloud" technique is a simple technique intended to capture what the participants are thinking while working. To implement this technique, have the participants provide a running commentary of their thought process by thinking aloud while performing the tasks of the test. Have them express their confusion, frustration, and perhaps even their delight. When done well, the technique assists you to "read their minds." It is especially effective for conducting early exploratory research (such as evaluating the participant's mental model of a product), because it exposes the participant's preconceptions and expectations about how the product works. While the technique has its share of advantages and seems to be an ideal means to capture all the implicit information of a usability test, it is not without some disadvantages. Therefore, do not use it indiscriminately. Following is a list of advantages and disadvantages of the "thinking aloud" technique.

Advantages of the "Thinking Aloud" Technique

■ You are able to capture preference and performance information simultaneously, rather than having to remember to ask questions about preferences later.

■ The technique can help some participants to focus and concentrate. They fall into a rhythm of working and speaking to you throughout the test.

■ You are constantly receiving early clues about misconceptions and confusion before they manifest as incorrect behaviors. These early clues help you to anticipate and trace the source of problems more easily.

■ Participants can reveal how they are thinking about doing a task and why things work or don't work for them.

Disadvantages of the "Thinking Aloud" Technique

- Some participants find the technique unnatural and distracting. Working with these participants may require you to encourage them to "think aloud."

- Thinking aloud slows the thought process, thus increasing mindfulness. Normally, this is a good effect, but in this case it can prevent errors that otherwise might have occurred in the actual workplace. Ideally, you want your participants to pay neither more nor less attention to the task at hand than they normally would.

- Regardless of personal styles, preferences, and other considerations, it is just plain exhausting to verbalize one's thought process for very long.

How to Enhance the "Thinking Aloud" Technique

If you decide to use this technique, following are some ways to improve its effectiveness.

- **Avoid using it for very short or pointed tests where the unusual aspect of the technique does not have time to wear off.** For example, Jeff was once testing whether or not participants noticed and understood one specific label on a hardware product. That objective comprised the entire test, and each session lasted for all of 10 minutes. He found that thinking aloud heightened the participant's awareness of a task that was usually performed on "autopilot." The very act of saying, "Now I'm loading the paper. Now I'm pulling out the tray," made the process unusually deliberate. Consequently, he stopped using this method after the second participant, because it was simply too artificial in this case.

  Fortunately, for most people thinking aloud becomes rote over time, and the participant's awareness returns to the less heightened, more customary state after a short period.

- **Demonstrate the technique first, so that participants feel less self-conscious.** Demonstrate a few seconds of thinking aloud while performing some unrelated task to make sure that the participants get the hang of it. Then let them try it and ask you any questions if they need to.

- **Do not force the technique if you encounter strong resistance.** If the participants resist adopting the technique by ignoring your cajoling and prodding to think aloud, or simply saying it is too distracting to them, take the hint. Do not push the technique, but instead probe as needed.

- **Pay attention to where participants become quiet.** This can indicate that they are concentrating on solving some problem. Rather than nudging someone to tell you what she is thinking, it may be better to note the incident and ask about it later.

- **Acknowledge that you are listening to your participant's comments by periodically repeating comments back and following up.** Reinforcing a behavior causes it to reoccur. Therefore, let the participants know you hear them and are writing down their comments.

- **Practice meaningful silences and patiently waiting.** It can be good in some situations to observe a behavior or ask a question and then wait. Count to 20 or 30 before asking for clarification. Often in that time, the participant will complete processing his thoughts and will begin to explain what he's thinking. It's almost always better if the participant verbalizes unprompted.

- **Consider a different technique entirely.** Test two participants together and encourage them to think aloud to each other. For more on this technique, see the variations on the basic technique section presented in Chapter 13.

Probe and Interact with the Participant as Appropriate

If you are conducting a true experiment or even a validation test, your interaction with the participant should be minimal. On the other hand, interaction, especially for a test occurring early or midrange in the development cycle, is mandatory in order to understand fully the "why" behind performance and preference. Interacting with the participant appropriately is a difficult skill to master and should not be undertaken lightly. In fact, it is one of the more advanced skills that a usability professional should possess. Even a sigh at the wrong time can influence results and render all or a portion of the results useless.

On a project with a tight schedule, where many design decisions hinge upon the test results, it is important to explore all ambiguous actions and situations. You haven't the luxury of letting things unfold without intervention.

If this is your first test, then proceed cautiously. Feel your way gradually and learn from your mistakes. Err on the side of interacting too little. If you accidentally divulge information, simply keep going, noting the point in the test where this occurred.

Following are general guidelines that present the basics of probing and interacting. Keep in mind that there is no substitute for sensitivity and practice. When probing:

- **Don't show surprise.** Keep in mind that you are creating an atmosphere in which it is perfectly acceptable and in fact expected to make mistakes. Therefore, reacting with incredulity may destroy that atmosphere because it puts a participant on the defensive. For example, suppose a participant accidentally destroys the file on which he or she is working. Rather than saying anything, let the consequences speak for themselves. If the participant becomes unduly alarmed, simply say something like, "How close was that to what you expected?" and give the participant a chance to recover.

Of course, your calm interjection of, "Tell me what is happening. Is there some problem?" while the participant is inadvertently destroying an hour of work often makes for humorous, incongruous situations, but it is usually best to play this situation "straight." Do not immediately let on that you are aware of what has happened. Even comments in jest, such as, "I'm sure there are more files where those came from" are liable to have a negative effect. (As an aside, set up the test so that files are never really deleted, and can easily be restored. You might need to begin again at the point where the file destruction occurred.)

▪ **Focus on what the participants expected to happen.** When the participants have obviously done something different from what was expected or are lost or confused, ask them what they expected to happen in order to understand the root cause of the situation. Do not feel the need to describe in any way what *you* expected to happen. Simply describe the events that occurred as if they were everyday occurrences and leave off any indication of expectation. Do not imply that anything is wrong necessarily. Do not imply "correct" results.

▪ **Act as a mirror to reflect back what the participants are saying and help them to express their thoughts in a useful way.** Do not say too much and do not volunteer information unless it is an administrative issue or logistical point. Don't interpret what you think happened. If someone is hopelessly stuck and needs a hint for the test to go on, then it is fine to offer assistance. Otherwise, you should not say anything. Do not imply to the participants that there is any right or wrong answer, or that their statement is similar or different from other participants. Most people do not want to seem different from others, so your comments could affect what they say.

▪ **Do not always ask direct questions.** The real challenge with probing is the subtlety required. You simply cannot always ask direct questions, especially if the participants sense that you are affiliated with the product in any way. Direct questioning of the type, "How did you get all the way over to that screen?" will tend to make the participants extremely defensive as if they were being grilled. A better approach is to ask, "How's it going? How close do you feel you are to completing the task?'' Alternatively, take the blame yourself by saying something like, ''I missed what just happened. Could you tell me?''

Ask neutral questions rather than ''loaded'' ones that imply an answer. An example of a loaded question is, ''Most people find this feature easy to use. How about you?'' A more neutral phrasing would be, ''Is this feature easy or difficult to use?'' or ''What were you thinking when you used that feature?'' (Of course, there is a lot to the delivery of the question, as well. So be careful about what your attitude or emotions might betray even with neutral, open-ended questions.)

Ask questions that do not imply right or wrong answers. Focus on the participants' preferences and the value they place on features and functions. Some additional examples of neutral questions are:

- What are you thinking right now?
- You seemed surprised/puzzled/frustrated, what happened?
- Exactly how did that differ from what you expected to happen?
- Would you expect that information to be provided?
- How close was that to what you expected?

- **During the session, limit your interruptions to short discussions.** Save longer issues for the debriefing session. Too many and too lengthy interruptions disrupt the thought process of the participants and affect their performance. Jot down topics on your data collection form concerning what you want to ask questions about. Then ask them during the debriefing session. This method is preferable to constantly interrupting the participants while they are working. Keep your probes short, sweet, and to the point.

- **Probe in response to both verbal and nonverbal cues from the participants.**   A good moderator pays attention to the reactions of the participants at all times. Very often, participants will make very subtle responses to what they are seeing or doing. A raised eyebrow, a biting of the lower lip, all can indicate a reaction to the product. You can take advantage of those moments as an opening to the thought process or feelings of the participants. For example, if a participant starts frowning or sighing while performing a task, you might want to probe with, ''You're frowning. Tell me what is happening.'' or ''What are you thinking right now?'' So, read the body language of the participants. This is one of the main reasons the authors favor being in the same room as the participants. *There is so much nonverbal implicit information that the participants express that is hard to read from another room.*

- **Look for opportunities to understand the rationale for a particular behavior or preference.**   If someone expresses that a particular aspect is interesting or valuable or problematic, however casually, probe to find out why. If a participant mentions other ways of performing or designing a function, ask for examples of what he or she means.

- **Handle one issue at a time.**   It is very easy for participants to become sidetracked on tangential issues. Focus on the task at hand. Avoid venturing off into several issues at once or revealing information that is yet to be covered. It is simply too distracting. Make a note to cover the other issues later.

- **Don't problem solve.**   Do not use the testing time to fix problems that are discovered. The vast majority of problem resolution should wait until after the participants leave for the day. This is not to say that you cannot ask the participants how they *would* have designed a feature. Obviously, that in itself can be revealing and sometimes helpful.

  More often than not though, participants are neither qualified as designers, nor are they aware of the constraints of the project. So their suggestions may be highly impractical and distract you from what they are more qualified to do than anyone else — reveal what they can and cannot do and what they like and do not like.

  If the participants offer design suggestions, do not discourage them. Write down the suggestions whether they have merit or not. But, if they are clearly impractical, do not waste valuable time exploring the ideas at length.

Stay Objective, But Keep the Tone Relaxed

Unfortunately, seriousness of purpose is often equated with taking oneself seriously. Too much solemnity in the interest of being serious inhibits people and limits the amount and quality of information that you gather. Remember that you are dealing with people who are performing with two or three sets of eyes (or more) on their every move. Humor can counteract their self-consciousness and help them to relax. If they are having fun, they are more apt to let their defenses down and tell you what is really on their minds.

Humor in this instance is the type that keeps things "light" and on an even keel. It is perfectly appropriate to laugh along with the participants when they find something humorous about the product, or to be nondefensive about the product's flaws. Of course, be sure to laugh *with* and not *at* your participants.

Don't "Rescue" Participants When They Struggle

There is a tendency to jump in and help participants too quickly when they become confused or lost. The authors have noticed this especially of inexperienced moderators. The tendency to rescue is due to our natural empathy and even embarrassment when watching someone struggle. Instead, at those times especially, encourage participants to verbalize their feelings.

By not letting the participants struggle, you lose the opportunity to understand what happens when people get lost and how they recover. Very often participants will venture into unexplored areas and open up entirely different issues. If you are using a "thinking aloud" technique (see the section "If Appropriate, Use the 'Thinking Aloud' Technique" later in this chapter), remind the participants to keep talking. If you have not set up such a technique beforehand, then probe the individual participants who are having difficulty to find out what caused the difficulty.

To counteract your tendency to rescue, remind yourself why you are there and why you are testing. It is better to watch the participants struggle now than to receive calls on the company's "hotline" later. Also, there is absolutely no replacement for a struggling participant to convince a skeptical developer that there actually *are* problems with his or her beloved product.

You may feel better if, at the very end of the session there is time, you take a moment to correct or teach something that you saw the participant struggling with, especially if she will return to a job or task in her real life that involves the situation you included in the test. It's a good way to close the session on a positive note.

If You Make a Mistake, Continue On

Do not panic if you inadvertently reveal information or in some other way bias the session. Just continue on as if nothing happened. At worst, you will invalidate only a small portion of the test. At best, your comment or action will not even be observed by that participant.

There are many possible ways that you can inadvertently reveal information. If you have conducted dry runs of your protocol and pilot tested with a user, the chances of something in your script revealing some bias is minimal. The mistakes typically happen in the un-scripted parts of the test, such as when you ask follow-up questions or ask participants to reflect on what they have done so far. Especially because you as the test moderator know the "right" answers, as you ask probing follow-up questions or if you decide to use graduated prompts (see Chapter 13), it can be very easy to lead the participant to the correct next step when what you want is for him or her to discover it as part of the problem solving process.

Ensure That Participants Are Finished Before Going On

If you are verbally presenting tasks to a participant one at a time, wait a few moments after you see the current task completed before moving on to the next one. Very often, especially if a participant is unsure of a task, there is a moment of indecision after completing the task when a participant is not sure if he or she has performed correctly. If you jump in too soon, because you notice the participant is finished, you are confirming that he or she has performed correctly and undercutting that moment of indecision. If you pause for a moment, the participant may actually redo the task incorrectly or do something else interesting or informative. If the participant appears to you to have stopped, is stuck, or you feel he or she may be finished, count silently to 20 or 30 before you intervene. At that point, you might say, "Tell me what you're thinking," or "How close do you feel you are to completing the task?"

Be especially careful if you are sitting close to the participants, because if they notice you making a mark on your data collection sheet, that can signal them that they have completed a task, even if they are not sure. The best way to prevent this problem altogether is to have the participants signal when they are finished, as part of the test protocol. This will help you to resist "rooting them home."

Assist the Participants Only as a Last Resort

Whereas probing is the act of soliciting information from the participants and is often an integral part of the test design, assisting the participants to complete a task is invasive and should only be done when absolutely necessary. Let's be very clear about this. *As soon as you assist, you are affecting the test results in a major way*. If you are tracking the number of tasks performed correctly, you need to differentiate between those that required assistance and those that did not. Never lump both of those categories together. As much as you want to avoid assisting the participants, there are times when it is unavoidable. Following are some suggestions for when and how to assist the participants during a test.

When to Assist

- **When a participant is very lost or very confused.**   Obviously, assistance at the first sign of difficulty is not advised. If you can, wait until the participant has gone beyond the time benchmark for the current task before providing assistance or offering a hint. At that point, you have already scored the task as "unsuccessful" anyway, and your assistance can no longer affect that compilation.

- **When performing a required task makes a participant feel uncomfortable.**   For example, the test may require the participants to perform an action that they ordinarily cannot bring themselves to do, such as deleting a file without having a backup system in place. (We're serious. Certain actions are so deeply ingrained that people refuse to do them even if they know it's a test.) Or, participants may feel that the task they are performing is just not realistic and requires some additional background information or context. In such cases you may have to provide a more in-depth explanation.

- **When a participant is exceptionally frustrated and may give up.**   People have their own thresholds of frustration, after which they will simply stop working. On the other hand, periods of frustration are often gold mines of information about the product's weaknesses, and much can be learned from letting a participant struggle. It is up to the moderator to gauge a particular participant's frustration level before jumping in. The key here, in terms of getting the most information, is identifying the frustration level at which the participant will give up and not exceeding it. Knowing when to jump in comes through experience. Letting a participant know you empathize with him or her and encouraging the participant to hang in there can help extend the time the participant will stay with a task before giving up.

- **When the product is in a "before-final" state and you need to provide missing information to the participants.**   Almost always, usability testing occurs before an interface or document is complete. This requires the moderator to fill in missing information that ordinarily would be there. For example, an error message should have appeared on the screen but did not. As moderator, you should provide the appropriate message and continue on.

- **When a bug occurs or a participant's actions cause a malfunction that requires repairs.**   Very often, making repairs to a product in the middle of a test involves actions that the participant should not see because the repairs could reveal crucial information or procedures that the participant is not yet privy to. If a repair is needed, the moderator must not only intervene, *but must remove the participant from the test room*. Have someone else take the participant to a predetermined waiting area, if you need to help with repairs to the product. Be sure to tell the participant that he or she has done nothing wrong, and that it is the tenuous nature of the product at this stage of development that caused the problem. Conveying the information is important because participants may become tentative if it appears that they have caused damage.

How to Assist

Having identified those times when it is appropriate to assist, the next order of business is discussing *how* to assist. There are some important considerations that will minimize the effect you may have on the overall test results.

- **NEVER, EVER blame the participants, even indirectly, for a problem.** The fastest way to lose and/or bias a participant is to blame the participant for problems during a test. Just as the "customer is always right," so is the adage, "mistakes are always the fault of the product." Do not lose your cool and react negatively even in the most trying of circumstances (e.g., when a participant's actions crash the machine or cause alarms to sound).

- **Clarify the concerns of the participants.** Ask questions that let the participants express what is happening and what, if anything, they find confusing. However, if they say that they are stuck, do not immediately take that as permission to show them what to do. You *want* to see what the participants do when they reach this point, not discover how quickly you can help them. Often, they make horrific detours (from the viewpoint of the consequences) and it is invaluable to see that take place. Do everything you can to avoid telling them *how* to do something.

- **Gradually provide more revealing hints to get the participants past an obstacle, rather than revealing everything all at once.** If the participants are lost or confused, provide them with hints, rather than "spilling the beans" all at once. Providing hints lets you ascertain the minimum amount of information required for error recovery and helps the development team design solutions later. Perhaps telling the participants to reread an instruction is all they need. For more on this technique, see Chapter 13.

- **Be aware of the tasks to come and the effect your comments could have on the performance of the participants.** In the course of helping the participants when they become confused and cannot continue, it is very easy to inadvertently reveal information that helps them to perform tasks that appear later in the test. Therefore, keep the rest of the test in mind when assisting on the current task. When in doubt about how much to reveal, the best thing is to err on the side of saying too little.

Checklists for Getting Ready

Having completed a review of the basics of moderating, you are now ready to begin the actual process of testing. Because of the myriad details to remember and coordinate when testing, it helps immensely if you develop a series of checklists to guide this process. The lists prevent you from forgetting any important points. The authors have included three generic lists to get you started. Over time, you probably will create customized versions that work well for your situation.

- **Checklist 1**, to be used a week or so before the test.
- **Checklist 2**, to be used about one day before the test.
- **Checklist 3**, to be used during the day of the test.

These checklists begin after all the preparation work has been accomplished. Use them as a starting point from which to create your own customized lists that include the specifics of your own testing situation. Your customized checklists should include those places in the test where you need to be especially observant or where you may even interact with each participant in some way. For example, one of your checklists might include:

- Places in the test where you need to mimic a realistic function that does not yet work on the software.
- Particular problematic sections of a web site where you want to ask questions while a participant is working.
- A reminder to record the search keywords used or count the number of times participants return to the beginning of a task path.

Now let's move through the generic checklists one at a time and discuss each item.

Checklist 1: A Week or So before the Test

The point here is to know what you're testing and to feel comfortable that your session script matches up with what you want to happen in the testing room. The checklist for the week before the text is shown in Figure 9-1.

Take the Test Yourself

Take your own usability test and look for design flaws. Try to assume the mind set of your prospective users. Take timings to ensure that the test is achievable in the time allotted. Make sure to use your own questionnaires and read them carefully. Revise the test before continuing.

Checklist 1: A week or so before the test
- ☐ Take the test yourself
- ☐ Conduct a pilot test
- ☐ Revise the product
- ☐ Check out all the equipment and the testing environment
- ☐ Request that, if possible, the product be "frozen" for the test period

Figure 9-1 Checklist for the week before the test

Conduct a Pilot Test

After you have made revisions based on taking the test yourself, conduct a pilot test. Ideally, you should use a "real" participant, perhaps someone who is on the lower end of the expertise scale for what you are doing in this test. Doing so should give you a good feeling for how long it will take most users to do tasks (a beginner being more likely to take longer). Then you can adjust your plan accordingly. In a pinch, using internal participants (employees of your company) whose background is similar to your end users can work for a pilot session. Conduct the entire test, including reading the orientation script and providing the test scenarios. Practice the various data collection techniques you will be using. Instruct the participants to fill out all questionnaires that are part of the test.

The importance of conducting one or more pilot tests cannot be overstated. Do not cut this step short, or you will find that your first one or two real participants will be used "to get the bugs out" of your testing process, essentially acting as the pilot test. Not only does pilot testing allow you to practice, it enables you to refine your test plan as a result of having discovered that certain tasks were not applicable, that questionnaires were misunderstood, and that other areas or sections you had not thought to explore could benefit from testing.

Revise the Product

Yes, revise the product or prototype or whatever it is you are testing. Do not be surprised when you identify areas of the product that obviously require fixing, based on the pilot results, without the need for further confirmation by the real test. After all, why waste valuable time testing those features and functions that you know are broken? Uncovering product problems is one of the reasons why conducting a pilot test well in advance of the usability test makes so much sense. If you should discover problems, you have time to correct them before the usability test.

A note of caution is in order though. Be careful about making too many product changes just prior to the start of the usability test, especially software or firmware changes. Too many changes without adequate QA may cause the product to crash, and you run the risk of jeopardizing the usability test altogether. Experience has taught us this the hard way. Against Jeff's better judgment, he once allowed a programmer to make changes to the product right up to the day before the usability test. When test time arrived, the product was buggy and would not work longer than five minutes without crashing. Needless to say, the test had to be canceled and rescheduled for a later date, and the team lost a window of opportunity in a tight schedule.

Having learned this lesson, we now take a much more conservative approach to allowing product changes before the usability test. Make sure to leave adequate time to debug and test the changes so that the chances of a product crashing during the test are minimized.

Check Out All the Equipment and the Testing Environment

If you will not be using an area dedicated solely to testing, check that the room you will be using is available for the entire time. Also make sure that the equipment you have reserved, leased, or borrowed is available and in working order. This includes everything from cameras to recorders to computers.

Request a Temporary "Freeze" on Development

If at all possible, development should be stopped during the period in which you conduct usability test sessions. Any changes may affect the participant tasks or the scenarios for the test. In addition, a "freeze" stabilizes the product to a known set of bugs that you can script around, if needed. However, the development team may decide that it must go on during the study. In that case, ask if a version of the product can be made available that isolates it from development or other types of testing. That way, you will have a snapshot version that is manageable for you, consistent among participants, and can still be used as a source on which to base findings.

Checklist 2: One Day before the Test

Now you line up all the ingredients you will need to have in place or at hand during each session (Figure 9-2).

Check That the Video Equipment Is Set Up and Ready

If your camera or recording software does not provide written titles or a timestamp that would identify the recording, acquire an erasable white board or slate to hold up in front of the camera to record the participant number and date. When the recording is complete, simply identify the participant number and date on the video label. In addition, check that you have enough media to store the recordings.

Checklist 2: One day before the test
- ☐ Check that the video equipment is set up and ready
- ☐ Check that the product, if software or hardware, is working
- ☐ Assemble all written test materials
- ☐ Check on the status of your participants
- ☐ Double-check the test environment and equipment

Figure 9-2 Checklist for the day before the test

If you are storing video and audio electronically, determine a file naming convention to use as you save each sessions recordings.

Check for power sources in the room you will be using, and ensure that your electrical cords are long enough. If you will use battery power instead of AC, ensure that you have plenty of fresh or recently recharged batteries available.

Check That the Product, if Software or Hardware, Is Working

Remember Murphy's Law here. It never fails. Make sure that it is installed or available exactly as you would like it for the session. Try it out; don't just log in or power up. Also check that any monitoring equipment, such as data logging programs and stopwatches, is working correctly.

Assemble All Written Test Materials

Assemble all written test materials including scripts, test scenarios, questionnaires, and data collection forms. Be as organized as possible, because you will be shuffling large amounts of paper during the test. Consolidate each participant's forms into an individual packet that you simply distribute prior to that person's session. Set up a filing system for yourself to store all the paper after each session, along with checklists to make sure you have received everything back that you should have. Remember, the less you have to think about logistics, the more you can concentrate on watching the test with undivided attention.

Check on the Status of Your Participants

If you are handling arrangements for the participants yourself, call the first wave of participants to verify that they will be participating. Continue to do so each day as the test progresses. If an agency or a colleague is handling the participant arrangements, then verify that everything is set up and a fallback procedure is in place in case someone does not show up.

Double-Check the Test Environment and Equipment

Murphy's Law returns. Power everything on, run a short shakedown test, and make any final adjustments.

Checklist 3: The Day of the Test

Finally, you organize yourself and your observers and step through one session with one participant after another. Figure 9-3 shows the checklist for the day of testing.

Checklist 3: The day of the test

- ☐ Scan your customized checklist
- ☐ Prepare yourself mentally
- ☐ Greet the participant
- ☐ Have the participant fill out and sign any preliminary documents
- ☐ Read the orientation script and set the stage
- ☐ Have the participant fill out any pretest questionnaires
- ☐ Move to the testing area and prepare to test
- ☐ Start recordings
- ☐ Establish protocol for observers in the room
- ☐ Provide any prerequisite training if your test plan includes it
- ☐ Either distribute or read the written task scenario(s) to the participant
- ☐ Record start time, observe the participant, and collect all critical data
- ☐ Have the participant complete all posttest questionnaires
- ☐ Debrief the participant
- ☐ Close the session
- ☐ Organize data collection and observation sheets
- ☐ Debrief with observers
- ☐ Provide adequate time between test sessions
- ☐ Prepare for the next participant

Figure 9-3 Checklist for the day of testing

Prepare Yourself Mentally

Mental preparation sets the stage for how open, alert and unbiased you are during the text. Let go of any expectations about test results. Remain as open as possible. The best analogy the authors have seen for the appropriate attitude when conducting a test comes from the Zen tradition, which speaks of "Beginner's Mind."

"Beginner's Mind" in that tradition refers to the discipline of always remaining in the present moment and not taking on the "all-knowing" attitude of an expert. In the context of testing, it describes the attitude of someone who knows very little about the product and has very few preconceptions. This is especially important in the case where it is necessary (but not recommended of course) for you to test your own materials.

- ▪ **Review the problem statements and overall test objectives**, which may have become obscured while you handled all the details. Remind yourself of the main issues you will be covering and on which you will focus during the usability test.

- ▪ **Once all preparation is complete, prepare yourself and your attitude.** Have confidence in the ability of the testing process to expose the product's deficiencies. Rather than embracing all the predictions of the "experts" on the development team, take the attitude that reactions of participants are closer to how the product will fare when released. Keep that in mind throughout the entire process to guard against becoming defensive when results are not what you expected.

- **Create an open, nonjudgmental environment.** This guideline is listed under mental preparation because it is less tangible than the physical environment that you create. However, it is every bit as important. It has to do with creating an environment in which participants feel completely at ease, even if they make mistakes. If the importance of creating an open, nonjudgmental environment is not immediately obvious, then recall how you personally have felt in the past when performing even familiar tasks in front of an audience. Participants should not feel the slightest sense of being judged or of having to obtain any particular types of results. Once they do, it affects their behavior and introduces a bias.

- **Be curious about what participants do and why.** Curiosity is simply the natural result of "Beginner's Mind." Do not be defensive about their actions.

- **Expect the unexpected.** *Every* test will result in the unexpected. If this were not the case, there really would not be much reason to conduct a usability test. Remember that it may be necessary for you to deviate from the original test plan should a participant uncover important issues that no one had previously considered and that require exploration.

Greet the Participant

Meet the participant or have the participant met outside the testing room in an area that is private, accommodating, and, if possible, stocked with refreshments. Relax, introduce yourself, make small talk, and help the participant feel at ease. Acknowledge and try to understand any nervousness the participant may feel. Perhaps there is something the participant was told that was upsetting and that you can address. If the usability test revolves around new or unfamiliar technology, the participant is very likely to feel especially nervous or intimidated.

Treat the participant with respect. Show appreciation for his or her willingness to come in and provide this research for you. It is important to guard against projecting an "ivory tower" or "think tank" mentality where this "poor little participant" is being allowed to enter.

Always begin by asking the participant to tell you what he or she was told about today's session by the recruiting person or agency. Often, you will find that the participant has been given information that is biasing and can seriously affect the test session. You need to know that in order to rectify it.

For example, Jeff conducted a test for which he used a temporary agency to recruit the participants. He discovered that when the participants expressed concern about the nature of their assignment, the agency's standard reply was, "Don't worry, even a baby can do it." Talk about getting off on the wrong foot!

This answer is a serious problem because it sets a false expectation about the ease of a product's use. During the test, encountering the slightest difficulty will confirm (in the participant's mind) that he or she is an absolute moron. As a result, the participant tries too hard and performs unnaturally and under extra pressure. If you find that your participants are being prepped in an unprofessional manner by an agency, you need to contact the offending party before the next test session and instruct them about what to say. Do not simply ignore the situation.

Have the Participant Fill Out and Sign Any Preliminary Documents

These documents, as discussed in Chapter 8, include:

- Background questionnaire
- Permission to record
- Nondisclosure document

Read the Orientation Script and Set the Stage

Yes, make sure to *read* the orientation script aloud to the participant each time you start a session. Explain and demonstrate any special techniques you will be using, such as "thinking aloud." Once again, relate to any nervousness on the part of the participant, and if it is excessive, do not just jump into the test, but see if there is a tangible cause. Clear up any misconceptions that may still exist about what is expected of the participant. Emphasize that it is *impossible* to really make a mistake. You can take your script sample orientation scripts in Chapter 8.

Have the Participant Fill Out Any Pre-Test Questionnaires

These pre-test questionnaires are intended to gather product-related information and not just demographic data about the participant. Unless there is a need for the participant to view the product first (possibly to give first impressions), the questionnaire can be filled out in the waiting area. Chapter 8 discusses why and how to develop a pre-test questionnaire.

Move to the Testing Area and Prepare to Test

If observers are present in the room, make brief introductions. Explain the setup of the room to the participant, and let him or her see the equipment if you feel it is appropriate. Never avoid the fact that the participant will be observed and recorded, even if he or she is very nervous. It is not ethical, and it will make things worse if the participant finds out later.

NOTE You may also tour the testing area while reviewing the orientation script, whichever seems more natural to you.

Position yourself and the participant according to the environment you have previously set up. Assuming that you are going to be working adjacent to the participant, *never set up in front of or directly behind a participant unless you are well beyond the range where the person will feel your presence without being able to see you.* Those locations, front and directly behind, create a sense of anxiety in most test participants and tend to accentuate a sense of self-consciousness. Your best bet is to be slightly behind and to the side, where the participant can just see you out of the corner of his or her eye. If you are too close, the participant will be concerned with what you are doing and may be distracted from the tasks at hand. The same holds true generally for additional observers — keep them away from the front and directly behind unless they are at a considerable distance. Because we strongly encourage you to have observers view the test sessions, more explicit guidelines for managing observers during a test are in the section "Debrief the Observers" later in the chapter.

Start Recordings

This is so easy to forget! (Even very experienced practitioners forget.) Put a prompt for yourself, or embed some keyword in your introduction to the session to remind you to start the software and or other equipment recording the session.

Set Decorum for Observers in the Room

Many usability researchers prefer to have observers watch the test through electronic observation from another room or through a one-way mirror. However, because some readers will not have the luxury of either option, yet will want to encourage direct observation, it is important to plan ahead how observers should behave. You want to reap the benefits (observers are more likely to abide by the test results if they have seen the test in person) and avoid the negative aspects (biasing the participant). The moderator must feel comfortable and capable of controlling the proceedings. If you have not been able to brief in-room observers on how they should behave before now, this is the time. See Chapter 8 for an example of guidelines for observers.

- **Introduce everyone to the participant.** Even if the observers will be well away from the participant during the test, but in the same room, it is still common courtesy to introduce everyone to the participant. This helps to make the participant feel less self-conscious, less like a guinea pig. First names are fine, titles are unnecessary, as are project assignments. For example, do not introduce an observer as, "Joe Schmidt, who wrote the user manual for the software you'll be working with today." It is an unusual participant who can openly criticize a user manual while the author watches from the other side of the room. An introduction of "This is Joe Schmidt" is sufficient. If the participant asks, just say that the observers are interested in the outcomes of the test.

▪ During the testing session, the observers should be as inconspicuous as possible, completely out of the sightline of the participant. The observers should be well away from the testing station, at least 10 to 15 feet. (If the room is not big enough to allow this much of a buffer, then limit the number of observers so the room is not crowded.) While this may interfere with their ability to see exactly what is happening, anything closer runs the risk of a group of people hovering over the participant like mother hens. If it is a very large room, have the observers watch the proceedings from a television monitor that is displaying the video camera feed, as shown in Figure 9-4. In that way they can remain in the room without crowding the participant or affecting the test.

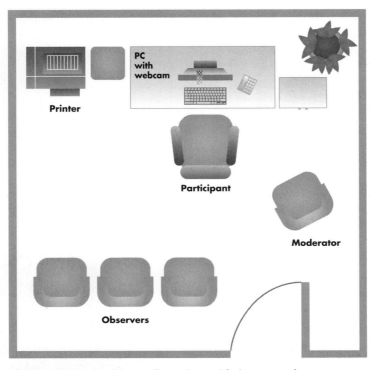

Figure 9-4 Monitoring configuration with in-room observers

- **During the session, the observers should not make any comments or ask questions.** The moderator should control the session with no interruptions from the observers. The only exception is if there are technical problems and the session must be interrupted or revised. Observers should jot down important topics and wait for the debriefing session to discuss them, not bring them up during the test.

- **During the debriefing, observers can be asked to join in the discussion.** The decision to have observers participate in the debriefing is the call of the moderator based on his or her confidence at being able to control the process. Especially where observers can provide an added dimension to the moderator's questioning (e.g., when products are targeted toward an extremely specialized audience), it is valuable to bring them into the process. Also, observers may raise concerns specifically related to their own component (e.g., the person who is responsible for the text messaging aspect of a cell phone may have very specific questions about getting and replying to text messages). For pointers on developing a debriefing guide, see Chapter 8. For more on how to conduct debriefings with participants and observers, see Chapter 10.

  Structure the debriefing session beforehand to minimize confusion to all concerned. The moderator should begin the debriefing and complete his or her line of questioning completely. At that point, have the observers join in and ask whatever questions they like, or ask the participant to expand upon subject matter already discussed. Be sure to prevent a sense of "shooting" questions at the participant from every direction, and when necessary, intervene to stop that from happening.

- **The moderator has final say on observers in the room.** Try it out with the express agreement that the moderator will ask the observers to leave if the participant is being affected by their presence.

One final word here on observers. If the observers will only be attending a limited number of sessions, it is important to remind them to withhold final judgments until the test report is complete or at least until a preliminary presentation is made to them by the moderator who has viewed *all* the test sessions. Rushing to judgment is one of the most common tendencies of observers who view a limited number of test sessions.

Provide Any Prerequisite Training If Your Test Plan Includes It

Prerequisite training may be required to acclimate? the participant to your product prior to the test or to bring the participant's expertise to a predetermined criterion. Prerequisite training might involve anything from a simple "20 minute tour" of the product to a full-day, in-depth session. In either case, the appropriate time to administer prerequisite training is after introductions and just prior to the actual test.

Either Distribute or Read the Written Task Scenario(s) to the Participant

If this is a test with little or no interaction required between the participant and the moderator, then provide written task scenarios for the participant. Because a very long list of tasks can be intimidating, you may want to present the scenarios in phases. After the participant completes one phase, simply present the next one. If the test is more exploratory in nature and there will be much interaction with the participant, then consider reading the scenarios one at a time to the participant or have the participant read the scenario out loud before beginning the task. This method provides better control of the pace of the test.

Record Start Time, Observe the Participant, and Collect All Critical Data

Finally, you are ready to begin collecting information. Everyone should be ready to go. Using your data collection instruments, begin to moderate and write down test events.

Have the Participant Complete All Post-Test Questionnaires

Once the main testing has been completed, take a short break if it is appropriate. Then, without further discussion of the test, have the participant fill out all written questionnaires. It is important to do this prior to any discussions with the moderator or other observers to minimize any biasing effects. For information about why and how to develop post-test questionnaires, see Chapter 8.

Debrief the Participant

Take a moment to peruse the questionnaires that the participant has just completed in order to ascertain if there are additional issues to raise during the debriefing. Skim through your notes to see if there are spots where you had questions that you want to follow up on with the participant before closing the session. A more in-depth discussion of debriefing can be found in Chapter 10.

Close the Session

Thank the participant, provide any remuneration, and show the participant out. If the participant is not being paid, it is always appropriate to give a token gift at the very least. Leave the door open for contacting the participant later to clarify any questions that may arise about the session.

Ask observers to write down the three most important things that happened in the session.

Organize Data Collection and Observation Sheets

Gather any data collection forms, comments, and so on, from other observers. Place all the information from the just-completed session into one file folder. If you are using an automated data collector, make sure the data is backed up and secured on disk.

Debrief with Observers

Ask each observer to read the points he or she wrote down about the most important things that happened in the session. Record this information in some way, either by continuing the video recording, making an audio recording, writing down what observers say, or gathering their "top-threes" on sticky notes. You can conduct this exercise within a few minutes. Doing so helps you see what observers are looking for and can help you focus your time later when you analyze and report the results. For more about debriefing with participants and observers, see Chapter 10.

Provide Adequate Time between Test Sessions

Do not rush yourself. Make sure you have some time to clear your mind between sessions. Moderating a test requires immense concentration. Pace yourself, especially if you will be testing for three, four, five days, or even longer. Clear your mind so you can treat the next participant with a fresh start. It is best if you can get completely away from the test area, if only briefly. Testing is mentally demanding on the moderator, so take it easy on yourself.

Prepare for the Next Participant

Onward, ever onward. Go back to the beginning of this checklist if you need to, and review for the next session.

When to Intervene

When testing, you will encounter many situations that simply cannot be covered by a guideline. Following are some frequently asked questions regarding two situations that occur quite often. The authors have also included some comments in the next section, often found at the tip of a moderator's tongue during a usability test, but which are better left unsaid for obvious reasons.

When to Deviate from the Test Plan

When is it appropriate to deviate from the test plan? This is one of the most difficult decisions for the novice moderator. Obviously, experimental rigor requires you to retain the same conditions from session to session. However, it is of little benefit to stick with a test design that is not meeting your test objectives. Testing is a serious undertaking. It is a waste of time and money to continue with something that is not providing you with the required data.

Following are some of the more common reasons for deviating from the initial test design. Keep in mind that if you are conducting the type of rigorous research that requires you to hold all conditions constant, your data and findings will be seriously affected by major changes to the test design. In the beginning, when you are first learning how to moderate a test, err on the side of sticking to the test plan as much as possible. With that said, you should consider changing the test plan under the following circumstances:

- **If the participants either do not understand or are not able to identify with your task scenarios.**   Consider revising the tasks to more accurately reflect reality. It is not unusual for the development team to lack a clear understanding of the end user and usage for a product, and you may not discover this until the actual test. This is one of the very good reasons to do at least one pilot session.

- **If you uncover additional areas that need to be investigated, but were not originally included in your test plan.**   If there is an aspect of your product that is unexpectedly problematic, it is important that you not stand on ceremony but explore it. For example, you may find that participants are having difficulty simply downloading your application and are taking three times as long as expected. Even though nothing indicated a problem with that module and you had not planned to devote much energy to probing it, you need to explore why it is taking so long.

- **If your questionnaires are asking the wrong questions.**   If the questions do not jibe with the problems or issues raised during the test sessions, change them. Ask questions that go directly to the heart of any problems uncovered.

- **If the participant(s) you expected does not show up.**   If the wrong person(s) shows up, with different experience and background than expected, consider changing the test design on the spot. For example, if you are expecting a participant who is experienced with the Internet and a complete novice shows up, you have two choices. You can ask the person to leave (but pay him or her first), or you can make the best of the situation. The ultimate decision depends on your schedule and whether you have time to acquire a different participant.

▪ **If the timing you set up doesn't work well.**   Another situation in which you might deviate from the test plan is when you find that the timing for the tasks is not working out. How should you let participants continue when they have exceeded the maximum time allotted to a task? This depends on the priorities of the test and how much time you have for the overall session with each participant.

If you have developed benchmark times representing the maximum allotted duration of a task, you need to decide what you will do when the participants take longer than the benchmark. You could stop them as soon as they reach the benchmark, of course, but not being allowed to complete a task can often be discouraging for the participant. If you have limited time with users, then you must stop them at the time limit for each task and move on to the next one. If you want to cover certain tasks, set limits for each, whether you are measuring time on task or not. If you want to see how many tasks participants can complete, keep track of their success, but end the session on time. What you do usually depends on how close the participants are to completing the task.

If the participants are close to completion and there is time in the session, let them continue, even though *that task will be graded as "unsuccessful."* After a few more minutes on the task, if they still are not able to complete it, we will ask them to move on to the next task.

If they are not at all close to completing the task, give them a hint to see if you can get them past whatever aspect is causing difficulty. Provide the minimum information that gets them moving toward a solution, and no more. Of course, as with the previous example, once a participant receives a hint, the task is graded as either "unsuccessful" or "required prompting." If need be, continue to provide hints in the interest of learning the precise information that does the trick. This can help in redesigning the product.

What *Not* to Say to Participants

We have discussed what you *should* do or say during a test. What you do not say is equally important. With all due respect to David Letterman, here then is our "Top Ten List" of Things *Not* to Say to Participants:

    10. Saying, "Remember, we're not testing you," more than three times.

     9. Don't worry, the last participant couldn't do it, either.

     8. No one's ever done *that* before.

     7. HA! HA! HA!

6. That's impossible! I didn't know it could go in upside down!

5. Could we stop for awhile? Watching you struggle like this is making me tired.

4. I didn't really mean you could press *any* button.

3. Yes, it's very natural for observers to cry during a test.

2. Don't feel bad, many people take 15 or 16 tries.

1. Are you *sure* you've used computers before?

CHAPTER 10

Debrief the Participant and Observers

Debriefing refers to exploring and reviewing the participant's actions during the performance portion of a usability test. When first sitting down to organize this book, Jeff was not sure whether to assign debriefing to its own stage of testing or to combine it with the previous stage of conducting the test. After all, one could argue that debriefing is really an extension of the testing process. Participants perform some tasks, and you interview them either in phases or after the entire test.

Because there is much to learn during the debriefing portions of tests, it seemed apparent that debriefing warranted its own separate treatment, or stage of testing. While the performance of the usability test uncovers and exposes problems, it is often the debriefing session that sheds light on why these problems occurred and how to fix them. Though a debriefing does not have to be formal or extensive, it is often not until the debriefing session that one understands motive, rationale, and very subtle points of confusion. If you think of usability testing as a mystery to be solved, in the debriefing session all the pieces come together.

Why Review with Participants and Observers?

Ideally, for every test that you conduct, your goal should be to understand why every error, difficulty, and omission occurred *for every participant for every session*. Debriefing with participants is your final opportunity to fulfill this goal before you let the participants walk out the door. It allows you to resolve any residual questions still resonating after a session. The debriefing session gets the participants to explain things that you could not see, such as what they were thinking when they accidentally deleted a file, or to communicate their personal preferences, such as where in a manual to place a specific piece of information. The participant debriefing session is intended to illuminate the thought process and rationale behind each participant's actions, especially for those actions about which the test moderator is unclear. If the task-oriented portion of a test indicates or exposes the "what" of performance, then the debriefing portion exposes or indicates the "why" of performance, especially if the performance portion did not include getting participants to think aloud.

Debriefing with observers is about getting them to help you see from different points of view what is happening in the sessions. By actively including observers in the ongoing discussion and analysis of impressions and trends gathered throughout the sessions, the moderator gains an expanded view of the performance of the participant by taking advantage of others' observations (not to mention the filling of gaps in memory or notes). When observers are included in the research and analysis activities, they are more likely to feel ownership of the issues and to buy in to the remedies. Perhaps as importantly, the moderator can take from interactions with observers some notion of the priorities of the stakeholders on the design team, a useful thing to know when it comes time to report results.

The following sections cover debriefing with participants. We'll cover reviewing and consensus building with observers at the end of the chapter.

Techniques for Reviewing with Participants

In a moment we will discuss the steps involved in conducting a post-test debriefing. But first we would like to review a couple of guidelines on questioning participants.

- **Never make participants feel at all defensive about their actions or their opinions.**   The debriefing session should have the flavor of a discussion among peers. By no means should it take on the flavor of a defendant on the witness stand being interrogated by a prosecutor or a defense attorney. For example, "As you reviewed your shopping cart, I noticed that you frowned when you clicked the Update Order button. Tell me about that. What was going on there for you?"

- **While questioning a participant, do not react to the participant's answers one way or another.**   This is very hard to do if you have a close affiliation with the product, because there is such a strong tendency to want the product to succeed. Consequently, it is very easy to lead the witness by communicating through body language and other non-verbal means that a particular answer is inherently better than another answer. The debriefing session is one aspect of the test session where a skilled and experienced test moderator and interrogator can make all the difference. Once a participant becomes defensive about any of his or her answers, or starts to get a sense of what you are looking for, that person's answers become suspect. Try something like this: "Fair enough. Thanks for answering that. I appreciate your feedback." And leave it at that.

Where to Hold the Participant Debriefing Session

Debriefing sessions can be held in the same area as the test, or they can be held in a different room entirely. If you feel that you will be referring to the product during the debriefing, then you want to conduct the session in the same location as the test. However, there may be times when you want to conduct the debriefing sessions away from the test location if the participant is extremely shy, tired, or distracted. At another location, the participant is more likely to open up than in the test location. This is especially true if your test location happens to be a very large room that is being observed by others either through a one-way mirror or from an electronic observation room. On the other hand, the participant may have become comfortable in the testing room, now that the work part of the session is over. For this reason, and because it is important for observers to view the debriefing, only move if there is no choice.

Basic Debriefing Guidelines

In this section, you go through a step-by-step process for conducting a debriefing session after the main performance test. These guidelines consider the needs of both the test moderator and participant.

1. **Gather your thoughts while the participant fills out any post-test questionnaires.** After the test, have the participant immediately fill out any post-test questionnaire(s). Help the participant know that you are getting close to the end of the session. You just have a few things you want to ask about. Take advantage of this time when the participant is filling out the questionnaire to gather your thoughts and think about how the session went. Decide which issues are resolved and which are still fuzzy to you.

   For example:

   ▪ Why didn't the participant notice the icon that communicated to place the cable "right side up"?

- Is it apparent why the participant never read the instruction that was integral to performing an entire task?

- What was the participant expecting to do when she tried to change the address associated with her account and ended up starting an online chat with customer service instead?

Review your debriefing topics guide, circling those issues that need to be moved to the forefront since the conclusion of the test. Cross off those topics that are no longer relevant or a concern. For more about developing a debriefing guide, see Chapter 8.

2. **Review the post-test questionnaire.**   Now reverse roles. Let the participant break while you review his or her just completed questionnaire. The questionnaire can also be used as "food for thought" for the debriefing session. Quickly glance over some of the participant's answers and ratings. Or, if there is no post-test questionnaire, skim through your notes or gather questions from observers.

   Look for unexpected answers that could benefit from exploration. For example, suppose that you monitored a test session where the participant obviously had great difficulty and seemed to exhibit quite a bit of frustration while performing. When you quickly scan this participant's post-test questionnaire, you notice that the participant rated the product extremely high. That is a discrepancy worth investigating during the debriefing session. Why would the participant rate the product so highly? Was the participant aware of the difficulty and just reluctant to give the product bad marks? Did the participant have an "easy" time compared to using a competitive product? Sometimes you might find that as difficult as the test session seemed, the participant's current product is five times worse. Or, was he just being nice?

3. **Begin by letting the participant say whatever is on his or her mind.**
   We like to begin by allowing the participant to say whatever is on his or her mind. Start with a very general open-ended question such as "So, what did you think?" or "How did that go?" This does two things. First, it allows the participant to vent, if he or she is feeling really frustrated. Second, because the question is open ended, it means *that the topic the participant chooses to speak of is usually the most prominent one to that person.* That in itself is an important piece of information.

4. **Begin your questions from general high-level issues.**   Use your debriefing topics guide, if need be, to help you remember your main concerns coming into the test. Focus on research questions. Come back to what you were trying to learn by doing this usability study.

5. **Move to the specific issues.**   Now you are ready to cover the specifics. Move down your data collection form to places where you have made

a notation to probe. Figure 10-1 shows an excerpt from a data collection form with "??" indicating a probe point.

The "??" indicates some action or comment by the participant that bears further exploration in the debriefing session, yet did not warrant stopping the test to pursue it at that point in time. You can use such a notation to indicate that there is a question about why a participant behaved as he or she did, and to probe later.

6. **Review those places in the participant's post-test questionnaire that you previously marked as areas to explore.**   Take your time. Give yourself enough leeway to think about the issues that you need to explore. Though many study moderators spend very little time debriefing participants in each session in a typical usability test, if you are doing retrospective review (or are "replaying the test with the participant," see the next section, "Advanced Debriefing Guidelines and Techniques"), you could conceivably spend *more* time in a debriefing than in the performance part of the test session. You might spend quite a lot of time debriefing someone for a relatively short test, especially if you are testing during the early stages of product or documentation development when your product is not yet set in concrete. By taking your time, you also help the participant to relax a bit and not necessarily answer with the first thought that comes to mind. Give the participant a chance to contemplate his or her answers, to really think through some of the issues and how these issues relate to the person's eventual use of the product on the job or at home.

Stay with one point until you feel confident that you clearly understand the basis for the problem, difficulty, and so forth. To be sure, ask yourself if you could explain a problem's cause to someone else who did not view the test.

Task	Elapsed Time	Notes
A	4:25	Clicked the wrong tab. Found his mistake. Clicked the wrong table again. Entered address incorrectly. Self-corrected after reading error message.
B	:30	Perfect. YES!
C	1:25	Very long hesitation. Pulls down the opportunities list and lean in close. Silence. Then selects and completes correctly. ??
D	2:30	Entered the wrong password. Very lost. "I hate it when that happens." Totally missed note after Step 8.

Figure 10-1 Data collection form showing probe location

7. Focus on understanding problems and difficulties, *not* on problem solving. A very common misuse of the debriefing time is to view it as

   ▪ **A time to solve the problems uncovered by the test.**   You do not need to understand how to *fix* the problem. In fact, focusing on resolution at this stage often undermines a more creative solution later when you have more time to think about the issue.

   ▪ **A time to solicit design ideas from the participant.**   Participants who are not experts in such disciplines as interface design, information architecture, interaction design, and technical writing should not necessarily be solicited for ideas about redesign. Sometimes, suggestions from the participants are well meaning but impractical. The participants are not able to take into consideration the constraints of the development team, especially time constraints. An exception to this would be when you want to show the participant some specific design ideas in development for feedback. You might say that this is a rather elitist and closed-minded attitude, but think about it. As end users of products, what participants know *best* is whether a product meets their needs or not. However, designing a product to meet those needs is an entirely different skill. That is why companies hire professional designers, engineers, writers, and training personnel. It's the job of these professionals to take the end user's needs into consideration and build the product. Please do not misunderstand. If a participant offers suggestions that make sense, of course you should note them. However, do not make the solicitation of ideas the main thrust of your debriefing session.

8. **Finish your entire line of questioning before opening up the floor to discussion by observers.**   We advocate letting observers with a vested interest have the opportunity to ask questions of the participant. *But it must be done in a structured fashion that allows you to maintain control of the process.* We *do not* advocate different people firing questions at the participant in random fashion. The two ways we would suggest accommodating observers depend on your physical setup.

   ▪ If observers are located outside the testing area, then it is best if they write down their questions on a piece of paper and have you ask the questions. Although you have told the participants they are being watched, it can still be a bit awkward when they meet the observers in person. You might also get questions through instant messaging if you are using a computer separate from the one the participant is using.

   ▪ If observers are located in the test room during the test, you can still ask them to write down their questions for you to ask or, if you sense that the participant is comfortable enough for the observers to ask their own questions, then allow it. However, have observers do so after you have completed your line of questioning. You can bring them over and even have a round-table discussion if you feel that such a discussion will not intimidate the participant.

9. **If appropriate, leave the door open to further contact.**   Once you have completed the session, you might want to suggest the possibility of contacting the participant to clarify any issues that might come up. Be sure to thank the participant for participating in the usability test, and then present the participant with any remuneration before sending him or her home.

Advanced Debriefing Guidelines and Techniques

Essentially, the steps in the last section represent the basic debriefing session. However, once you have mastered the basics, there are other advanced guidelines and techniques that are worth learning and practicing. The following sections examine a few of them.

"Replay the Test" Technique

Replaying the test (sometimes referred to as *retrospective review*) is an excellent technique for jogging the participant's memory and helping the participant to remember important points that he or she would otherwise forget to tell you. By actively recalling events that occurred, the participant reexperiences his or her thoughts and feelings at the time of the usability test.

There are two methods associated with the "replay the test" technique, the manual method and the video method.

The Manual Method

After the test session, go back to your data collection form on which you should have taken cryptic but descriptive notes of the participant's actions for each major scenario. An example might be "Chose the wrong tab." For those tasks for which you still have questions, describe to the participant his or her actions with enough detail so that the participant can visualize what he or she was experiencing at the time. Once you have succeeded in "returning to the scene of the crime," so to speak, ask whatever question you have about the particular circumstances.

It this technique very helpful in both getting the participants to reexperience what was happening and to reconnect with their emotions and reactions at the time that events occurred. There are some caveats though. You really need to pay attention during the test, take excellent notes, and have a good memory. The test should also be of moderate length, or else you will not be able to remember what happened during the early tasks, and it will be a stretch for the participant as well.

The Video Method

An even better variation of the manual replay method is simply using technology to replace notes and memory. In the video method, rather than simply describing past events, you and the participant watch a video of the relevant portions of the test session that was just recorded. When participants see themselves and their own expressions, they are better able to recall their own feelings at that moment.

Using the video method provides little reason to interrupt the participant to probe during the test portion. You should still make notes about potential problems, so you know which portions of the tape to access. The downside of this method is the inordinate amount of time to shuttle through the recordings. In addition, the test session is literally experienced twice, which is time-consuming.

Audio Record the Debriefing Session

Another way to enhance the productivity of your data collection is to audio record the debriefing session and have it transcribed later. This enables you to give the participant your full attention because you need not take comprehensive notes. It's also much easier to pull important remarks out of the transcript than from the audio recording itself. There are other ways to use the transcription, as well, such as for content analysis.

Reviewing Alternate Designs

During the early stages of development, use the debriefing session to review alternate versions of the product and collect information about participant preferences. You might show two or three working prototypes of a web page or web application, or alternate high-level designs of a user manual, and solicit opinions from the participant. This is a much more practical and effective way to solicit design preference information from a participant than asking the participant to come up with his or her own ideas from scratch.

"What Did You Remember?" Technique

Very often, one of the objectives of your test is to ascertain whether specific design elements are contributing or inhibiting or even having no effect at

Test moderator:	When you opened the cover to replace the transverse hippleklammer, did you notice anything in the vicinity?
Participant:	Why yes, I vaguely remember seeing a label.
TM:	Great. What was on the label?
P:	I haven't any idea. I didn't really look at it carefully, or even read it.
TM:	So you didn't feel it would be helpful in replacing the hippleklammer?
P:	Well, I suppose if you are asking me, it probably means that it would have helped, but at the time, I guess I was just really focused on the hippleklammer. Remember that it was stuck. So, what did the label say?
TM:	Oh, nothing that important. Let me read it to you: "WARNING: Replacing the hippleklammer before checking that the tootenpleeber is securely fastened can result in serious injury."
P:	AHHHHHHHH!

Figure 10-2 "What did you remember" dialogue

all on end user performance. Perhaps a label on a machine, a key note in a user manual, or an important error message on a screen represents an area of concern. For example, did the participant notice a special message on the address page while performing a task? Because you cannot really question a participant about such items during the test itself because you will bring his or her attention to the object. (Q: "Excuse me, you didn't happen to notice that note over there, did you?" A: "Oh, you mean this one over here. Why no I hadn't until you just mentioned it. Thanks.") You need a more subtle approach.

The way the technique works is as follows. During debriefing, show the participant the web page, or section of the user manual, or machine part with the particular element in question either removed or covered up. Then ask the participant if he or she remembers anything in that spot. For example, in the case of a machine label, your questioning might proceed as shown in Figure 10-2.

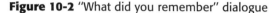 **TIP** All kidding aside, in reality, you would never place the participant in jeopardy during the test, and you would explain that at the appropriate moment during the test if asked. However, on the job, it's a different story. There is a real problem to be solved here, and if the label is not working, you need to know that.

Here is how Jeff used this technique while conducting a study. A crucial part of the test was whether a participant would notice a label attached to a print cartridge on a printer, which helped the end user to insert the print cartridge correctly. Jeff was testing the effectiveness of two different types of labels: graphic labels and word labels. He wanted to see whether one of these types was more effective than the other. After finishing the test, he would hide the print cartridge in his hand and ask the participants whether they remembered seeing the label and, if they did, what was on it. Jeff found that for this particular situation words were remembered much more often than graphics — a somewhat counterintuitive finding. Users tended to ignore the graphic version. Jeff has found that this technique and line of questioning is extremely valuable in ascertaining which design elements are actually being noticed and having an effect, if simple observation does not reveal the answer. Often developers spend inordinate amounts of time refining elements that the end user never even notices.

"Devil's Advocate" Technique

There are times when you really want to challenge the intellectual positions of the participants on a particular issue to establish just how strongly they feel about it. It may be a particularly critical or vulnerable aspect of the product, and you might feel that a particular participant is not being completely candid.

This last technique, which we both use rather consistently, is one of our favorites. It is also one of the more advanced data collection techniques. In this technique the test moderator drops his or her neutral demeanor and takes a position diametrically opposed to the participant's, to ascertain the participant's true feelings about a product. The main reasons for adapting this technique are:

- Your participants seem reluctant to criticize the product, even if they have experienced difficulty using it.

- You are testing a particular feature/section that is known to be problematic or controversial and that may jeopardize release of the product, depending on the severity of the problem. In other words, there is a lot riding on the outcome of the usability test, and you have to be extra sure that the test is "exposing all the bad news" before release.

If either of these situations is the case, then the "devil's advocate" technique is very helpful in providing that extra bit of confidence in your results. It is normally done during the debriefing session, after the participant has completely finished the usability test. It is especially appropriate to use this technique if the participant had a difficult time during the test but downplays the problems during the debriefing.

How to Implement the "Devil's Advocate" Technique

The technique is simple but should be used with great discretion and serious caution. Here is how it works:

- Mention that you are surprised at the discrepancy between the participant's performance and his or her comments. Ask the participant for specific reasons for his or her feelings. Tell the participant that you sense reluctance on his or her part to offer criticism, and you want to make sure the participant is not just "being kind."

- An even more assertive approach is to tell a "white lie" and mention that other participants have offered quite opposite criticism to this particular participant's comments, and you want to be absolutely sure how he or she feels.

The following are some examples of the types of questions you might ask or the types of statements you might make:

- It's interesting that you say you liked it, since it seems as if you had great difficulty.

- I'm rather surprised by your answer; are you sure you don't consider this unusually difficult to perform?

- Gee, other people we've brought in here have responded in quite the opposite way.

- You're the first person who has felt this way.

- Don't you think that the manufacturer of this product is doing you a disservice with this design?

Sometimes just asking these types of questions will cut through a participant's hesitation, and the participant will say that he or she has been reluctant to criticize, almost with a sigh of relief. More often than not, though, participants will simply restate their position because that is the way they truly feel about the product. Being challenged, however, forces them to look more closely at why they feel as they do and often results in a more thoughtful and comprehensive rationale. However, *it is very good news indeed* when participants continue to respond positively even after being challenged in this way.

Example of the "Devil's Advocate" Technique

Let's provide an example of this technique in action. Jeff was testing a hardware product for a client. The product required a participant to run a manual adjustment routine (a fix) to overcome a problem on the assembly line. The routine adjustment would take an end user about 3 minutes to run and would need to be performed every 3 months or so. The manufacturer did not want to delay release of the product, because it would be very costly, but would do so if the usability test showed a strong adverse reaction to the fix.

The manufacturer was very concerned that the adjustment would be seen as a blemish on the company's sterling reputation.

The results of the performance test were very positive. Participants were able to perform the fix, and even enjoyed implementing it. Because the true feelings of the participant were so crucial in this case, Jeff began to challenge each participant by intentionally asking *extremely* leading questions, such as, "Don't you find it insulting that the manufacturer is making you perform a fix that should have been resolved at the factory?" He gave them every possible opportunity to change their position.

Time and again, the participants said that performing the fix was not insulting because they appreciated that the company was advising them of the problem and providing them with an easy fix that was even fun to do. This reaction convinced everyone that the fix was truly acceptable. In fact, so strong was the positive reaction that, by the time testing was complete, the company was ready to market the new routine as a "feature" rather than a fix.

Perhaps you are thinking "Isn't it a bit risky to challenge participants this directly because you might cause them to change their minds?" Certainly that is possible, but if the interview is conducted assertively but without aggression, using the appropriate target participant, very rarely will you intimidate the participant. If you do, it becomes rather obvious anyway, and you can back off and factor that into the person's comments.

In reality, it is much more likely during a test that the product will get treated with "kid gloves" and go out the door with a better reputation than it deserves. Many organizations, even those committed to testing, are still loath to admit the truth about product problems until it is too late. Also, any risk of biasing the participant's *performance* data is negated by the time this technique is conducted because the participant has finished that portion of the test already. You can only affect the participant's comments.

There are, however, some participants on whom this technique will not work well because their opinions are more easily swayed:

- Very young or some very old participants who have difficulty drawing inferences.
- Participants who are overly ingratiating.
- Participants who mistakenly see the testing situation as a possible job opportunity and will say anything to please you.

One final note: If you should use this technique, be sure to warn observers and team members about your intentions beforehand. They may misunderstand your intentions and get downright testy when they feel the test moderator is taking sides. Only use this line of questioning as a means of getting at participants' real feelings and thoughts about their experience with the product and *not* as a way to *influence* their thinking in any way.

Reviewing and Reaching Consensus with Observers

By the time you have reached this chapter, you probably have briefed your observers about how to behave during a usability test session — whether they are in the testing room with you and the participant or not — and what to observe for. Now, imagine that you're at the end of a session. You have collected data and observations. You have debriefed with the participant and taken final follow-up questions from the observers to ask the participant. What's left before you either go on to the next session or start to analyze the data from the entire study? Work with the observers to make them co-researchers.

Why Review with Observers?

When you include observers as "co-researchers," there are great benefits to you and to them.

- You have other people to talk to about what happened in each session.

- Observers become more engaged and invested in the test if they know there will be discussion with the goal of reaching consensus on what the usability issues are.

- You begin to see what things the team considers high priority and this gives you indicators for what to include in your reporting and in what order.

- You get the team to agree on what the issues are, which should make remedying the problems easier when the redesigning gets under way.

In the debriefing with observers, they also receive tacit training about usability testing from you as you help them interpret and make inferences about what they observed. You become the expert and an even more valuable resource to the team.

Between Sessions

When you spend a few minutes debriefing with observers between test sessions, you start at the same place you did with participants: by asking "How'd that go?" The idea here is to get to talk with all the observers before they leave for a bio-break, return phone calls, or get absorbed in email. Keep them together for just 10 minutes to get their impressions of what just happened in the session. Using a flip chart or a white board, write down each of the issues that the observers bring up in a "rolling issues list."

Then ask, "What surprised you?" Note everything each observer says; try to group the observations and insights in some way, if you can. If you can't, don't worry about it. You'll get a chance to sort things out later.

Now, back up and ask, task by task, what issues observers saw. Or, if you have logged problems in a data logger or have other data that you can get to quickly, step through that together. Go through each point to ensure that everyone in the room understands what the real finding is and how important it is. Get the people in the room to come to consensus on what the issues were and — very importantly — how to describe them. Ask if the others agree with each item raised. If they don't, ask the originator for clarification until there is general agreement. Document the item on something visible and accessible to the observers. Ask everyone in the group if they agree on the wording of each issue. Next to each issue, note which participant had the issue. There's an example in Figure 10-3. As you complete sessions, add participant numbers for each applicable issue. As we discuss in Chapter 12, to protect participants' privacy, you should refer to them by numbers rather than names.

Nothing on the site seems seriously broken; there were no show-stoppers.

It seems a bit easy to get lost on the way to completing a reservation; participants didn't seem to recall where they've been.   P1, P3, P4

Participants had remembered features, but couldn't find them again and didn't see clues in the site to tell them how to find them.   P2, P3

Some of the features participants asked for were there, but they didn't see them.   P2, P3, P5

Comparing properties on the search result page is not effective—it's hidden at several different levels. For example, participants don't notice the checkboxes and the call to action button is invisible.   P1, P2, P3, P4, P5

Participants didn't notice the guided navigation; they did not use the links to narrow the search results.   P1, P2, P5

Participants went to the hotel property sites.   P4, P5

There seemed to be a set of core amenities that participants were interested in:

       Internet access.   P2, P4, P5

       Near attractions.   P1, P2, P3

       Nice looking room.   P2, P3, P4

Participants talked about location, but scrolled past the map without interacting with it to get to the search results (the map may not look clickable).   P3, P5

Find and Reserve holds some confusion—participants aren't clear what to expect when they click on it. P1 thought it would take her to search results, P3 called it a "Home page of sorts."

Figure 10-3 Rolling issues from one day of testing

Continue like this until all the observers have talked about their main insights. Repeat the process at the end of every session. The rolling issues list will also help you in reporting if you plan to deliver "top 10" or "top line" reports, which are very brief summaries of the day's (or study's) issues.

At the End of the Study

When you have completed all the sessions, have one last debriefing session with observers. Step through the rolling issues list to review. Ask the observers if there are any revisions they want to make to the consensus issues.

Finally, it's time to set priorities. There are a few ways that we can think of to get the group to rank the issues in order of priority. You could:

- Ask for the top 10 items, just called out verbally.

- Ask the observers to vote. The items with the highest number of votes are the top priorities.

- Write up the issues on sticky notes or on cards and ask observers to sort them into priority lists.

Again, it is important to get the observers to take part in the ranking and classifying exercise. Doing so provides you with a sequence to consider for organizing your findings in the final report. It also helps ensure that no one is surprised when your report is issued. They already know what to expect because they have been engaged in the study as co-researchers.

One or two cautions here: It is extremely tempting to start talking about how to remedy the agreed issues. Don't do it. Do everything you can to stop any discussion of how to redesign the user interface at this stage, especially because most observers will not have seen all of the sessions.

Although you all have agreed on issues, these issues are only accumulated impressions and memories that are weighted by personal and (perhaps) political precedence, not data. You do still have to go back through the data collected and analyze it. When you review the data, you will see these same issues but with subtle effects that may reveal answers or even conflict with what happened in the debriefings with observers. That analysis and transformation is covered in the Chapter 11.

Analyze Data and Observations

Finally. You have completed the testing and are now ready to dive in and transform a wealth of data into recommendations for improvement. Typically, the analysis of data falls into two distinct processes with two different deliverables:

- The first is a preliminary analysis and is intended to quickly ascertain the *hot spots* (i.e., worst problems), so that the designers can work on these immediately without having to wait for the final test report. This preliminary analysis takes place as soon as feasible after testing is complete. Its deliverable is either a small written report (which you could deliver by email, as a short slide deck, on a blog, or to a groupware site) or a verbal presentation of findings and recommendations. The steps for performing this preliminary analysis are covered in this chapter:

  - Compile data.
  - Summarize data.
  - Analyze data.

  Generally, the point is to get out the weeds to be able to see the larger trends and patterns.

- The second is a comprehensive analysis, which takes place during a 2- to 4-week period after the test. Its deliverable is a final, more exhaustive report. This final report should include all the findings in the preliminary report, updated if necessary, plus all the other analyses and findings that were not previously covered. The steps for generating the final report are covered in Chapter 12.

A word of caution is in order regarding preliminary findings and recommendations. Developing and reporting preliminary recommendations creates a predicament for the test moderator. Your recommendations must be timely so that members of the development team, such as designers and writers, can begin implementing changes. However, you also need to be thorough, in the sense of not missing anything important. Once preliminary recommendations are circulated for public consumption, they quickly lose their *preliminary* flavor. Designers will begin to implement changes, and it is difficult to revisit changes at a later time and say "Oops, I don't really think we should change that module after all."

You could simply avoid producing preliminary recommendations, but if designers viewed the tests, they are sure to act on what they saw prior to your final report. Therefore, not providing *any* preliminary recommendations is not a satisfactory option. The best compromise is to provide preliminary findings and recommendations but be cautious and err on the conservative side by providing too little rather than too much. Stick to very obvious problems, such as ones that prevented completion of the task by all or the majority of the users. If you are unsure about a finding or a recommended solution without performing further analysis, simply say so.

As outside consultants, we typically meet with the development team immediately after the test for a debriefing and informal report, and then follow up with a formal report later. The informal report will only include obvious items that do not require further analyses, and if possible, come out of consensus debriefings that we held throughout the study or after the last session. In addition, we always qualify our preliminary recommendations as *"preliminary,"* and if we leave any paperwork behind, it is clearly marked **PRELIMINARY** in large letters. This gives us the option of changing a recommendation later based upon further analysis.

Now let's move on and discuss the steps involved in analyzing test data and developing recommendations. There are four major steps to the process.

1. Compile and summarize data.
2. Analyze data.
3. Develop recommendations.
4. Produce the final report.

This chapter covers compiling and analyzing data. The next chapter describes how to turn the results into insights and findings for reporting.

Compile Data

Let's look at the process of compiling and summarizing the data you have collected. The following is a step-by-step process for compiling data, although in all honesty it never goes as smoothly and as linearly as described here. It tends to be circular and iterative, as some answers lead to more questions.

Begin Compiling Data as You Test

The process of compiling involves placing all the data collected into a form that allows you to see patterns. The compilation of data, whether you are creating a preliminary report or not, should go on throughout the test sessions. Not only does this speed up the overall analysis process, but it also serves as a checkpoint to see that you are collecting the correct data and that the data matches the problem statements in the test plan. Compiling data as you test also helps you to see if you are missing anything important, and that you understand what you have collected during one day before moving on to the next day.

At the end of each day, gather all the data for that day's session. Make sure that all data is legible, especially if others are helping you. If observers are assisting with collection, make sure that you can read their notes, too, and that they are collecting data as you expect. Begin to get recordings and data files backed up and audio recordings transcribed. It is much easier to work with digital recordings than analog ones. Having transcriptions can be helpful for protocol analysis or studies where you are particularly concerned with vocabulary or information architecture.

Transfer handwritten notes to a computer, and transfer times and other quantitative data onto a master sheet or computer spreadsheet. If you like, keep a running summary of the data, which you update each night. For example, tally errors and successes by task on a spreadsheet and recompute the average after each day's data is added.

This ongoing compilation of data takes advantage of the fact that the test is still fresh in your mind so that you can remember odd quirks and events that happened during the day. Even with the best note taking, keystroke or mouse click recording, and so on some events simply are not captured, except in your memory, and they will fade unless you record them. That is why we recommend doing some compiling each day of a study. The ongoing compilation also prepares you to move faster on any preliminary analysis that you provide.

If you happen to be conducting an iterative, fast-turnaround test (e.g., changes are made to the product after every few sessions), compiling data each night will be a necessity. You and the design team will have to decide which changes to the product to implement for the next day's session, and there should be a record of what those discussions were. In this situation, you may want to update your test plan, session script, and debriefing guide (see Chapter 8 for more about each of these) to reflect the revisions in the product.

Organize Raw Data

When you complete the sessions from a study, you probably have several types of data at hand, from recordings to notes, to questions and comments from participants, to issues lists from observers. The toolbox for organizing the raw data has many offerings. There are, of course, transcriptions of sessions, especially if you have conducted a "think aloud" study (see Chapter 9 for more information). There are various types of recordings to review (even the audio recordings can offer hints at emotion that can help you determine a severity rating for a problem). In addition, you may have used monitoring software that collected other data such as mouse clicks, and that should generate tables and spreadsheets for you.

At some point, though, you simply have to start going through your own notes or the notes you get from your assigned data gatherer and/or observers. The tools are simple but many: lists, tallies, matrices, stories, storyboards, structure models, flow diagrams, and so on. Use any tool that helps you get a handle on how the data looks. Break out highlighters, yellow sticky notes, and flip charts if you do better with moving things around physically rather than virtually.

One of our favorite tools is also one of the simplest and most available: a spreadsheet program. Whether you are defining and quantifying everything to be able to get statistical significance or you just want to know what the dominant task path is, you can drop text or tallies into the cells of a spreadsheet and then use its tools to help you with analyzing the data. A spreadsheet program helps you generate counts, averages, medians, means, and percentages. Obviously, it's good for helping with number-related analyses. However, it will also help you sort and filter data, which can lead you to recognizing important patterns that you may not be able to represent statistically.

Even laying text out in a spreadsheet — such as answers to interview questions — can help you see true duplication as well as near matches that reveal useful insights. For example, in one study Dana asked participants "When you tried to use the site before but couldn't find what you were looking for, what did you do then?" In reviewing a dozen responses, she could see that the ultimate answer wasn't "go to the site map," as the team had hoped it would be, but instead was "ask someone else" because the participants said things like, "I ask my manager," "contact the help desk," or "email a coworker." To analyze the text, Dana skimmed through the first few transcribed responses in a spreadsheet, looking for key words. Finding two or three, she used the Find and Replace feature of the spreadsheet to search for each keyword in turn, and changed that cell to a different color. The software automatically told her how many instances it had changed, and she could see which participants said what. Over the next few Find-Replace steps, Dana could track trends to user groups. Pretty simple, but efficient and effective.

See the web site that accompanies the book (www.wiley.com/go/usability testing) for full-color examples of analysis spreadsheets and tallies.

Of course, you could also use outlining programs, data visualizers, or mind-mapping software. Use whatever works for you to be able to recognize trends and patterns. As those trends and patterns are revealed, you should be able to draw inferences about what the usability problems were.

Summarize Data

After all sessions have been completed, finish compiling the data. Transfer information from data collection sheets onto summary sheets. Or, if you are using an automated data logger that summarizes data for you, print out those files and review them. *By aggregating the data measures you have collected, you get a snapshot of what happened during the test — where participants performed well and where they performed poorly.* These summaries are also used to indicate if there were differences in performance of different groups, such as novice and experienced users, or differences in performance of different versions of a product. It is at this point that you begin to have what you need to determine whether the test met its objectives and to answer the original research questions outlined in the test plan.

Summarize Performance Data

You will want to summarize performance data in terms of errors and task accuracy. You may want to use timings, too. The most common *descriptive* statistics for these types of performance data are shown in the sections below. (We talk about inferential statistics later in this chapter.) Descriptive statistics are simply techniques for classifying the characteristics of your data that help you see patterns that may review problems or insights. All of the statistics use simple formulas that are available on most computer spreadsheet programs.

Task Accuracy

For task accuracy, you have several different statistics at your disposal. You could simply count the number of errors made per task. Or, you could go further and categorize the errors by type, such as errors of omission (leaving something out), errors of commission (doing something not needed), and so on. Or, as described in the following discussion, you could track the number of participants who performed successfully, either within the time benchmark expected or outside of it. You can also track those participants performing successfully but requiring some assistance. This statistic, however, is not all that helpful unless you have kept the type of assistance consistent from session to session and know where in the task and product the assistance was given.

Following are three types of statistics that relate to task accuracy:

▪ **Percentage of participants performing successfully, including those who required assistance.**   This task accuracy measure includes every participant who completed the task successfully, regardless of whether the task was completed within a time limit, or if participants needed assistance. If this number is very low, say 50 percent, it indicates *very* serious problems with the product because participants could not perform successfully even with assistance and extra time.

▪ **Percentage of participants performing successfully.**   This task accuracy statistic indicates the percentage of participants who were at least able to muddle through the task well enough to complete it successfully. If the participants made errors, you know they were eventually able to correct themselves and perform successfully.

▪ **Percentage of participants performing successfully within a time benchmark.**   This task accuracy statistic is an indication of correct performance and efficiency. If 7 of 10 participants achieved success within the allotted time, then the task accuracy would be 70 percent. You and your team should have determined ahead of time what the benchmark should be (see Chapter 8). If you are conducting multiple usability tests over time as the design is iterated for elimination of usability problems, the team may allow that 70 percent success rate is acceptable in the first couple of rounds of usability testing. (For a discussion about whether 70 percent success is good enough, see Chapter 3.)

Figure 11-1 shows an example of a combined summary of task timings and task accuracy scores from a hypothetical test.

Note that one can look across any line on the table and see the timings and score for each task. For this particular summary, a score was considered correct only if it was performed within the benchmark. Note also the use of footnotes to indicate any discrepancies that occurred during the test. This provides a historical record without having to reference a second table or the raw data itself.

See the web site that accompanies the book (`www.wiley.com/go/usability testing.com`) for additional examples of analysis spreadsheets and tallies.

Task Timings

Task timings relate to how much time participants require to complete each task. Common statistics that describe task timings include mean,

Module	Tasks	Percentage of participants performing correctly (within benchmark)	Mean time (minutes)	Standard deviation (minutes)
A	Set temperature pressure	83	3.21	4.38
	Set gas flows	33	12.08	10.15[1]
	Ignite the QRC	83	2.75	2.68
	Bake out column	100	0.46	0.17
	Set oven temperature program	66	6.54	2.56
	Run QRC checkout	100	0.83	0.34
	Program pressure and temperature	66	5.17	3.46
	Rerun checkout	100	0.29	0.09
B	Load the sample tray	100	0.88	0.28
	Create a subdirectory	33	8.00	3.92
	Create a sequence	66	9.42	7.70
	Start the sequence	66	1.00	0.92
	Stop the sequence	100	1.30	0.89
	Check the report	100[2]	1.38	0.58
	Reintegrate and print report	66	11.67	5.15
	Modify the method	100[3]	2.67	1.86
	Save the method	83	2.92	5.41
	Modify the sequence	66	3.46	3.96
	Restart the sequence	83	1.08	0.89

1 Participants 4's timings are not included. Participant had great resistance to performing the task and had not attempted it on the job in more than 18 months. Participant was also given misnformation during the task.

2 Participant 4 did not perform this task due to running the wrong method and having the test plot run.

3 Participant 1 did not perform this task to time constraints.

Figure 11-1 Performance score summaries and mean times ($N = 6$)

median, range, and standard deviation, each of which is explained in the following discussion.

- **Mean time to complete.** For each task, calculate the average time required by all participants to complete it, using the following formula:

$$\text{Mean} = \frac{\text{Sum of All Participants' Completion Times}}{\text{Number of Participants}}$$

The mean time to complete is a rough indication of how the group performed as a whole. It can be compared to the original time benchmark developed for the task to see if users, in general, performed better or worse than expected. If it turns out that task times are very skewed either left or right — that is, the highest or lowest times are very different from the other times — consider using the median score, instead of the mean, as a comparison tool.

- **Median time to complete.** The median time to complete is the time that is exactly in the middle position when all the completion times are listed in ascending order. For example, if the times to complete a task (in minutes) for nine sessions were:

SESSION NUMBER	COMPLETION TIME (IN MINUTES)
1	2.0
2	2.3
3	2.3
4	3.0
5	**3.0**
6	3.2
7	3.8
8	4.0
9	16.0

Then the mean time to complete would be 4.4 minutes. However, the *median* time to complete would be 3.0 minutes (bold above), which because of the aberration in session #9, seems more typical of the scores.

■ **Range (high and low) of completion times.**   This shows the highest and lowest completion times for each task. This statistic can be very revealing if there is a huge difference between these two times. Especially for small sample sizes, where each participant's performance is crucial, you would like to know why there is such a huge difference between the high and low scores. Did the poorest performer view the task in an unusual way, one that a significant minority of the target population might share? Or, did that participant simply lack some important skills possessed by the target audience?

USING RANGE TO DETERMINE "OUTLIERS"

For performers who fall outside the range, the question is always if this is representative of the majority or if the participant lacked a skill. This sometimes happens, as it did in on particular test that Jeff did. The very last participant of eight performed much more poorly than the other participants on a task yet fit the user profile exactly. The design team was forced to decide if this poor performance was an aberration (sometimes called an "outlier") or if other end users might perform the task similarly.

■ **Standard deviation (SD) of completion times.**   The standard deviation, like the range, is a measure of variability — to what degree the times differ from each other. It reveals how closely the scores, in this case the completion times, are clustered around the mean time. Because the SD takes into consideration the middle as well as the end times, it is a more accurate indicator than simply using the longest and shortest completion times. The basic formula for calculating the standard deviation for a group of scores is:

$$\text{Standard Deviation (SD)} = \frac{\sqrt{\Sigma x^2 - \frac{(\Sigma x)^2}{n}}}{n-1}$$

Where $\Sigma\, x^2$ the sum of the squares of each of the scores.

$\Sigma\, x$ the sum of all the scores.

n the total number of scores.

As an example of a calculation, let's assume that you have the following series of four completion times, where x is the value of each time:

X (MINUTES)	X^2
6.0	36.00
5.5	30.25
4.0	16.00
5.0	25.00
$\Sigma\, x = 20.5$	$\Sigma\, x^2 = 107.25$

Then the standard deviation would be calculated as follows:

$$SD = \frac{\sqrt{107.25 - \frac{(20.5)^2}{4}}}{3} = \frac{\sqrt{107.25 - 105.06}}{3} = 0.73 \text{ minutes}$$

The SD is always stated in the original measurement units, in this case, minutes. Fortunately, the SD formula is included on almost any current computer spreadsheet program.

How can you use the SD? Suppose that you calculate a mean time of 6.0 minutes for a task, with an SD of 0.5 minutes. This represents a tightly clustered distribution around the mean, which implies that users performed very similarly to one another. If, however, the SD is 3 minutes with the same mean time of 6 minutes, that represents a much broader distribution of times. This much broader distribution could warrant a second look at users' performance to understand why they performed so differently from each other. Were there identifiable differences in experience that could cause this wide variation in scores? Or did some users simply miss an important piece of information?

Summarize Preference Data

In addition to summarizing performance data, you will also want to summarize the preference data that you collected. Preference data may come from multiple sources such as surveys, post-test questionnaires, and post-test debriefing sessions. Following are some guidelines for summarizing different types of preference data.

- **For limited-choice questions.**   Sum the answers to each individual question, ranking, rating, and so forth, so that you can see how many participants selected each possible choice. You may also want to compute the average scores for each item, but for a small sample size this may not even be necessary in order to view trends.

- **For free-form questions and comments.**   List all questions and group all similar answers into meaningful categories. For example, sum all positive and negative references to a particular screen or particular section of a document. This method will enable you to scan the results quickly for a general indication of the number of positive and negative comments.

- **For debriefing sessions.**   Have all interviews transcribed, and pull out the critical comments. It can help to have interviews transcribed because it is so much easier to skim through written comments or search the electronic versions and pull out the essential information from a transcription than it is to listen and categorize the information while you are listening to the recording. In addition, a written record of these interviews makes the information much more accessible for later reference by others.

List the comments and observations from data collection sheets, both your own and those of participants. Organize these comments and observations in some workable form that makes sense for your test. For example, group them by task or by product component, such as a screen or section of a manual.

Figure 11-2 shows an example of a preference data summary. The summary includes the questions and choices that were provided to participants, as well as a summary of their responses.

Figure 11-3 provides another example of a data summary. The data in this example is even more compressed because, instead of including participants' comments, it shows only the number of times a participant referred to a particular product component or aspect. Especially for tests with more than 10 participants, this more compressed summary gives you a quick means of identifying those aspects that are of greatest concern and those that are of least concern.

Preference questionnaire

I thought the information I got from this web site was useful.

answer options	Strongly disagree	Disagree	Neither agree nor disagree	Agree	Strongly agree
count	0	0	1	6	5
percentage	0	0	8	50	42

What two things did you like about it? (As entered by participants themselves)

Candidate statement, and the opportunity to change my address and info.
Showed all locations for ballot drop off and easy to follow maps. Also showed information about all candidates current and running.
Information on upcoming elections and drop off places for the ballots.
Getting into the system easily and the fact that the forms are protected from copying.
Easy to navigate, Simple colors, concise, quick reference, learned things I didn't know, embedded map-handy!
The knowledge I gained from it. The ease of going through the web site.
Candidates' bios for upcoming election. Ease of changing address.
One–Stop Shopping. Intuitive.
Gave option to change address. Option to print registration from.
The candidate statements are available. I like that I can vote from home on the web.
Organized, easy to use.

I can do everything I would expect to be able to do on a web site for voters.

	Strongly disagree	Disagree	Neither agree nor disagree	Agree	Strongly agree
count	1	0	1	8	2
percentage	8	0	8	67	17

What two things are missing from the site?

Better descriptions of where the drop–off places are and the ability to click on candidates' names for info.
Like to see my current address so I don't have to change it to make sure its right.
Being able to vote online.
I'm not sure if anything I would need is missing.
I can't think of anything at this time. I need to spend more time checking out the web site.
Future election dates.
More in–depth information. Low Tech.
Candidate info. Broader view of district info.
Being able to look at other election going on in the city, past election results.

Figure 11-2 Usability survey data summary

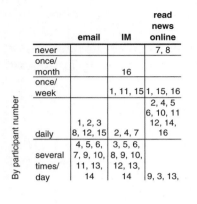

By participant number

	email	IM	read news online
never			7, 8
once/ month		16	
once/ week		1, 11, 15	1, 15, 16
daily	1, 2, 3 8, 12, 15	2, 4, 7	2, 4, 5 6, 10, 11 12, 14, 16
several times/ day	4, 5, 6, 7, 9, 10, 11, 13, 14	3, 5, 6, 8, 9, 10, 12, 13, 14	9, 3, 13,

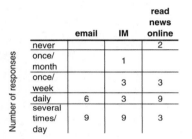

Number of responses

	email	IM	read news online
never			2
once/ month		1	
once/ week		3	3
daily	6	3	9
several times/ day	9	9	3

Figure 11-3 Compressed data summary

Compile and Summarize Other Measures

Above and beyond the standard set of descriptive statistics just discussed is a variety of other measures that may be of use. For example, you may want to note the following if appropriate for answering your research questions and the measures you planned for when you designed the usability test:

- Number of times returning to main navigation unnecessarily
- Number (and type) of hints or prompts
- Number of times the site map was accessed
- Points of hesitation (and for how long)

Compile and summarize these measures in your report, as needed, to diagnose problems and address test objectives.

Summarize Scores by Group or Version

If your test design included more than one user group, you will want to summarize the data separately for each distinct group to see whether one group is performing differently from the other. For example, Figure 11-4 shows a comparison of task accuracy scores (e.g., percentage of participants completing a task successfully) for two groups — novices and experienced users.

Percentage (and number) of participants completing a task successfully

Group	Task 1	Task 2	Task 3
Novice users	83% (10)	50% (6)	66% (8)
Experienced users	66% (8)	100% (12)	100% (12)

Figure 11-4 Task completeness by group

Similarly, if you tested different versions of a product or materials, you should compile summaries of performance on each different version. For example, Figure 11-5 shows a comparison of the number of errors made by participants on three different versions of a manual.

Figure 11-6 shows a more comprehensive comparison summary from an exploratory usability test that compared two product prototypes, one a "radio button" type interface, prototype A and the other a graphic representation of the product, prototype B.

Number of errors by version

Group	Version A	Version B	Version C
Novice users	6	6	15
Experienced users	9	20	12

Figure 11-5 Number of errors, compiled by version

Summary of performance and preference

Participant	Group	Version A # tasks correct	Version B # tasks correct	Liked best	Prefer to teach a novice	Version A Ease of use (1–5)	Version B Ease of use (1–5)
P1	N	*12/15	11/15	A	B	4	3
P2	N	12/15	*11/15	B	B	3	5
P3	N	*12/15	10/15	A	B	5	2
P4	N	10/15	*13/15	B	B	2	4
P5	E	*11/15	10/15	B	A	4	3
P6	E	11/15	*13/15	B	A	5	4
P7	E	*12/15	10/15	B	B	3	4
P8	E	13/15	*11/15	B	B	4	3
P9	N	*9/15	13/15	A	A	4	3
P10	N	12/15	*11/15	A	B	3	4
P11	E	*11/15	13/15	B	B	4	4
P12	E	14/15	*12/15	B	B	4	4
					Avg.	3.8	3.6

Key:
N = Novice
E = Experienced
* = Participant saw this version first

Figure 11-6 Summary of performance and preference rankings

One note of caution about using percentages with small sample sizes: If you only have 8 or 10 participants in your study, talking in terms of percentages can sometimes seem to inflate an effect. For example, an 83 percent success rate sounds like a big deal. But saying that 10 of 12 participants completed tasks on prototype A grounds the finding in reality.

Analyze Data

After you have transformed the raw data into more usable summaries, it is time to make sense of the whole thing. Please note that the decision to summarize by task was a deliberate one, because the task represents the viewpoint or goal of the users and what they would like to achieve. Staying task-oriented while summarizing and analyzing the data forces you to look at the situation from the viewpoint of the users, which is the ultimate reason for testing. Can the users perform their tasks using your product? If they cannot, you then need to determine which component, or combination of components, is the culprit — and to what extent. To begin the analysis, identify the tasks on which users had the most difficulty. That will keep you focused on the worst problems.

Identify Tasks That Did *Not* Meet the Success Criterion

Going into your study, your team defined "success" for each task (see the section "A Description of Successful Completion of the Task" in Chapter 5), by specifying criteria for proper completion. Simply put, a task that does not meet a criterion is one that a predetermined percentage of participants did not complete successfully within a specified benchmark, if one was specified. As mentioned in Chapter 3, we have come to use a 70 percent success criterion for a typical assessment test. If at least 70 percent of participants do not successfully complete a task, then it is "difficult" or "problematic." It then gets attention in analysis and reporting. Essentially, such tasks represent the vulnerable portion of the product and its support materials. If you do a preliminary report, tasks that participants had difficulty with or completely failed to be able to do are the ones on which you should focus first.

The 70 percent criterion represents a reasonable balance between being too demanding and too lax, especially in a test of an early version of a product. Assuming that you are doing small tests and iterating design in between them, as the tests go on, the likelihood of reaching (and surpassing) the 70 percent success criterion should grow. Eventually, you would like users to approach a 95 percent success rate, but if you demand that for the first usability test in a planned series of tests, you will often flag almost all tasks. The difference between 95 percent and 70 percent is what the design team has to bridge by its improvements to the product. Conversely, if you make the criterion too low, such as 50 percent, then too many product deficiencies are being assigned to a lower priority.

In Figure 11-7, the eight non-criterion tasks are shaded, that is, the eight tasks from the data summary (originally shown in Figure 11-1) that have success rates below 70 percent. If this data had been collected during a validation test, you would flag these eight tasks in exactly the manner shown in Figure 11-7.

While the 70 percent criterion rule works quite well for providing a snapshot of problem areas, you may have a completely different method for identifying the most difficult tasks. For a test with few participants, for example, the most difficult tasks will usually jump right out at you, without need for much analysis. However you do it, you must make a distinction between levels of performance, rather than just listing and lumping all the results together into one long table. Distinguishing between different performance levels allows you to focus on the problem areas.

Module	Tasks	Percentage of participants performing correctly (within benchmark)	Mean time (minutes)	Standard deviation (minutes)
A	Set temperature pressure	83	3.21	4.38
	Set gas flows	33	12.08	10.15[1]
	Ignite the QRC	83	2.75	2.68
	Bake out column	100	0.46	0.17
	Set oven temperature program	66	6.54	2.56
	Run QRC checkout	100	0.83	0.34
	Program pressure and temperature	66	5.17	3.46
	Rerun checkout	100	0.29	0.09
B	Load the sample tray	100	0.88	0.28
	Create a subdirectory	33	8.00	3.92
	Create a sequence	66	9.42	7.70
	Start the sequence	66	1.00	0.92
	Stop the sequence	100	1.30	0.89
	Check the report	100[2]	1.38	0.58
	Reintegrate and print report	66	11.67	5.15
	Modify the method	100[3]	2.67	1.86
	Save the method	83	2.92	5.41
	Modify the sequence	66	3.46	3.96
	Restart the sequence	83	1.08	0.89

1 Participants 4's timings are not included. Participant had great resistance to performing the task and had not attempted it on the job in more than 18 months. Participant was also given misnformation during the task.

2 Participant 4 did not perform this task due to running the wrong method and having the test plot run.

3 Participant 1 did not perform this task to time constraints.

Figure 11-7 Non-criterion tasks shaded

Identify User Errors and Difficulties

After you highlight the non-criterion tasks, identify the errors that caused the incorrect performance. An error in this case is defined as any divergence by a user from an expected behavior. It is very helpful if you can define what an error is before conducting the study. You must do this in a validating or summative test. (This is where doing one or more pilot sessions can be extremely useful.) The purpose of an exploratory or formative test may be to understand what the possible errors are. For example, the user was supposed to enter a customer ID in field 10, but instead entered it into field 11. Or, the user was supposed to delete a backup file, but instead deleted a working file. Or, the user simply omitted a step. These all represent errors that resulted in unsuccessful completion of a task.

Conduct a Source of Error Analysis

Now the real fun begins. Identify the source of every error, if possible, by noting the responsible component or combination of components, or some other cause. *This is your transition point from task orientation to product orientation.* This type of analysis is the ultimate detective work and is the most labor-intensive portion of the post-test regimen. Your objective is to attribute a product-related reason for user difficulties and/or poor performance. Essentially, one has to be clear about why user errors occurred, otherwise the recommendations cannot be accurate. Therefore, take your time and do a thorough job here. This is the point at which you might go back and review the recordings. But don't just go off and do this by yourself. You can use this analysis as a framework for workshops with others who had observed the test. Together, you can review the data in light of who the participants were. Together, you can agree on what the sources of problems were.

Of course, some sources of error will be *dead-on* obvious, and will take very little probing. For example, if a user's task was to enter a 20-character customer record identifier within a field on a screen and the field was only long enough to contain 11 characters, the reason for the problem is obvious.

Other determinations will be much more challenging. For example, if customers of a health insurance company were unable to perform a complex decision making process that took them through three sections of web application, four different sections of a benefits handbook, and two online chats with a customer service rep, identifying the source of error is an order of magnitude more difficult. Each of the aforementioned components probably contributed in its own way to the problem. However, there is usually a primary and a secondary culprit, and you should so note. For example, when multiple components are involved, confusing navigation may be the primary problem, followed by the content of the documents, and last by the information from the service rep. Clearing up the primary problem invariably simplifies the changes required to the secondary sources.

To perform the source of error analysis, you have many areas to review and consider. You have your notes and memory, the notes and memories of others, your understanding of how the product works, possibly the video recordings, and, equally as important, your understanding of user-centered design. You also need to consider the background of the users who made errors.

For particularly challenging or critical errors, such as the situation described above, go back to any data collected by monitoring software and/or review the video recordings of several users who erred. You may have missed something important during the actual test.

Try not to solve the problem prematurely and recommend a fix before you have identified *all* the sources of error. In terms of thoroughness, you should ideally perform a source of error analysis for every task performed by every user. In this way, you will account for every deficiency and recommend action for each one as well. Figure 11-8 shows an excerpt from a source of error analysis. Note that there are two sources of error: the flow of the transaction (which did not match how the users thought of the task), and the information architecture (which used domain-specific language unfamiliar to users).

Task	Source of error
Use points to reserve a hotel room	• Nothing in the web site said users must be logged in before starting the reservation process to be able to use points.
	• Participants expected to be able to sign in to see how many points they had after Step 3 (Check availability), but there was no way to log in there.
	• After the home page, the search widget that included an option to redeem points was in the lower–right corner of the page, and none of the participants noticed it.
	• Participants looked for a link to FAQs; they should have selected the Customer Service link, but participants inferred that the Customer Service link would lead to a phone number or online chat.

Figure 11-8 Excerpt from source of error analysis

Prioritize Problems

There are many ways to rank usability problems. Criticality is one. After you identify the specific sources of errors, the next step is to prioritize these problems by *criticality*. Criticality is defined as the combination of the severity of a problem and the probability that the problem will occur. If you represented criticality as an equation, it would look like this:

$$\text{Criticality} = \text{Severity} + \text{Probability of Occurrence}$$

The reason for prioritizing problems by criticality is to enable the development team to structure and prioritize the work that is required to improve the product. Obviously, you want the development team to work on the most critical problems first, assuming that there is time prior to the next release. Here is one way to prioritize problems by criticality.

First, categorize a problem by severity. We measure severity on a four-point scale, with each problem ranked. Figure 11-9 shows one severity rating system; Figure 11-10 shows another.

Severity ranking	Severity description	Severity definition
4	Unusable	The user either is not able to or will not want to use a particular part of the product because of the way that the product has been designed and implemented. Example: Product crashes unexpectedly whenever it is powered on at altitude.
3	Severe	The user will probably use or attempt to use the product, but will be severely limited in his or her ability to do so. The user will have great difficulty in working around the problem. Example: Synchronizing the device to another device can only happen when certain files are not in use. It isn't obvious when the files are in use.
2	Moderate	The user will be able to use the product in most cases, but will have to take some moderate effort in getting around the problem. Example: The user can make sure that all complementary applications are closed while syncing the two devices.
1	Irritant	The problem occurs only intermittently, can be circumvented easily, or is dependent on a standard that is outside the product's boundaries. Could also be a cosmetic problem. Example: The message area of the device's small screen is at the very top, dark blue, and often shaded by the frame of the screen.

Figure 11-9 Problem severity ranking

4 = Task failure–prevents this user going further

3 = Serious problem–may hinder this user

2 = Minor hindrance–possible issue, but probably will not hinder this user

1 = No problem–satisfies the benchmark

Figure 11-10 Problem severity ranking

Frequency ranking	Estimated frequency of occurrence
4	Will occur ≥90% of the time the product is used
3	Will occur 51–89% of the time
2	Will occur 11–50% of the time
1	Will occur ≤10% of the time

Figure 11-11 Frequency of occurrence ranking

Next, rank the problem by estimated frequency of occurrence. That is, estimate the probability that a problem will occur in the field, and convert that estimate into a frequency ranking. See Figure 11-11 for a table of frequency rankings. (Don't get nervous if this is hard — this is only an estimate.)

To arrive at your estimated frequency of occurrence, you need to account for two factors:

■ The percentage of total users affected

■ The probability that a user from that affected group will experience the problem.

Therefore, if you feel that 10 percent of the target population will encounter this problem about 50 percent of the time, then there is only a 5 percent estimated frequency of occurrence ($0.10 \times 0.5 = 0.05 = 5\%$). Do not worry about the exact precision for your estimated frequency of occurrence. Your best guess will still be quite meaningful.

Ascertaining a problem's criticality is then a simple matter of adding the severity ranking and the frequency ranking for that problem. For example, if a particular problem is ranked unusable (severity ranking = 4), but will only occur 5 percent of the time (frequency ranking = 1), then that problem would receive a priority of 5 (4 + 1). Similarly, if there were a problem that was simply an irritation but affected almost *everybody*, then that would also get a 5. Using this method, the very highest priority are assigned to problems that made the product unusable for everyone. These priorities can then help you and the development team decide how to focus resources, concentrating on fixing the more critical problems first if there is a time constraint. In an ideal situation, every problem would be fixed before release, but that rarely happens. Keep in mind that you can develop your own hierarchy and definitions for criticality based on your organization's objectives and the particular product you are testing.

For simple tests, there is an easier way to ascertain which problems are most critical and in most need of attention. *That is to simply ask participants during the debriefing session to tell you what was the most problematic situation for them*. If you find that several participants are in agreement about priorities, then that is an important indication about where to focus your resources.

Analyze Differences between Groups or Product Versions

If you have conducted a comparison test, you may want to compare the differences between groups or between different versions of your product. For example, you might compare the difference between the use of an old versus a new checkout sequence for an e-commerce web site or the difference between the performance of novice and experienced users.

You will do this by analyzing the amount, types, and severity of errors that users made for the two (or more) versions or groups, as well as users' preference ratings, rankings, and general comments. This analysis can be very challenging especially if there is no clear-cut "winner," as in the following example.

Figure 11-12 summarizes the results of a comparison test of two prototypes (previously compiled in Figure 11-7). A simple review of the number of errors and the ease-of-use rankings reveals that the two prototypes are very close in user performance and preference. There is a slight advantage in performance for the A prototype and a clear advantage in preference for the B prototype. That much is clear.

What is not clear and what can only be deciphered from notes and observations are the *types* of errors that participants made, the assumptions they made even when they did perform correctly, and what they said about using the product. As it turns out, the reason that the B prototype did not perform as well as the A prototype was that it was unfamiliar to this group of participants. The participants were much more familiar with the interaction elements on A, which will also be true for the intended customers.

However, the B prototype resulted in more positive comments, especially as users mastered its subtleties. It also seemed more intuitive for new users. Almost all of the participants said they would prefer to teach the graphic interface to a novice, due to its particular representation of the product. Participants felt that novices could see relationships of different parts of the overall system on the B interface, while these relationships were only inferred on the A interface.

Lastly, the source of error analysis was very revealing. Most of the B prototype errors occurred because of the poor quality of the visual elements. The participants simply misinterpreted the graphic representations of system parts, such as ports and buttons. Had the graphics been more realistic, the error rate might have been nil.

For all these reasons, the decision was made to move to a graphic interface such as the one in the B prototype for the initial top-level screen, with radio buttons used for lower-level selection screens, such as those used in the A prototype.

Summary of performance and preference

Participant	Group	Version A # tasks correct	Version B # tasks correct	Liked best	Prefer to teach a novice	Version A Ease of use (1–5)	Version B Ease of use (1–5)
P1	N	*12/15	11/15	A	B	4	3
P2	N	12/15	*11/15	B	B	3	5
P3	N	*12/15	10/15	A	B	5	2
P4	N	10/15	*13/15	B	B	2	4
P5	E	*11/15	10/15	B	A	4	3
P6	E	11/15	*13/15	B	A	5	4
P7	E	*12/15	10/15	B	B	3	4
P8	E	13/15	*11/15	B	B	4	3
P9	N	*9/15	13/15	A	A	4	3
P10	N	12/15	*11/15	A	B	3	4
P11	E	*11/15	13/15	B	B	4	4
P12	E	14/15	*12/15	B	B	4	4
					Avg.	3.8	3.6

Key:
N = Novice
E = Experienced
* = Participant saw this version first

Figure 11-12 Summary of performance and preference rankings

The previous example illustrates how such comparisons usually work. There are many types of data to analyze and sift through before solid conclusions and recommendations can be formulated. Typically, the source of error analysis is especially important for comparisons. This is because each version usually has distinct advantages and disadvantages. Only by understanding the types and sources of errors in depth is it possible to ascertain the best version. Because neither of the versions being compared is a clear winner, that is, neither ever has all of the advantages or all of the disadvantages, a comparison test inevitably results in a hybrid version that incorporates the best elements of the prototypes.

Using Inferential Statistics

To this point, you have analyzed the test data using simple descriptive statistics. For example, the means, medians, and ranges of times all *describe* the characteristics of your data in ways that help to see patterns of performance and preference and ascertain usability problems. You have also reviewed the strictly qualitative data such as specific comments made by participants. For the vast majority of tests that we conduct, and for the vast majority of readers of this book, such analysis is sufficient to make meaningful recommendations.

Occasionally though, the development team or whoever has commissioned the usability research may insist that one obtain statistically significant results. Most often, this situation arises when two versions of a product are being compared with each other and much is riding on the outcome. To obtain statistically significant results requires the use of inferential statistics. That is, we *infer* something about a larger population from the smaller sample of test participants. If the results of a test are statistically significant, then you can assume that if you conducted the study over again with different people with similar experience and background, you would get the same results. However, the use of inferential statistics opens a huge can of worms, and we recommend extreme caution.

First of all, many of those involved in usability tests have not been sufficiently trained in the use and interpretation of inferential statistics. Even among seasoned professionals, there can often be much disagreement about exactly which statistical test to use and what the results imply afterward. Deciding which statistical technique to use is not trivial and depends on the following factors:

- The scale or measurement used for the conditions (variables) being tested
- The number of conditions and the number of levels in each condition
- The number of conditions that will be analyzed at the same time
- The way in which participants were assigned to groups
- What you will infer from the statistical method

Second, those using the results of the test to make decisions about the product are rarely trained in interpreting such statistics, and can easily misinterpret the results. It is important that they receive an explanation of what the statistical results "prove" and "disprove."

Third, and probably most relevant, the way in which you conduct the test will vary greatly depending on whether you are trying to obtain statistical results or not. Obtaining statistical results requires a more rigorous design and probably a fairly large sample of participants.

For example, when comparing two or more versions of a product, you must have rigorously controlled the conditions that differ in each version during the test. If you were testing to see if the *format* of a new version of a document was easier to use than the format of an old version, but in addition to a revised format, the new document had additional content and an improved index, you would find it very hard to isolate the effects of format on performance. To support a hypothesis that one format will result in improved performance, the versions should differ in *format* alone and nothing else.

Also, if you conduct a test with much probing and interaction between test moderator and participants, then it is very easy to bias the results of one of the versions to the detriment of the other for the purpose of proving a hypothesis.

Your sample size is also crucial. If your sample size is small, as in the previous example of the two prototypes (see Figure 11-12), you will have difficulty obtaining statistical proof that the results were not due to chance. As a very general rule, all things being equal, you should have sample sizes of at least 10 to 12 participants per condition before considering the use of inferential statistics.

To summarize, the appropriate use of inferential statistics is both a complex and subtle topic. While there certainly is a place for their use in usability research, only those with a thorough grounding in experimental design and statistical theory make use of this tool. For the vast majority of practitioners, we suggest avoiding the use of such statistical techniques for the reasons mentioned previously. If you would like to learn more, we recommend reading one of the many introductory books on probability and statistics, such as *Statistics for People Who (Think They) Hate Statistics* by Neil J. Salkind (Sage Publications, 2007) or *Statistics in Plain English* by Timothy C. Urdan (Erlbaum, 2005). Depending on your study goals, you may want statistics oriented to behavioral sciences, social sciences, or market research — or something else.

An even better plan, if you are genuinely interested in learning more, is to enroll in a university course on statistics offered through either the university's social science or behavioral sciences department.

CHAPTER 12

Report Findings and Recommendations

As discussed in Chapter 11, there are four major steps involved in analyzing test data and developing recommendations. These are:

1. Compile and summarize data.
2. Analyze data.
3. Develop findings and recommendations.
4. Produce the final report.

The last chapter discussed the first two items on the list above. This chapter shows you how best to produce a final report that thoroughly covers findings and recommendations.

What Is a Finding?

The results of a usability test are not merely tables of data and lists of issues. The results of a usability test comprise the discoveries made while observing real users performing realistic tasks using a product. Results document the data you collected and analyzed. Findings are inferences you and your team draw from the observations you have made along with analyzing the data.

Shape the Findings

By now you should have a pretty good start on understanding what the findings from the study are. As you and your team reached consensus on the issues in your debriefings, together you drew inferences about what the problems were, based on what you had observed in each of the sessions. Later, as you went away and compiled, tallied, and summarized the data, you noticed patterns or connections that gave you further insight about why certain types of users had difficulty or success (probably by user group or cell), while performing particular tasks or at specific points in the product. After you recover from the epiphany of discovery in your analysis, you have to figure out how to express that "ah-ha" to someone else. That specifying of truth revealed is a finding.

Findings are often expressed in headline fashion or one-sentence statements that encapsulate the essence of the usability issue. They are the centerpiece of the report. For example, "The 'Go' label did not suggest 'refresh' or 'reload' to participants."

Start documenting your usability study by approaching the final report in layers. In the next section, we suggest an outline for organizing the overall report, but most of the work comes in expressing the findings and developing recommendations:

1. Write out the findings.
2. Expand the discussion of each of the findings with narrative, participant quotes, and illustrations (such as screen captures).
3. Go back to the beginning of the results section of the report to write a section describing global findings and overall conclusions.
4. Sort through the findings and group them in some way that makes sense. Here are some possible groupings:
   - Task
   - Research question
   - Product section
   - How the team is organized (information architecture, visual design, interaction design, database, technical communication or information design, etc.)

Dana often uses the research questions as the top level of headings. This accomplishes a few important things. By reiterating the research questions as a way of grouping findings, you can:

- Ensure that you have answered the original questions, thus accomplishing the goals of the test.
- Tie the data gathered to the final findings and recommendations.
- Educate the team by connecting the plan and design to the outcomes.

Within each group of findings, you can then think about ordering them further in any of these possible ways:

- Local versus global (an isolated problem versus a more general or fundamental problem)
- Impact on users (time or data loss, injury or possible loss of life)
- Frequency
- Ability to work around or not
- Where in the product the problem occurred
- Task
- Visibility (a clear problem or one that occurs two weeks later because of something you did that you didn't realize)
- Cost to fix
- Level of embarrassment to the user

You may find that a combination of these ideas — and others — work well for any given test.

We typically create a section in the beginning of the results section of the report, which covers the global or general usability problems.

We recommend focusing your *first* efforts on simply listing the findings.

Draft the Report

The reporting process is one area that can benefit immensely from user-centered design expertise and knowledge of usability principles. The whole is often more than the sum of the parts, and it is not always obvious which component is responsible for problems. Even if one identifies the problem's source, solutions are often extremely subtle. Knowledge of how people read and learn, how they process information, how human performance is affected by short-term memory limitations, and so on is critical to understanding your data, detailing findings, and reaching reasonable conclusions. Therefore, if you have not already done so and if you're not an expert in this area, this is an excellent time to confer with someone experienced in cognitive psychology, human factors engineering, or human-computer interaction.

While the compilation of data should occur immediately after the testing process, we advise the opposite for reporting results. The testing and analysis process can be arduous. It is very labor intensive, requires long periods of concentration, and, in general, tends to wear you down — not exactly the ideal frame of mind for thinking creatively and in new ways.

Therefore, before reporting findings and drawing conclusions, try to get away from the project for a few days. Work on something else and do not even think of the project. Of course, if a great idea strikes you, write it down but let it go after that. Providing this "gap" for "creative forgetting" can help you recharge and approach problems from a fresh perspective.

It is typical of most development environments that the development team begins revising the product well before the final test report is distributed. However, this is no excuse for not producing a report or for doing less than a stellar job on its content. Always produce a report, even if it is brief and even if its recommendations are after the fact. The report will serve as the only historical record of what occurred.

With this in mind, be aware of the useful shelf life of the report. If you are just beginning a usability program, you will find it useful to go back to reports from your first studies later. Doing so will remind you of steps you went through, what the priorities were, and what the important deliverables were. You can use your first reports as templates for reports of later tests. And, you can remind yourself of earlier problems as you do your next studies, thus tracking improvements in the product as well as building your expertise on product usability.

The reality is that most of the team will probably not return to a long, written report, no matter how thoughtfully and beautifully written. You want to give them what they need and no more.

So, you want to serve several purposes with a report:

- Document findings, recommendations, and agreements.

- Record that the study happened and what its goals and objectives were.

- Explore methodological issues or protocol burps that may have influenced the outcomes.

- Give direction to designers and developers about how to remedy design problems.

- Report to management the highlights related to business concerns.

Create a report that is accessible, portable, and understandable on its own. If it is unlikely that your team, indeed people in your company, won't read a written report explaining each finding and recommendation, don't waste your time. Instead, consider "top 10" reports that are basically lightly expanded bullet points from the consensus debriefings or from a final design direction workshop. Deliver your report in a slide deck, in a company blog, or even an email if that way works best in your situation. Know *your* audience. Be creative but mindful about how your report will be received, reviewed, and reacted to.

Why Write a Report?

The quality of the report and how it is viewed will be a direct reflection of how you view it. If you see the creation of the report simply as a *mopping-up* exercise intended to pull together all the loose ends, then that is what it will be. If you view it as a vehicle for impressing others with the sheer volume of statistics and minutiae collected, it will impress no one but you and the two coworkers in your organization who revel in reading such documents.

What the test report *should* do is support and initiate change, direct action, provide a historical record, and educate — all at the same time. Above all else, it should *communicate* to people. There is no reason that reports need to be stuffy, boring, and overly technical. Do not use the report as a way of creating job security for yourself, by ensuring that you are the only one who can decipher its mysterious findings and revelations. This approach will backfire in the long run. Think a moment about the incongruousness of receiving a report on a usability test that itself is hard to use. Such a report sends a very mixed message indeed, and one that you should avoid.

When writing the report, approach it as if you were basically telling a story, and make sure that all the sections of the report relate to that story. Thinking of the report in this way makes it easier to pull the disparate sections together so that they make sense and support each other.

Organize the Report

There should be a threefold logic to the report. That is, the report should have a beginning, a middle, and an end. The beginning is composed of why you did the test, and how you prepared. The middle is composed of what happened during the test. The end is composed of the implications of what happened, that is, what you recommend doing about what happened. Following is a suggested outline for a report, showing the major sections and each section's intended purpose regardless of delivery method. The critical element is usability, not brevity. General consensus among usability practitioners is to keep a formal written report in the range of 20 to 25 pages.

Below we present a very general outline that serves as an all-purpose report format, assuming that most of our readers are working on formative or exploratory tests. If you are very interested in standards and are working on a validation, comparative, or summative test, you may want to consult and use the Common Industry Format (CIF) report format that is part of the ISO Standard 25062.

Executive Summary

This section should contain a brief synopsis of the test logistics, the major findings and recommendations, and further research required, and the overall benefits of the test. Keep it to one page if you can, as its purpose is to enable readers to quickly scan for high-level information. Dana sometimes simply creates a table of the research questions on the left with one- or two-sentence answers on the right, describing the highlights of the results. Figure 12-1 shows an example.

Method

In this section describe the nature of the research, how it was set up, participant characteristics, and the data collection methods used. If this sounds suspiciously like the test plan, go to the head of the class. If your test plan is comprehensive, simply paste it in as is (updating the verb tenses, of course), with one exception: Update it with exceptions to the original plan. That is, describe any events that occurred that forced you to change your procedure,

We conducted the study that this report covers to answer these questions:

Question	Summary Insights
What types of information do they expect to find on the site? At what depth?	Because the tasks were outside the experience of most of the participants in the study, we don't really have the answer to this question. I recommend further study, in the field with participants who are in the mode of researching conditions they've recently been diagnosed with.
How easily and successfully do participants find the tools? Where in the site do participants look for them?	Finding the tools was fairly easy for about half of the participants. However, once inside the site, finding the tools is difficult and it is not simple to move between the HCT and the TOT. Most participants looked for the HCT in Find a Provider. Most participants tried to find information about the condition when looking for treatment options rather than looking for a tool.
How easily and successfully do participants use the hospital comparison tool and the treatment options tool to answer questions they come to the session with?	With the HCT, the further in participants got, the more questions they had—they started with general questions and drilled to the specifics as they learned more. However, interpreting the ratings across the categories on the Summary page was very difficult. Using the TOT, most participants imagined questions they might have and said they had the impression they would be satisfied that with some study they could answer those questions in the Treatment Options Report.
How satisfied are participants with their experience of using each of the tools? **What comments do participants have about the value of the tools? Are the tools useful and desirable, as well as usable?**	About half the participants saw no reason to research hospitals and didn't find much value in doing so even after using the HCT. Many of the participants were not confident that they were interpreting the ratings correctly. Most of the participants said they thought the TOT would be useful if they were in the situation of having been diagnosed with one of the conditions in the tool. One participant thought it was too much work to get information that she thought was available publicly on the web.

Figure 12-1 Executive summary example with table of research questions

such as the system crashed repeatedly, no participants showed up one day, you dropped a question or adjusted a task scenario after the second participant, and so on. Of course, because you were so diligent about noting this information as it happened, you will have no trouble documenting it now.

Results

In this section display both the quantitative and qualitative summaries, using the most concise and readable form possible. Quantitative summaries are task completion, errors, prompting needed, ratings, and so forth. Qualitative summaries are free-form questions, types of errors, and the like. You need not include the raw data (e.g., copies of individual questionnaires or data collection sheets), although you could place these in an appendix. However, we have found it useful to leave out the raw data, and we suggest that you do the same. Simply mention in the report the name of the person who holds the raw data or the location where it is stored, for those interested in perusing it. Also, mention where the recordings are stored.

Findings and Recommendations (Discussion)

At last we come to the raison d'être for the entire process of usability testing. It is time to take all the information you have analyzed and translate it into specific findings. This is neither a simple process nor a precise scientific one in the sense of a cookbook approach. In fact, it is similar to that stage in product development where one moves from characterization of the user and development of functional specifications to the design of the system. At that point, 20 different designers might conceivably come up with 20 different interpretations of the specifications, resulting in 20 different designs. Drawing inferences and articulating findings is similar, in that any single individual might read the implications of the test a bit differently from the next person.

In this section are the findings, along with a discussion and explanation of them as well as recommendations, if appropriate. The design of this section should enable someone to quickly pick out and grasp the findings and recommendations *without* having to read the supporting text. Especially design this section for usability, by having the findings in boldface or separated by space from the discussion. Just as with good documentation, do not make people read through a whole lot of extraneous information to get to the things they need quickly.

Beyond that, the number of issues to address may seem overwhelming, and some readers may not feel that they get a payoff for the amount of time it takes to read and digest the report. It is not necessary to leave out anything important, and you should explain findings in as much detail as is required to make your point. But do lay out the information so that readers can easily

P1 used quotation marks and demonstrated using asterisks. P5 used asterisks as wildcards in her searches.

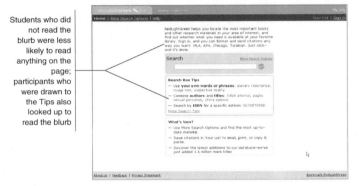

Round 2 participants rarely used More Search Options

P5 liked being able to search by date

P5 also searched for sources by date, and found that doing so was quite useful.

? What comments did students have about the search examples on the home page?

Participants didn't have a lot of comments about the examples in the Tips box. They simply seemed to read the tips and make use of them. PP said, "It says I can search for anything." P1 said about the blurb, "Oh, that's cool..." and then about the Tips, "So this has all the really fast ways to do it."

Students who did not read the blurb were less likely to read anything on the page; participants who were drawn to the Tips also looked up to read the blurb

Figure 12-2 Report with screen captures and callouts to usability insights

bypass explanations if they choose to. Including illustrations such as screen captures with explanatory callouts may help with usability but will add to the length. Figure 12-2 shows an example.

You may find that you want to divide this section into *general findings and recommendations* followed by *specific findings and recommendations*. The general findings and recommendations section would include a high-level discussion of important global issues (for an example, see Figure 12-4), possibly in paragraph form. For example, this section might include a discussion about what you learned about the abilities and expectations of the end user from viewing the participants at work. (For example, "We expected that behaviors and preferences would be the same in undergraduates and graduate students. However, grad students were more willing to and interested in going to the library to review a book than undergrads were.") The specific findings and recommendations section would contain a listing of the nitty-gritty changes that are required. (For example, "The format for entering dates in the advanced search was not obvious to participants. Consider allowing any date format to be entered, or add an example to the field to show the acceptable format.")

Be sure to include positive findings. The nature of usability testing is to reveal problems so as to inform design, it's true. But seasoned usability specialists try to include at least some positive findings. Doing so makes the "negative" findings more palatable for the team by softening the blow and rewards them for putting in their best efforts going into the study. It may not always be easy to find positive things to say, but try your best. As you develop positive findings, you will gain further perspective about where the product was going into the study and how much improvement is required to make it more usable.

Develop Recommendations

While you can report findings and conclusions on your own, making recommendations should not be a solo effort. While one person has primary responsibility for the report, the design team should be an integral part of the process of creating recommendations. This is true whether one is part of the organization or an outside consultant, although the degree of collaboration will vary. Here is why a group effort is beneficial.

- **Different perspectives are essential.** There is no "right" answer when it comes to design recommendations. Rather, there will always be a variety of alternatives as seen from different perspectives. The development team will have experts from a variety of disciplines, such as engineering, technical communication, marketing, and hopefully human factors. Each discipline will provide a unique perspective, which can help in making informed judgments. Often, if you can simply and clearly identify the issue, the design team can help you to come up with an elegant solution.

  Also, it is amazing how the same test can be viewed so differently by several different observers. Even impartial observers will interpret what they see differently. Very often, this results in a unique perspective or insight that triggers a creative recommendation.

  However, we caution that this process is not a democratic one. It is important that those who observed only a session or two do not have a major say in recommendations. Seeing only one or two sessions, while helping to provide a sense of value to the testing process, does not give a wide enough perspective to interpret results. The test moderator who attended each session clearly has the broadest perspective, all of the data at hand, and the final say.

- **You need buy-in.** *For optimum success, it helps if designers and developers have a personal connection with the results and recommendations.* Recommendations are only as good as the degree to which they are embraced by the people who must implement them. Simply reading a recommendation in a report will rarely convince anyone to make a dramatic change. The most sterling ideas may sit on the shelf or in someone's drawer if they do not make sense to the people who incorporate them into products.

As you draft the final report, it behooves you to find out what those who will be affected by the report think of the preliminary test results (as we talked about in Chapter 11). It is better to have discussions of conflicting perceptions and opinions and identify shortcomings of certain recommendations before the final report rather than afterward. Also, remember that it is much easier to ignore a report than it is to ignore a flesh-and-blood person making a particular point. Do not underestimate your ability to persuade people to your point of view by holding discussions, whether formal or informal.

The rest of this section discusses a systematic approach to developing recommendations when you:

- Focus on solutions that will have the widest impact.
- Ignore political considerations in the first draft.
- Include both short-term and long-term recommendations.
- Talk about where the team should do further research.
- Cover all of the issues thoroughly.

Focus on Solutions That Will Have the Widest Impact

Obviously, recommendations will interact with each other. A recommendation to change a field on one screen will have very limited impact. A recommendation to change the navigation scheme for the entire user interface will have a decidedly greater impact. Similarly, a recommendation to change the wording of a paragraph will have limited impact, but the decision to change the entire format for procedural instructions has a far greater effect. The point is, global changes affect everything and need to be considered first.

Therefore, in determining solutions to problems, begin by looking at the global usability level first to make sure that those bases have been covered. For example, shown in Figures 12-3 and 12-4 are some global usability issues/principles for software and for documentation. These high-level issues will have profound and wide-ranging effects on the usability of the whole product. In a sense these are the foundation or building blocks of usability. Addressing such issues first will provide the most leverage for improving the product. That is why conferring with a usability specialist can be so helpful at this point. He or she will be familiar with the common global issues.

There are also global usability issues that are not necessarily associated with a broad principle, but rather are due to discovering a finding with broad

General Findings

The organization of the manual reflects the user's on-the-job tasks rather than being system-oriented.

The layout and format support skimming and scanning.

While the headings, tabs, and table of contents help make the document accessible, the index does not incorporate common terms that should be mapped to terms used in the product.

Illustrations are clear and helpful on their own, but have been allowed to float to fit rather than being anchored near the relevant text.

Figure 12-3 Example of global issues for documentation (courtesy of Rolf Molich and CUE 6)

Overview of Test Findings

- Too much industry jargon throughout the site
- Aesthetics are not inviting and look unprofessional.
- The progress bar is confusing.
- Sessions time out too quickly.
- The layout of forms is confusing.
- Optional services are not obvious.
- Search results include vehicles that are not available to rent.

Figure 12-4 Example of global issues for user interface (courtesy of Rolf Molich and CUE 6)

implications. For example, on a software test that Jeff conducted, he discovered through testing that users were divided into three distinct levels of expertise, with a huge difference in abilities and knowledge, almost a chasm, between the least and most sophisticated level. This discrepancy had not been known before the test, and had the most profound implications of all test results.

Jeff and his client team found that it was impossible to adequately support all users from the same screens. Therefore, it was decided to have two distinct tracks for the product. The least sophisticated users would use the simple track, which simplified decision making drastically and the functionality of the product as well. The second and third user groups, who were more sophisticated, would use a more comprehensive track with different screens, different choices, and full functionality. This finding set the stage for all other findings and recommendations, because the implications affected every screen and, of course, the documentation as well.

The main point is to recognize and begin developing recommendations at an aerial rather than ground level. In the anecdote just discussed, the finding had little to do with a specific difficulty on a certain screen or even with a certain task. Rather, it affected the entire approach to using the product. Perhaps the best way to summarize this point is not to lose sight of the forest for the trees.

Ignore Political Considerations for the First Draft

By political considerations, we mean what may or may not be possible, doable, and acceptable to management and the team, and whether or not your findings are a major departure from the past. You *will* need to consider political issues later, since there is little point in making recommendations that have no chance of being implemented. However, if you concern yourself with politics prematurely, you lose your objectivity, limit your recommendations, and get sidetracked.

Proceed initially as if there is only one concern, the user. This approach results in the most creative solutions, and avoids presupposing that some constraint is in effect, either technical, financial, time, or otherwise. If you are writing findings and creating recommendations to be reviewed with the team, by all means include solutions that are clearly the right thing to do but may not be politically correct or even feasible for one reason or another. As one famous design firm practices, "reality bats last." At the review session, it is amazing what happens when seemingly unacceptable solutions are discussed, rather than immediately suppressed. (Of course, if you have consensus debriefings throughout the study, the review should be a review of the results and any recommendations should not be surprising to anyone.) Solutions often get revised but end up further along than if you had simply avoided including them. It is important to remember that usability testing is one of the most potent forces for change within organizations, because the user is able to influence the process. By all means, take advantage of that opportunity.

Provide Both Short-Term and Long-Term Recommendations

A test will often result in recommended changes to the product that cannot be addressed in time for the scheduled release. Do not be satisfied with just recommending band-aids for deep-seated problems, simply because there is no time to implement full-blown solutions. Instead, state in the report that your recommendations fall into two sections:

- **Short-term recommendations** are the types of changes that can be made without slipping the schedule.

- **Long-term recommendations** are the types of changes that are really required for long-term success. It is important that the organization be aware that stop-gap changes are just that, an attempt to get the product out on schedule with minimal problems.

Indicate Areas Where Further Research Is Required

Usability testing, as with almost all research, often results in new questions that require answers. This should not be considered a *defeat*. Rather, it is simply the norm if you are doing a good job, and you should not shy away from raising these questions. The questions might require further testing or the application of a different research technique, such as a formal experiment, survey of the user population, or on-site observation. Ambiguity is the wellspring of change, and no one will fault you if you honestly point out the limitations of the current study. You might even have a section in the report titled "Future Research" to emphasize the point.

Your findings and recommendations probably will introduce new elements that should be tested to ensure that the remedies really do correct the issues and not just create new ones. By conducting regular, small usability tests, you can help ensure that the product continues to improve. Recommendations for follow-on validation testing should be included in this section of the report. Consider a program in which you are conducting some kind of usability test every two to six weeks.

Be Thorough

Cover all bases. Even though you begin by focusing on the most critical global problems, eventually you will want to cover everything. Again, review the research questions and the issues you wanted to explore when you designed the study. Make sure that each problem related to those has been identified and addressed (and if it has not, say why). Remember that the final report becomes a historical document, referred to by others who were not privy to your constraints. You want to make sure you have addressed all the objectives and captured all the revisions required.

Figures 12-5, 12-6, and 12-7 contain suggested formats that you can use for showing specific findings and recommendations, which is probably the most important part of the report. The format you choose will depend on the amount of explanation you provide, your personal preference, and your intended audience.

Format 1 shown in Figure 12-5 is the format we favor because of its cause-and-effect logic. This format reveals the specific finding (the cause), and follows it with a recommendation (the effect). Figures 12-6 and 12-7 are variations on the same theme. Figure 12-6 takes advantage of your source of error analysis by simply adding another column — Recommendation — to that analysis.

Overview of Test Findings

- Too much industry jargon throughout the site
- Aesthetics are not inviting and look unprofessional.
- The progress bar is confusing.
- Sessions time out too quickly.
- The layout of forms is confusing.
- Optional services are not obvious.
- Search results include vehicles that are not available to rent.

Figure 12-5 Sample Format 1: A finding with its recommendation

Finding 3

The "Go" label did not suggest "refresh" or "reload" to participants.

Recommendation: Add a "Refresh" button on the bottom of the screen next to the "Reset" button.

Figure 12-6 Sample Format 2: Findings first, recommendations after (excerpt courtesy of CUE 6)

Task	Source of error	Recommendation
Use the web site to reserve a car at the San Francisco airport.	**Policy information and specifics are not clearly communicated to users making reservations** The primary source of policy information is the Verify Information page, which contains the specifics of the rental (rate, time, etc.), as well as any policy information specific to that rental. Users tended to skim all content on this page, looking only at the far right and left columns containing the specifics of their rental.	**Redesign the Verify Your Information Page** Consider changing text that is in all uppercase text to mixed case or title case. Expand the columns slightly so users are less inclined to skim but instead will be slowed down. Break up **one** large page of solid content into smaller visual areas to make viewing easier and simpler.

Figure 12-7 Sample Format 3: Findings with source of error, in three columns (excerpt courtesy of CUE 6)

Make Supporting Material Available to Reviewers

Most of the time, it is unnecessary to include supporting material, raw data, or copies of the earlier deliverables from the study in the final report. If you think it is useful to readers to do so, you might consider including this in the *appendices*. There is one exception. In the interest of providing additional protection for the identity of participants, don't list their actual names in the report, simply their backgrounds and other important information. Their names are of no importance, and this is simply an added precaution against misuse (see Chapter 7 for more information on protecting the participants' privacy). Instead, refer to them as Participant 1 or P1 in anything that will be distributed for review. Anyone needing to contact a participant can contact the test moderator directly.

Refine the Report Format

If you will be conducting tests on an ongoing basis within your organization — as you should do and we hope you will be able to — it is important to get feedback on how well your test report communicates to people. You need feedback not only on the content but also on the report's usability and value. Ask the readers of the report (using whatever format works best in your organization):

- Were you able to get the information you needed?
- Was the type of information you needed all there?
- Was the format easy to use?

Then incorporate that feedback into later reports until you come up with a format that really works in your organization. Once you do, stick to it as a template for future tests and reports, and let it guide your analysis as well as the writing of the report. Why reinvent the wheel if you have found something that works?

In addition to the report, you may want to make a presentation of your findings, especially if your efforts are part of an overall usability program. Setting up such a program is the focus of Chapter 14.

Create a Highlights Video or Presentation

If you have made video recordings of the usability test sessions and you're close to the end of writing your final report, somewhere in that process you may have found yourself reviewing the recordings. For the person who moderated the sessions, reviewing the recordings can be invaluable for finding clarity on points that may have eluded you or your note takers during the sessions. You can also review the recordings to gather participant quotes or even to improve your own performance as a moderator.

Giving others a glimpse of the videos may be appealing. You may even have received requests for a compilation of video clips to summarize the test. Producing a "highlights" video can illustrate the typical usability problems uncovered in the study powerfully and succinctly. Or not; developing an effective highlights video is difficult and time-consuming. Although mechanically it is relatively easy to create a video using Morae or iMovie or other tools, many experienced usability professionals avoid producing highlights videos (as discussed in the next section). However, if you find yourself in the right place (a new account, or a start-up company) at the right time (a skilled change agent has made him- or herself known, or decision makers show interest), and the video is done well, it *can* be *part* of a compelling case for moving forward with building usability and user-centered design into the development process. In the next sections, we will talk about how to decide whether to create a video of test highlights. And then, if you decide to go ahead, we provide the steps we use for producing highlights videos.

Cautions about Highlights

We have heard it a hundred times: "Showing management (or development or marketing or product management) the videos from the test would be so powerful! Done right, it could really get their attention and make our case for making important changes to the product." The operative phrase here is "done right."

It's very easy to string together 10 or 15 minutes' worth of video clips that you can present to the doubting audience. It is not so easy to do it well.

If a video compilation is done well, it can help persuade the dubious. It can inspire further support of user-centered design practices. It can influence organizational change. This is a lot to ask of a 10- or 20-minute mash-up of carefully selected video clips. And it is rare that a) there are all the resources necessary for producing a high-quality highlights video, and b) it is a highlights video that convinces management (or development or marketing or product management) to change the product or the way the company operates. But such a convergence has been known to happen.

There is no doubt that observing real people using a product is the best way of gathering data to inform design. Many first-time observers have a near religious experience as they sit through their first session or two. Unfortunately, there is no substitute for actually being present during a usability test session in real time. If it is your hope to try to duplicate the original experience of observation in miniature through a highlights video, we encourage you to rethink your approach to this very optional deliverable.

A highlights video can give "sound bites" and samples of what happened in a usability test as a patchwork that, if fitted together carefully, can offer a flavor of the critical problems and important victories from a study. It can also artfully misrepresent and be manipulative. Consider: By the time the video is complete, you are several steps away from the original event. First, you have a recording of the original event. Next you have small bits of the recording. Then you put several of those bits together from different sessions. You will have cut a clip of between 30 seconds and 3 minutes from a session that lasted for at least an hour (and you may have spliced things together within a "clip" that move it further away from the original event, as well). Retaining any sort of context around the original event for someone who was not present during the session is difficult.

Typically, highlights videos are directed toward people who were unable to attend the study sessions. That audience probably is not as familiar with the product as you now are. Neither are they likely to be familiar with the process of usability testing, the goals of the study, and the thorough analysis you conducted and presented in the final report. To give them as much context as possible, you may have to produce a longer video than is optimum. Or, you may want to consider a different format. For example, some practitioners create ''narrated reports'' that walk viewers through screen captures or reconstructed videos of interactions with the user interface as a voice (probably yours) narrates what participants did at each step and explains the implications. Another option to consider is to integrate clips at key points within your written report. If the report is delivered in any electronic form, it is fairly simple to capture short clip files that get ''packed'' with the report file and will run automatically in the appropriate player when the reader clicks a link.

All that said about loss of context, whatever your intentions for showing the highlights video, it *will* take on a life of its own. That life may consist of storage in some archive. Or, more likely, it will be distributed in ways you could never imagine to people you probably won't even know about. (This *can* be good, but it might not be.) Keep this in mind as you make your decision about whether develop a highlights video.

Steps for Producing a Highlights Video

Having given you every caution we can think of regarding the design, production, and viewing of highlights videos, we realize that you may feel your situation is not typical and you decide to create one anyway. Here we lay out our steps for developing a passable highlights video.

Properly producing a highlights video that truthfully reflects what happened in the study takes mindful review, which, in turn, takes time. If, from the beginning of your study, you plan to produce a highlights video, you may have built in ways in your note taking instruments to capture moments you want to include in your final production. Some data capturing or logging software also includes tools for marking or flagging points in the recordings to review later.

In any case, you will have to review the recordings again. And throughout the process we're about to outline for you, you will look at the same clips over and over again as you select them, catalog them, capture them, put them together, rearrange them, edit them, and connect them in a final cohesive piece. You can expect to spend 60 minutes or more for every minute of the final recording.

Consider the Points You Want to Make

Regardless of your purpose in doing the highlights video, you'll want to narrow the number of topics you want to cover in the video and limit the running time to no more than 20 minutes. (You may want to make smaller, shorter videos if they will be streamed over a corporate network or delivered as podcasts.) We recommend that you focus your efforts on three to five topics.

Set Up a Spreadsheet to Plan and Document the Video

Dana uses a simple Excel spreadsheet to plan the video. This step of planning prevents you from having to do more extensive editing of the clips themselves, which can be tedious. The spreadsheet sets out from left to right:

- The topic the clip supports.
- The type of element (title, clip, subtitle, or other).
- The start time on the recording of the beginning of the clip.
- The first few words (or actions).
- The last few words (or actions).
- The approximate ending time in the recording of the clip.
- The total time of the desired clip; at the bottom of this column, create a formula to total the times of all the clips you plan to use.

This approach is especially helpful if you have conducted sessions with six or more participants. Figure 12-8 shows an example of the beginnings of a clip list as it is outlined in a spreadsheet.

You can see the full clip list from the example above on the web site that accompanies this book: www.wiley.com/usabilitytesting.com.

Pick the Clips

If you or your observers were unable to flag particular points in the recordings as candidates for inclusion in a highlights video, you'll have to go back through your notes to find hot spots that relate to the topics you have chosen to cover in the highlights. If you are lucky and were smart, you have given yourself a clue in your notes that you wanted to use particular quotes or events in a final video. If not, you'll have to spend some time re-reviewing your notes. Because the topics for the video are the same as the main findings in your report, it should be easy to identify which participants had the issue you want to cover. And, if the sessions proceeded in basically the same order from participant to participant, you should be able to guess the point in the videos where you can find the clip you want within a minute or two.

		Seq	Tape	Task	Start time	Stop time	Begin Dialogue/Title	End Dialogue	Time	Cum.Time
Issue / Topic										
2			Title				Usability		0:10	3:31
Redundancy issues	negative	Clip	S12	fishing	0:26:00	0:26:40	Dana: How would you use the website to update that?	... if I didn't know whrer to go, if I just wasn't finding the update address.	6:00	9:31
	negative	Clip	Sg2	review of printout	0:59:00		Tish: I think I'd rather see these main topic areas more prominent, the ones on the left.	Mary Jane: I personally don't mind this.		
	positive	Clip	S11	member event	1:15:30	1:15:15	Dana: Tell me what you're looking for...	So I'd click here to find out more about it.		
Desire for cascading menus	neutral	Clip	T3	U1	0:35:30	0:36:10	Probably the Social Security issue	It's just one less step to make it a little bit easier.	5:48	15:19
	neutral	Clip	S3	home page	0:19:30	0:19:53	Here it would have a little caption	I like those secondary menu that you can see right away... it just comes up when you put your cursor.		
How readers read a page	negative	Clip	T12	magazine	1:32:47	1:33:26	I don't like to scroll a whole page to see single page.	I don't know you do it, but I don't care for that.		
	positive	Clip	B9	begin			scrolling home page.		0:00	15:19
	positive	Clip	T5	home page	0:21:44	0:23:28	Dana: Give me your impressions of the page	Discounts, senior discounts, which are great.		
Difficulties with dropdown menus	negative	Clip								
	negative	Clip	B9	voluteer			Holy cow! Would take one forever.			
App-based tasks: successes	positive	Clip	T12	contact congress	1:39:26	1:39:37	And here, I put in this, ooh! I'm guessing I put in my zip code and it'll bring up an email that I could send to my congressman.	[stop before:] Dana: you wanna do that?		
		Conti-nue	T12	contact congress	1:40:03	1:44:18	Let's see what happens if I'm right.	Now, they have to get the information out to the people that have email to know it's available.		
	positive	Clip	T4	message boards	1:06:05	1:07:02	We need to condense it some way.	24 message found. Okay, we can handle 24.		
App-based tasks:	negative	Clip	S4	member update	0:37:30	0:43:00	Change membership address...	Now its giving me the		

Figure 12-8 Example video clip list in a spreadsheet format

We have found that the most efficient way to gather clips is by participant across topics. For example, if one of the topics is the difficulty of finding the gray button to compare hotels, start with the recording for the first participant that had the problem or demonstrated the behavior. Continuing to work with the recording for that participant, review your notes about him or her against your topic list for the highlights video to see if there were illuminating moments from this participant on the next topic. If there were, you can shuttle to the place in the full recording for a clip for that topic. This is easier than going from recording to recording, because it often takes significant time to open each recording and render it for the screen. As you find a snippet you want to use, do a "rough cut" of the clip and save it off in the appropriate place in the software tool you're using. Document the clip in your spreadsheet.

Review Timing and Organization

When you have gone through the recordings for each participant to capture clips, you'll find that eventually you have much more video than you have allowable run time. Now is the time to take another look at your clip list. Are there very long clips? Which clips show best the point you are trying to make? Are your topics still valid? Do the clips you have listed support the other reporting you developed?

Why do this in a clip list rather than just a rough cut of the video? We have found that it is simpler to move things around in the clip list than to move clips around in a pre-production video. Also, like other drafts or prototypes, the clip list is a sort of model of what the video will become. If you are working with something that does not look like a final product, it will be easier psychologically to edit bits that otherwise might beg to be left in when reviewing a rough cut of a viewable video.

In addition, a clip list is much more portable than an incomplete video. If others should review the plan for the video, the spreadsheet will usually be enough to remind the reviewers of the event or quote you want to include.

Draft Titles and Captions

In your clip list, you included rows for titles (and timings for them, too) that capture concisely the topic that the clips that follow illustrate. It's time to revisit those topic titles and revise if needed. The topics might be the name of the task, or the words taken directly from findings in the report, or a combination of both.

You may find yourself thinking at various points in the gathering of clips about whether some of them need more than just the visual or the participant talking or thinking aloud with the visual. This is the context that will be important for viewers who are not familiar with the idiosyncrasies of the product or the goals of the test. These are excellent points at which to add captions or subtitles.

Again, document these in your clip list before going on to create them in the movie-making software you're using. It'll be easier to revise from the clip list, because the spreadsheet will show you much more at a glance. Soon you'll get to watch the video you sew together — over and over and over as you refine the points made.

Review and Wrap

You must now work on tightening up the video to tell the story efficiently. Remember that you want to keep the running time for the video (regardless of the number of participants or problems illustrated) under 20 minutes. This process is iterative — as design always is. As you review the video, you probably will find yourself stopping to make changes. Dana starts at the beginning each time through. While this can feel tedious, it does help ensure continuity and consistency.

As with your other deliverables, informally usability test your video by having at least one person besides you watch it. Ask for critical feedback and incorporate changes.

Finally, depending on the software you're using, you'll have some rendering steps to go through that may include compressing the file and writing it out to some drive so you can show it to others, later.

Congratulations. You have taken a product and its design team through one very important part of any good user centered design process: a usability test.

The next chapters look at the steps beyond conducting a basic usability test. Chapter 13 describes a few of the variations on the basic usability testing methods. Chapter 14 discusses how to expand the practice of usability and user-centered design in your organization.

PART

III

Advanced Techniques

Variations on the Basic Method

Having previously described the basic method for conducting a usability test, with one participant and one test moderator, this chapter describes some variations of that technique. It discusses some common variations, with tips about implementing them, such as testing with special populations, working with prototypes, and techniques for conducting sessions inside and outside a lab, including remote and automated testing. Ultimately, your testing methodology is limited only by your imagination and the types of questions you need to have answered in testing. We include many references to books and articles that expand on the techniques in this chapter on the web site that accompanies this book: www.wiley.com/go/usabilitytesting.

Who? Testing with Special Populations

Chapter 7 is all about recruiting participants, but following are some special considerations for people who you may want or need to include in your usability test.

People Who Have Disabilities

You probably have sought out this section of the book because your company wants to meet U.S. federal requirements for accessibility, such as the Americans with Disabilities Act (ADA 508). Or perhaps your company is particularly enlightened and understands that there is a huge potential target market in which there are people with disabilities who use technology regularly. If either of these cases rings a bell, you should be including people with disabilities in your usability tests. In our experience, people who have disabilities love to be included in usability studies. The extra effort it takes for you to bring them into the study will be well worth it.

Including recruiting requirements for specific types of disabilities and the use of assistive technology (such as a special screen reader or other equipment) can mean that it will take additional time to find and recruit people with disabilities, so plan ahead. If finding a typical recruit takes about two weeks, give yourself another week or possibly two. It is not uncommon, however, that once you find one or two people who qualify, the word gets out among their community and the response is great.

This is why it is important to make personal contact with organizations and support groups that work with people with disabilities — in order to get leads, yes, but also to establish relationships in the event of future studies. You can also find usability test participants through programs for students with disabilities at colleges and universities, rehabilitation programs, and independent living organizations. If you can find one person in the administration of these groups who is interested in your efforts, that person can help you get the word out and, in effect, prescreen candidates.

To take advantage of the tightness of many of these communities, you may want to stage your study to do one or two sessions with early volunteers. Encourage them to tell people about the session. Then wait for word of the positive experience your first participants had to get out among their friends, family, and colleagues. This sets the stage for you to make contact again, now with a more open pool of possible candidates.

A note about logistics: Many people who have disabilities have very particular tools and setups to use technology. You may be able to imitate the setup, but it won't be exactly the same, which may mean recruiting for particular types of assistive technology use. An alternative is to hold the usability test sessions at the place where the person normally interacts with the technology you want to test.

It can work well to communicate your recruiting needs and scheduling information by email rather than by phone. For example, if you need participants who are deaf, "phoning" them would have to happen on a TTY device. Other people with disabilities may have difficulty articulating clearly enough for you to understand them on the phone. Ask your contacts at the organizations that you have connected with for advice on this. Send a description of the session, consent forms, and recording waivers ahead of time to the organizations and to the scheduled participants. Some folks may need to be accompanied; include those assistants or interpreters in the design of your sessions. Speaking of that, you may need to cover expenses for the helpers as well as for special transportation or other services.

Scheduling and Reminding

Be sure to schedule extra time before, during, and after sessions. It may take longer for people with disabilities to do pre-session paperwork and to complete post-test questionnaires. In addition, it may take more time for people with disabilities to perform tasks, partly because of the disabilities of course, but also because your product may not be highly accessible or the participants may never have used something like it before.

Be conscious of possible energy level limitations. Some participants with disabilities may need breaks or may fatigue easily — but lots won't.

Once you have found the best way of communicating with these participants, use that method to remind them about the time, date, and place of the session. If transportation must be arranged, you may have to do the reminding and arranging well ahead of the day before the session. Find out whether helpers (human or animal) will accompany the participant. If a human helper is planning to come along, ensure that that person understands the study and the session by sending him or her the same instructions, consent forms, and waivers that you sent the participant. To a great extent, helpers may be just as much participants as your main target user, because they regularly work so closely with the person you want to be your test participant.

During the Session

Be sure to make room for assistants, interpreters, or service animals, as well as wheelchairs and other equipment, as appropriate. Clear obstacles out of the way and ensure that you have arranged for appropriate escorts to and from the session.

Depending on the types of disabilities your participants have, you may need to make test materials available in different formats. Or for some participants, you may need to read instructions or tasks to them, rather than having the participant read them.

Just as you used pilot sessions to help you recruit, you can also use them to help you gauge the length of the sessions and the timings for tasks. Otherwise, the guidelines for working with people with disabilities are very similar to those for working with older adults.

Older Adults

Older adults are the fastest growing segment of the population, worldwide. Our experiences with recruiting older adults as usability testing participants showed us some important differences in the patterns of use of the web for older adults, especially those in their 60s and 70s. These differences have important implications for where to find participants and how to recruit, schedule, and work with participants.

Life experience teaches us many useful things. It often also leads to caution and skepticism. If you intend to include older adults — by this we mean people over age 50 — in your studies (and you should), the best sources are personal networks. Cold calling just puts up red flags. ("Hi. You don't know me, I got your name from a list. . . .") Many older adults assume that you're trying to sell them something, even if you swear you're not; older adults are especially wary of scams. You might think that posting flyers at senior centers or other places where older adults congregate would work. Unfortunately, it does not, basically for the same reason: You are unknown and your purpose appears dubious. Most people over 65 are not familiar with the term or the concept of usability testing, and they are suspicious of marketing focus groups.

The best way to reach older adults is to start with personal networks from which you can gather letters of introduction (literally or figuratively) and thus, make connections. One great advantage is that much screening happens before you ever reach your ultimate participant because you have had to say to friends and acquaintances, "Do you know someone who . . ." already. One disadvantage is that it can be difficult to send an elder away if he or she doesn't really qualify for your study.

One important aspect of screening probably will be around expertise in using the technology you want to test. Especially with this group, it is not sufficient to ask for a self-rating or to assume that numbers of hours per week describes expertise. Those hours could be spent doing specific and limited tasks that are not necessarily indicators of wider knowledge that may be needed for your study. Also, be sure to differentiate between experience using email and experience surfing the web or using web applications.

Scheduling and Reminding

The personal contact continues after you have identified people to take part in your usability test. Although people in their 60s and 70s are the fastest growing audience for the web, they generally aren't as attached to email as younger people. And they are vigilant about spam. If older adults don't recognize your email address, or if they simply forget that you were going to send them something, they will not respond to your email. You probably will have to do scheduling and reminding by phone.

Something to keep in mind for scheduling sessions that you might not think of for other types of participants is the optimum time of day for attention. The oldest adults–people in their 70s and beyond–are often more alert in the mornings.

Also note, they *will* arrive at the session early, sometimes an hour in advance, and often with a spouse or friend in tow. Absolutely do call your older participants the day before their sessions to remind them. When you do, also remind them to bring reading and/or computer glasses and to eat before they come. Be sure they understand that the session they'll participate in is a one-on-one session; if they do bring a friend, the friend will need to wait the length of the session.

Allow extra time during the sessions. Older adults are often slower at performing tasks — as much as 25% slower. So, you may have to extend the length of your sessions or simply expect to get less done in the allowed amount of time.

During the Session

Respect your elders. To many older participants, this is a very special event, and you are a perfect stranger. Be respectful and polite without being patronizing. Be clear and detailed about how the session will work and what you expect up front. We recommend that you:

- Clearly explain the session plan, timing, and what they can expect.
- Warn participants that you'll interrupt them and that you may stop them before they have completed tasks.
- Schedule breaks for long sessions (and tell them they can take breaks whenever they need to).
- Have them practice thinking aloud. (For more about this technique and its advantages and disadvantages, see Chapter 9.)
- Consider including a practice task to help participants understand how the session will work.
- Take account of beliefs that participants may have learned or created about how to work with computers.
- Remember that older participants often are not versed in computer and web terminology, so avoid using this jargon when working with them.
- Be extra patient with older participants; wait longer than you normally might to prompt; consider giving participants permission to ask for hints.
- If participants stop talking, consider letting them continue that way; try reflecting on the task later.
- Teach participants something at the end of the session. Doing so wraps up on a positive note, and you may be able to dispel some myths that are causing the participant unnecessary effort and frustration.

- Although it's natural for people to blame themselves for difficulties they experience while interacting with a new product, older participants may do so more than is typical.

It can be challenging to keep older participants on track, as nearly everything reminds them of something else that has happened and there is a story to tell about it. Some of the stories can be pertinent; many stories will not be. You may have to gently interrupt stories to go back to tasks. Be kind but firm.

Children

Working with people under the age of 18 can be great fun; however, finding the right kids and getting them to your sessions can be challenging. Sources can be difficult to uncover; here again, it may be best to start with personal contacts: soccer or other sports teams, Parent-Teacher Associations, church groups, and Boy Scouts or Girls Scouts are all good starting places to put the word out among the adults involved.

Be clear about what is required of the child *and* the parent or guardian leading up to, during, and after the study. If there are secrets to be kept about the product after the session, say that. Don't make them sign NDAs (nondisclosure agreements). If your legal people insist on nondisclosure agreements, and parents will be observing the sessions, ask the parents to sign — not the kids!

You are recruiting the parents as much as you are the kids, even if the parents do not actually take part in the sessions. Winning the parents over with information about how the session will be conducted, what the children will do, who else will be in the room with them, and so on, are integral to getting their approval and cooperation.

Laws about protecting the privacy of children apply in situations like usability testing. Likewise, child labor laws must be respected in studies. Make yourself aware of those laws and work with your legal department to ensure that the rights of the children are protected. For example, you may not be able to collect personal information about children through a web site. Child labor laws may prevent you from paying children for the time they spend with you. Other incentives may work better, anyway. You could offer games, toys, or gift certificates instead of cash. Or, you may offer a small cash stipend to a parent (enough to cover gas and/or parking) who was required to stay through a session and give a toy or game to the child who participated in the study.

Scheduling and Reminding

It may work best just for logistical reasons to schedule sessions with two or more children at a time. Co-discovery (see the section about this technique later in this chapter) can work well with children. It may work better for one parent to deliver two or more children — as long as you don't mind the kids knowing each other. Siblings who get along well can deliver excellent data, as can best friends. But you may want to see more of the dynamic between children who do not know each other well; in that case, scheduling can be a bit more difficult.

If you want to hold sessions with individual children, but children in the study know each other, you may want to schedule sessions back to back so that parents can coordinate car pooling and so that the children don't have the opportunity to "tip" their friends about the session.

Working with children takes a lot of reminders — for the adults involved. Stay in close touch, and schedule extra sessions to make sure that you end up with the data you need, because last-minute cancellations are common due to illness, injury, or basic confusion of very busy schedules.

You will definitely need to schedule around school hours, of course. Weekends can sometimes work well for sessions, especially if you can hold them near a location where the families would be going anyway, such as sporting events, or shopping malls.

During the Session

Knowledge and interest combine to make motivation, which figures large in testing with children. Children who are age 8 and younger tend to be very literal, and attention can be limited for children of all ages, so be sure that you have carefully designed your test to test specifically what you want to test. That is, make it easy for children to focus on your purpose for testing by removing distractions from the test design, the product, and the room.

Children *get* usability, but most are not patient with complexity. Rather than persisting, the typical reaction is to stop and do something else. They are also highly aware of what is appropriate for their age and abilities and will tell you quite clearly. Expect high-energy sessions and frank comments.

What: Prototypes versus Real Products

The great advantage of conducting usability tests of prototypes — that is, early versions of a product that may not be completely operable — is that no one has invested much in the way of time or other resources to reach a complete product yet. By its nature, the prototype is disposable: the team should be willing to at least make extensive revisions and even be willing to throw out the first one and go back to the drawing board to create another prototype that works better for users. In iterative testing, each prototype tested and then improved on is simply design "practice," leading up to better and more robust versions.

It can be difficult to prototype entire products, especially for large web sites or web applications or other software. In those cases, we recommend that you concentrate your efforts on developing prototypes of the riskiest areas or functionality — those areas that would be "show stoppers" if they don't work for users.

Paper and Other Low-Fi Prototypes

A paper or low-fidelity prototype is just that: Something hand drawn or hand formed that has few or no working parts. It is only a representation of what *could* be implemented. Paper prototypes of web sites or software are done using — wait for it — *paper*, markers, Post-it® notes, and transparency film. You or someone on the team sketches or prints each element of the user interface on a separate piece of paper or a sticky note so that planned elements of the user interface can be moved around, added to, or changed on the fly between, or even during, testing sessions. Figure 13-1 shows an example.

Testing of prototypes would, naturally, be done very, very early in the design process. Your team may even want to create a paper prototype to test the *concept* they are thinking of developing to determine usefulness and feasibility before any further monies are expended in design and development.

With this super-early testing, your team will get quick feedback about design elements, labeling, and the position of items in the layout of a screen or page. All of these decisions are based on evidence — real, hard data — because target users will have been involved in the testing and the design as you and your team iterate on the design. And so, testing a paper prototype gives the

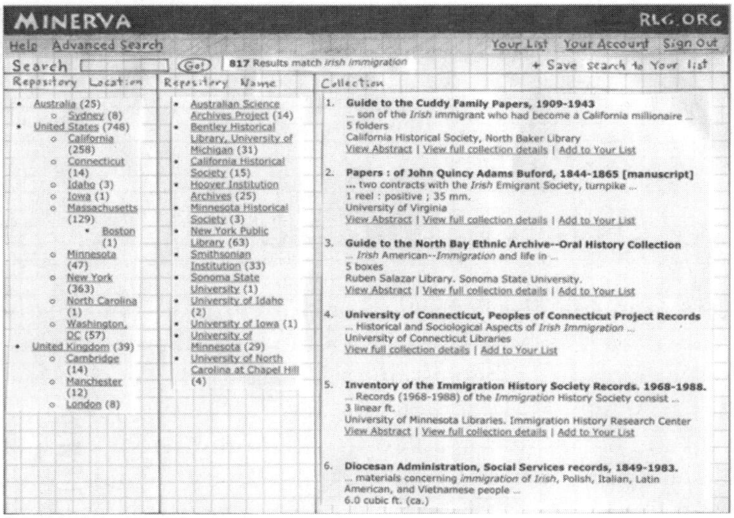

Figure 13-1 Example of a paper prototype of a web page showing search results

team exceptional design agility at a stage in the life cycle when there is very low risk to experimentation. Participants often respond very positively to paper prototypes, as well, feeling that their input is more valuable because it is considered so early in the design process.

Test your paper prototype using the same method you would with a product that is closer to being final. Use participants who have the same characteristics as your target users. Ask them to think aloud while they use the prototype to do real tasks or work. Get your entire design and development team to observe the sessions.

You may need two people to work with the participant, one to be the test moderator and one to be the "computer." This arrangement leaves the moderator free to conduct the session, make observations, and take some notes. The "computer" makes items in the user interface appear at the right times. For example, a participant "clicks" a dropdown menu by pointing to it; the "computer" places the sticky note that lists the choices on the prototype in the place where it is planned for the menu to appear. And so on.

Because it is a lot of work for the "computer," you will probably find that you cannot test an entire product this way. Choose to first test those sections or functions that the team considers high risk. You should be able to generalize findings to other parts of the product, but do plan follow-on studies to prototype and test some other sections or functions before proceeding to code anything. Remember, this is meant to be an iterative process of design, test, and refine.

Now, rather than debriefing with observers at the end of a day or the end of a test, debrief between each session. Collaborate and agree together what changes to make. Cut some new pieces of paper and make the changes. On to the next session.

Clickable or Usable Prototypes

The next step after testing a low-fi prototype is to create a prototype that is closer to the real thing but still basically disposable. For web sites and software, at least some parts should be clickable or interactive. The prototype could be constructed with a "static path" — that is, only part of the user interface is actually interactive; other parts will look properly live, but nothing happens if they are clicked. Managing the testing session in this situation will take a bit more skill from the moderator than it does when everything works the way it was specified. You will get the opportunity to utter statements such as, "in real life, what you did would work, but in this prototype, there is another way to accomplish that." This just means that you have learned something about the interface, perhaps that it does not quite match the user's mental model of the task. Figure 13-2 shows a page from a clickable prototype, which resulted from testing the paper prototype shown in Figure 13-1.

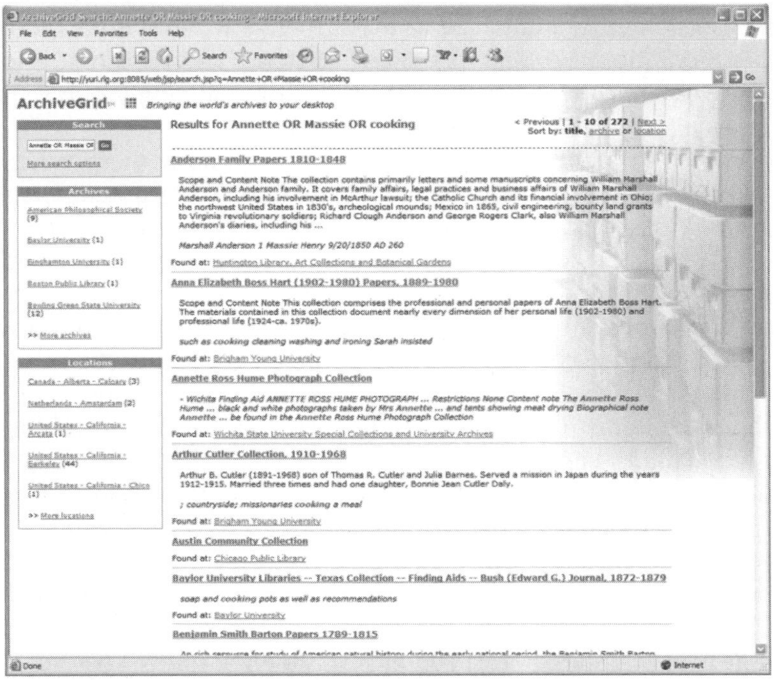

Figure 13-2 A clickable prototype of a web page

For other products, such as pointing devices, cell phones, or other physical devices, designers may want to mock up paper, Styrofoam, or clay "shells" or models that suggest what the final product will look and feel like but that are easy to change.

The closer to realistic the prototype appears, the more realistically the participant will try to use it. This may be good; it may not be because the closer to realistic the prototype appears, the more attached the design team gets to it, too.

How? Techniques for Monitored Tests

A standard, sit-by session implementing the same task scenarios for each participant while having them think aloud may not suit the objectives of your study. In that case, we suggest some options that can help you get to data that may otherwise be difficult to obtain.

- Flexible scripting to develop task scenarios on the fly
- Gradual disclosure to supply appropriate hints
- Co-discovery to get two participants talking to each other to solve problem or do a task

- Alpha and beta testing to get early, typically unstructured reports from favored customers

- Play testing to gather data about how fun and frustrating technology-based games are

You'll find links to articles, papers, and books related to these techniques at www.wiley.com/go/usabiliytesting.

Flexible Scripting

Also called interview-based testing, this is a technique in which the test moderator conducts a structured interview at the beginning of a usability test session in order to form tasks that are specific to the participant. This works best in usability tests where participants search for some piece of information or specific item on a web site. But it may be appropriate for other products that have highly flexible options or content.

What You Get

By customizing the task to the participant, you can generate scenarios that are based on specific experiences of the individual participants, which makes the scenarios more realistic and meaningful for that person. In turn, the data you get from observing a participant in this case is better because the participant is more motivated and better able to judge the outcomes of the task.

Although all of the participants in the study do not need to be doing exactly the same tasks (but perform similar tasks), the data generated should help the team gain an understanding of how users approach a searching task and what information they need to do the task at a higher level than a typical task scenario offers. Having a better view into how users model a task in their minds can inform refinements, expansions, or corrections of task scenarios that you use in future sessions in this study or in your next usability test.

How to Use It

Rather than starting out with a very specific task scenario for this type of usability test, use this method when these factors are important:

- The participant must be highly motivated to do the task (they won't cooperate if the task scenario doesn't fit them precisely).

- The participant must understand the outcomes of a task, and so must relate to the result to be able to understand whether he or she has completed a search-like task successfully.

Start the session by interviewing the participant. Ask about his or her interest in the domain that the product is used in, or about the product itself. For example, Dana used interview-based tasks in a usability test of a web site for older adults. She asked her age 50+ participants what they would expect to find on a site for that audience, what types of information they searched for on the web recently, and other questions related to what they might be able to do on the site.

Next, using the information gathered about the participant's experiences, you — as the moderator — and participant agree on a task together. Note carefully the wording that the participant used to describe the task as well as what the goal of the task is so you can know what it means to successfully complete the new, personalized task. Using this approach, Dana learned about frequent, high-priority search tasks, along with the language the target audience normally used to describe those tasks.

Gradual Disclosure or Graduated Prompting

Not to be confused with "progressive disclosure," which is an interaction design concept implemented typically in wizard-like interfaces, this technique uses hints or prompts to help participants along when they get stuck. This approach is usually used early in the development cycle, but it can be used carefully in testing at any point in design or development.

You might use this technique if you want to:

- Conduct a test that requires support material or embedded assistance but none has been developed yet.

- Ascertain the amount of support material, such as training, documentation, help, on-screen instructions, and so on, that is required to support a product. For example, you might want to find out what level of detail is required for a written procedure.

- Determine the degree to which a user interface is self-evident.

What You Get

Using these techniques, you can collect feedback from participants to get direction for where in the interface instructions or messages should be added or changed, as well as indications for whether the product needs further support materials, and what those might be. In addition, this technique can help reveal insights about where the design should be adjusted (to possibly prevent having to develop additional support materials) and the severity of the usability problems.

How to Use It

There are two ways to work this technique: with someone helping the test moderator and with the test moderator alone. If you are moderating the test but are not an expert on the subject matter (DNA electropherograms, anyone? Chemistry chromatographs?), it is best to bring one in.

First, let the participant attempt to perform tasks without any assistance, relying on his or her own abilities and the self-evidence of the product. If the participant becomes stuck and is at a point where he or she would normally give up, asks for help, or says he or she would access documentation, you (as the test moderator or the subject matter expert) provide information orally to get the participant started again. Whoever provides the information says only enough to get the participant working again and not one word more.

The information you provide could be either product-related, such as which key to press or button to click, or task-related, such as the relationship of the number being entered to the result in a tax worksheet.

If you include a subject matter expert (SME), the tricky part is controlling what the SME says to the participant, because the SME is usually as pleased as punch to talk about the product or his or her area of expertise, and may not be sensitive to the potential biasing effects of what is revealed. After all, if you simply tell the participant explicitly what to do, you've learned nothing. If you do use this technique with a SME, you must first brief the SME on how the technique works and make sure that you practice working together during the pilot session.

Jeff tells the SME that he or she is the first human user guide in history, and must be sensitive to the fact that the participants are only going to "read" what we tell them. During the test, you can call a time out to huddle with your SME to discuss how he or she will answer the question. The participant, of course, will have been briefed about the nature of the test methodology and be aware of what is transpiring. Some of the most enjoyable and humorous tests have resulted from this type of interaction, as well as some of the most fruitful.

Gradual disclosure is most valuable when the test is observed by the people who will be responsible for creating the embedded assistance, on-screen instructions, documentation, help, training, and so forth. They can see and hear for themselves what was said and what was most valuable to the user. This technique is an excellent one for establishing the raw content requirements of user support and in keeping a lean and mean approach. Only necessary information is documented, and the product's weak points that need extra help are exposed. Of course, an added benefit is that the interface designers can also see how intuitive and self-evident their product really is or is not, because the user must always try to work without support first.

Keep in mind that you need not run an entire test in this fashion. Perhaps you are unsure of only the more advanced functions of a product and want to see just how little or how much needs to be said to support them. Or, maybe you need to understand how much prerequisite information a user is required to know in order to perform without any help. Simply change the rules of the test at that point, remove any documentation that has been used, and tell the participant to ask questions when he or she is stuck or confused and ordinarily would access some type of user support.

You can also use this technique to identify the depth of a design issue rather than endeavoring to write support material to compensate. A slight variation of this technique is to graduate the level of detail you give in the answers to questions. This way, you can quantify the number and level of moderator interventions when participants need assistance. For example, you might just say "try again," or "try another way," if the participant simply needs a nudge to persist or if you feel that he or she is close to the goal. Next you might give a generic indication of the right approach, for example, "you have been in the right place," or "try a different area of the screen." Finally, you may have to give specific instructions if a task must be completed to be able to continue with the session. Keeping track of the hints at each level and where they were needed should help you determine where design problems lay and how severe they are, as well as what type of solution will be necessary.

Co-Discovery (Two Participants at a Time)

This technique uses two participants simultaneously during a usability test instead of a single participant. The participants are encouraged to communicate with each other during the test session, and it is this communication that is the key difference during a session. Their dialogue becomes the focal point for understanding how users attack problems using your product. It is useful when a product is normally used in the field by more than one person who might work through tasks together.

This technique is useful in early stages of design through to the middle of development for early prototypes of products where there is still time to change the basic design.

What You Get

The act of participants talking to each other offers an alternative to a moderator prompting one participant to think aloud. Some practitioners believe that this exchange between peers to be more natural, and therefore more reliable, than the typical moderator-participant relationship. Though you still may have to ask participants to verbalize occasionally, generally the technique generates rich verbal data that can reveal subtle problem-solving and usage patterns in ways that you may not observe in single-participant sessions, as the two people work together.

How to Use It

Rather than using the "thinking aloud" technique or test moderator interviewing to explore thought processes, the exchange between participants serves that purpose. Participants can be allowed to work together in any way they see fit, but usually one person will work on the product, while the other offers advice. At scripted points during the session, they should trade places.

This is a natural for those types of applications where different users normally work together as a team. For one test that Jeff conducted for a client, he used this technique with two participants who normally work together to perform chemical analyses. One person usually develops the analytical technique, while the other uses the software product to run the technique. Interestingly, when solicited for the usability test, these customers *insisted* on appearing as a team, and they worked well together during the test.

Because the dialogue is so meaningful, you will probably want to record and transcribe the communication between the two participants. You may also need to encourage them to talk to each other if there is little communication occurring.

This technique can be especially effective with some special audiences, such as children. Whether they know each other or not, children may be more willing to play together or work through using a product together than to try something alone with an adult who is a stranger to them.

That said, exercise some caution when matching participants; you may want to take extra steps to ensure that the personalities of the pair are compatible. No matter how careful you are, you may have to intervene in a session if one person is dominating the session.

Alpha or Beta Testing with Favored Clients

In this technique, you and your company work closely with an actual customer to help develop your product. Existing customers, or even potential customers you are wooing, provide their expertise throughout your product development life cycle. A secondary benefit of this technique is that it can cement your relationship with your largest customers.

You can use this technique throughout the product life cycle, although the earlier you implement it, the more beneficial it will be.

What You Get

By reaching out to customers early and often in a longer-term partnership, you can reap contextual data about how the product is used in place and create opportunities to follow up with customers as the team makes iterative improvements based on feedback directly from these favored clients.

How to Use It

Set up relationships with one or more customers who either exemplify your typical customer or who represent a large portion of your revenue base. Call on them at key points to get both input and feedback on your product. For example, show them preliminary concepts, have them meet with the design team, or have them act as participants for usability tests. The possibilities for gathering information are nearly limitless.

Alpha testing puts the customer or user on your company's physical premises giving input on concepts, prototypes, or parts of products in development. Beta testing is done after alpha testing. In beta testing, your company would release very early versions of the product to favored customers. Beta testing is usually done to get assistance from realistic installations in identifying bugs and to get early feedback. You can insert usability testing or other ways of gathering usability data into this process, as well.

Some companies go so far as to make the client part of their development team. Others, depending on the type of product, bring the customers in to try out the product for a week or two at a time to perform real-world functions, similar to a "residency" program. The best customers to use are often ones who also use your competitor's product, because their feedback is more well rounded and helpful in getting at where the advantages and disadvantages lie.

The advantage to your client is the ability to be on the cutting edge of product development in his or her field. The advantage to your company *in addition to the obvious usability benefits* lies in establishing a strong relationship with your best customers. By paying such close attention to them, you keep them away from your competitors.

There are, however, some things to watch out for. Be careful about letting the customer get *too* close to the team, so close that he or she begins to think like a developer. Chumminess breeds a lack of critical intelligence, and the last thing you need is a cheerleader instead of a critic. Also do not completely ignore the rest of your customer base who may work for a smaller company, be less skilled, and so forth.

In recruiting participants, look for customer representatives who are outspoken and knowledgeable, yet fair. Make sure that you have them sign a very binding nondisclosure agreement in which you stipulate that they may not serve in a similar capacity for your competition.

Play Tests

These sessions are set up specifically to test games. The games may be anything from board games or crossword puzzles to Halo™, but most play testing is done with electronic games. During a play test of computer-based games, participants — either single, pairs, or groups — try the games out in a lab so that they can be observed and asked questions before, during, and after play.

What You Get

Besides some useful quality assurance testing, play tests on games can net early feedback about the target audience, such as their interest and level of engagement while playing. You can get a measure of how fun participants feel the game is. You can also learn about how easy or difficult it is to win the game — although you want it to be a little challenging, you do not want it to be *too* frustrating.

How to Use It

There are many possible setups for play tests. For example, if you are testing a game on a console that would normally be played at home on a television, you may want to set up a living room–like setting. Much play testing occurs in a lab, where several players are situated together in an arcade-like setting. In major gaming companies, the lab is set up with elaborate video and data-capturing systems. But, like other testing, it can be done more informally and with less gear.

One person moderates the session. If there are multiple players present, the dynamics can be somewhat like a focus group, while other observers are assigned to listen to and observe specific participants. If testing single players, the approach is just like any other usability test. Observers may be in the testing room rather than an observation room. Ask participants to think aloud. But the data you gather is very likely to be different from the measures you look for when testing a web application or a cell phone. For example, you probably want to check in at scripted points about what players think their goal is and to get them to talk about what's exciting and what is frustrating.

Where? Testing Outside a Lab

In addition to taking your usability test to the field — that is, someone's office or home — there are options for gathering data about the usability of products that include:

- Remote testing with you in one geographic location and your test participant in another
- Automated testing over the Internet with hundreds or thousands of participants

▪ Surveys and diary studies in which study participants report their experiences to you without your observing them

The following sections discuss the basics of these techniques. There are links to tools and further information at www.wiley.com/go/usabilitytesting.

Remote Testing

By taking advantage of high-speed data lines and tools available on the Internet typically used for collaborating among people in workgroups over distances, you can conduct usability test sessions with participants who are distant from you. Remote testing generally uses a combination of phone and computer to test user interfaces that are screen-based, that is, web sites, web-based applications, and software. Although there are some fine tools available specifically for mediating remote usability testing, you can conduct sessions through tools that are downloadable from the web or that may even be available internal to your company already, such as NetMeeting, LiveMeeting, or WebEx.

What You Get

With remote testing, you can expand your participant sample geographically at very low cost. While you will not be able to observe the participant's body language because you won't be able to see him or her, you will hear as he or she thinks aloud. You will also to see what is happening on the participant's computer screen. You can still record the sessions, if that is important to you. This technique is not good for benchmark testing in which you seek to collect data about time on task because it demands that the participant think aloud and there may be slight delays in system response time.

How to Use It

Recruit participants who are like your target users. In this case, participants can be anywhere that they have access to a phone and a high-speed data line attached to a computer. You can either set up a conference calling number or arrange to phone the participant yourself. In either case, set up an appointment in the same manner that you would for an in-lab usability test session. If you are using an online meeting tool, be sure to send instructions to participants ahead of time and ask them to be set up in time for the session to start. Otherwise, you must build time into the session to help the participants get set up. Honestly, you probably should leave some time to ensure that everything is as it should be before the official start of the test session, anyway.

In the case of both the conference calling number and the online meeting tool, you can configure the session so that observers can hear and watch the sessions from wherever they are, as well.

Automated Testing

In this case, the usability testing is completely unmoderated by humans. Instead, an underlying program collects data as the participant uses the product that he or she is testing, and the participant is prompted for feedback at specific points in his or her session. The participant supplies feedback by answering scripted multiple choice or yes-no questions.

What You Get

Because licenses for automated usability testing software are generally quite expensive (in the tens of thousands of dollars, at least), the purpose in conducting automated testing is to gather very large amounts of data from hundreds or thousands of users in one go. These automated services compile data from click-throughs, timing, and answers to questions that you supply. Interpreting the data does take some particular expertise; what is most valuable is the quantitative data from this technique. Collecting qualitative data relies on participants' writing skills (because they will type their answers into a text field in an online form) and takes a lot of work to comb through to gain meaning. Some services supply text analyses, but we urge caution in relying on these. And, of course, you miss the emotional information that can be gathered by directly observing someone use the product that helps you gauge how severe a problem might be.

This can be an effective technique to gather lots of data about the usability of a specific part of a product. It is a good *complement* to usability tests in which you are observing someone up-close-and-personal. However, we do not recommend using this technique alone or as a substitute for the classic usability testing method.

How to Use It

Obviously, this is a method for web sites and software that runs under a web browser, rather than physical devices that don't use web browsers as part of the interface. The ideal time to use it is for summative or validation usability testing, in which case what you care most about is lingering error conditions that you may have been following through earlier, moderated tests.

The company that licenses the testing service usually also has access to large panels of people who have volunteered to participate in usability tests. It can be difficult to be too specific about the selection criteria here; automated testing works best with broad, general consumer audiences.

A pilot test is as necessary in automated testing as it is in any other technique, perhaps more so, because the tasks presented and the questions asked must be absolutely crystal clear to participants. If participants don't understand what they are being asked to do, they will skip tasks or questions, or give you data that cannot be used.

Be careful about using time-on-task as a measure, because you are adding reading time for the participant as overhead for doing the test.

Testing In-Home or On-Site

The idea is that you conduct usability test sessions with individuals in the environment where they would normally use the product. In some companies, this is called "follow me home" testing. The founder of Intuit, Scott Cook, coined the phrase when he encouraged designers and developers at Intuit to watch people buy the product in stores and then ask permission to follow those customers home as they installed and used the product.

What You Get

While conducting usability testing in a lab gives the researcher great control and an excellent opportunity for team members to observe sessions, testing where the user uses the product is much more realistic. By doing testing on the user's premises, you gain knowledge of the environment in which users engage your product and your company. This knowledge can inform design in ways that being in a lab cannot: You learn about the physical and social factors that may influence the ease of use. In addition, you can gather details about usage patterns and tasks that help you present more realistic scenarios when you get back in a more structured setting.

How to Use It

You can certainly try — if you have a consumer product that is sold in retail stores — to follow buyers home. The tradeoff for rich data is that you will spend a lot of time trying to get customers to take home a surprise guest. Most on-site studies are much more structured. You must design the session in the same way that you plan a usability test that takes place in a lab: Determine the goals and the research questions, determine how best to answer the questions, recruit participants, set up appointments with them, script the sessions, and so on.

There are additional logistical steps when testing on-site. You must learn where the person lives or works, and include time in the study for traveling there. There should be two people on the research team who go to each session (partly for safety). One person interacts with the user, while the other sets up and takes down any equipment brought along. On-site, you may encounter surprises, such as an unruly (or smelly) pet, rambunctious children, or coworkers who chime in over the cube wall or across the workbench. These are just some of the considerations. For more about whether to test in the field and some tips for doing so, see Chapter 6.

Self-Reporting (Surveys, Diary Studies)

This technique involves gathering preference information from the participant via a questionnaire delivered either in phases as the participant completes a series of tasks using the product or at the very end of completing all tasks. The former approach makes it easier for the participant to remember his or her perceptions and feelings about using the product. The tricky part of designing the test is to make filling out the questionnaires unobtrusive as possible, so it does not overly distract the participant from performing the tasks.

Use this technique when you want to compare how satisfied participants are in using versions or prototypes on such variables as ease of access, organization, intuitiveness, and so on.

What You Get

Here, the prize is snapshot data and impressions from participants' lingering memories of their interactions with the product. If you use questionnaires in a typical usability study, either at the ends of tasks or at the ends of tests, participants can quickly articulate their preferences in reaction to their very recent interactions with the product. If you use questionnaires or collect diary data in a longer study, you can learn much about context, frequency, and relationships that may influence participants' performance with the product as well as their preferences about how it works.

How to Use It

It is critical that the questionnaires be short and designed for ease of use. Fill-in questions, ranking questions, Likert scales, and list-choice questions are preferred over essay type or similar questions that require much thought to complete. It is imperative that the test be piloted to ferret out and eliminate leading and confusing questions. (See the section "Common Question Formats" in Chapter 8.)

Alternately, the participant can be asked to simply write down confusing terms or processes to jog his or her memory for a post-test debriefing session, although obviously this would require more time and effort by a test moderator.

You can also use this technique in longer field studies — lasting days, weeks, or months — in which you are not constantly present to moderate the test by asking participants to keep detailed records or diaries about their interactions with your product. These diaries can be free-form, or you can supply questionnaires or structured feedback requests at various points.

This is by no means a complete list of the improvisations possible on a standard usability test methodology. You may create variants of one of those we have described, or you may find you need to combine techniques in order to answer your research questions. This increased sophistication of test design will help you reach the goal of the next and last chapter: expanding user-centered design throughout your organization so it begins to think of the whole experience users have with your product.

Expanding from Usability Testing to Designing the User Experience

Up to this point, we have covered the technical aspects of planning, designing, conducting, and reporting the results of a usability test in great detail. We have also placed usability testing within the context of a user-centered approach to product development. In this final chapter, let's revisit the larger picture and discuss how to expand the influence of user-centered design and user experience design within an organization. These suggestions are primarily intended for an individual who has been given (or would like to take) primary responsibility for usability within his or her organization, with minimal formal training in user-centered design.

We suggest a phased program, extending over years, to emphasize the need to build such a program gradually. Let's be very clear: Implementing a user-centered approach to product development for organizations that have not embraced such a program previously is a major undertaking, fraught with the same difficulties, risks, excitement, and political intrigue of any major shift in the corporate culture. It requires much forethought and attention to the "human" issues within your own organization. However, depending on the degree of management support and the amount of resources assigned to usability, you may want to move faster or slower, implement these suggestions in a different order, or avoid those that simply do not make sense for your organization. The important point is to understand and account for the dynamics operating within your own organization and to act accordingly. In talking with people who have done it, we have found that the arc of building a program tends to be more organic than it is formal or planned. There is no magic formula that can be adapted in "cookie cutter" fashion to every organization, and any attempt to do so will jeopardize a program. This chapter reflects the collective experiences of several people and groups who

Year 1-2 Stealth Mode: Establish Value	Year 2-4 Build on successes	Year 3-6 Formalize Processes and Practices	Year 4-10 Expand UCD Through the OrganizationPractices
Status			
• 1-2 visible usability tests with publicized results • 1 person doing usability tests, 1 champion, using surrogates or "friends and family" for participants • Probably no usability budget: money is scrounged or "donated" for participant incentives and other costs	• Usability tests are scheduled a few times a year • Usability resources may be overextended as demand grows • Small budget for overhead: may have set up a charge-back system within the company to fund test and other projects • Scrounging for space to use as a center usability area	• The organization knows that there are usability specialists in the company • A few product groups do usability testing regularly • Budget covers 2-3 staff, dedicated equipment, and possibly space • Methods expand from usability testing to include field research for user and task analysis • Usability projects have demonstrated return on investment, savings	• The organization values user-centered design and strives to attend to the overall customer experience • User research and usability activities are assumed to be part of every development project • Methods are combined to reveal the richest, most realistic data • Funding and projects are coordinated with R&D, market research, others
Next Steps			

• Make friends in the company: get buy-in to new projects
• Talk about this cool new stuff you're doing and how it might be applied to other products and departments
• Educate yourself
• Volunteer your services
• Create a strategy and business case
	• Set up long term relationships with as many product groups as you can support and do research for them directly
	• Gather more champions and friends
	• Sell your services internally
	  o Deliberately market successes
	  o Train and coach product teams to do their own research
	• Strategize
	  o Use real customers as participants
	  o Implement iterated usability tests
	  o Bring in a vendor for special projects that need objectivity or specialized skill
	  o Create a budget based on a business case for user centered design
		• Set up central residency
		• Begin working with product teams and IT to build usability testing and UCD into processes throughout the product development lifecycle
		• Continue training and coaching product teams
		• Distribute videos or podcasts about your findings and successes
		• Expand your business case
		• Increase your budget request
		• Add: another usability specialist, an interaction designer, a recruiter
		• Set up standing dates for doing usability testing in a central location and invite observers
			• Get more education
			• Standardize processes
			• Align with other groups
			• Implement more research methods, expanding the scope and reach of research
			• Evaluate your efforts
			• Expand your UCD reach beyond proirity products to looking at the larger customer experience of researching, buying, installing, using, troubleshooting, etc. or from venue to venue (e.g., from web site to retail site)
			  o Add: more researchers, more designers, prototypers, recruiters – interdisciplinary group
			  o Increase your budget, revise your business case
			  o Organize internal conferences on UCD projects, practices, and outcomes
			  o Keep making friends
			• Look for groups to start coming to you for services and advice

Figure 14-1 Timeline of progress

have implemented usability, user-centered design, and/or experience design in small and large, start-up and mature companies.

Figure 14-1 shows a timeline of the progress you might experience in expanding user-centered design in your organization. When we conducted interviews with usability specialists, user researchers, and user experience designers in companies small and large, start-up and established, we found their common experience reflected in the process below. The corresponding next steps are in the second row in the table. We discuss the steps in detail in the following sections. Your results may vary.

Stealth Mode: Establish Value

You may be in this phase now: quietly conducting usability tests and other user-centered design activities to demonstrate the value of these efforts without threatening or scaring anyone, just working on making friends. We call this "stealth mode" because, while you probably have someone in management who is a champion for your usability cause, you probably have little or no budget to conduct regular studies and little or no access to real users.

Appraise the current situation within your organization and search for opportunities to contribute. The overall goal at the beginning is to make steady progress, while educating the organization about the benefits of usability and user-centered design.

Choose the First Project Carefully

If you have been charged with selecting or carrying out an initial "kick-off" project, choose one with moderate to high visibility within the organization and with a high probability of success. Success will come more easily if the first project has a champion(s) besides you and if there are minimal obstacles for carrying out a test or evaluation. A champion is someone within management with influence, one who is committed to the philosophy of usability and has a personal interest in seeing such a program blossom and flourish.

A documentation project can be a good kick-off project with which to begin, because it may be seen as less threatening to others in your organization (and technical communicators are often excited to take part). Begin with manageable objectives, such as testing only a portion of a manual or user interface. An assessment test midway through the development life cycle is probably the simplest, most straightforward test for the beginning usability specialist to conduct. For example, you could test early instructions for activating a cell phone or the installation poster for a wireless router or for changing printer cartridges. We recommend earlier involvement, which will have the greatest effect on the product. However, later involvement seems to be more politically acceptable and initially less threatening. Once the project is completed, play up and publicize the initial success as much as possible across the organization.

By the time you read this, you may be planning or conducting your first usability test already. Not to worry. The current usability testing project was probably chosen for some very good reasons, and you should be able to exploit it and its results regardless of how carefully or casually the project was chosen. The point is, you're getting to *do* a usability test, and that's good.

Begin Your Education

Begin your education by becoming familiar with the abundance of information available. Although much of it can seem quite technical and overwhelming for the beginner, you should start with those sources that teach usability principles and guidelines in simple English. The first edition of this book recommended three books and a few journals. There weren't many introductory titles or other information options for new usability practitioners then, in 1994. Today, we include a baker's dozen books, but the titles now available make up a much longer list. (A search on `Amazon.com` in November 2007 on the keyword "usability" turned up over 1900 results. Seriously. Nearly two *thousand*.) Also below we list a number of journals, conferences and seminars, and web-based sources.

Books

The following books are excellent for an introduction to the field of user-centered design, either for yourself or for those you wish to educate:

- *Cost Justifying Usability* by Randoph Bias and Deborah Mayhew
- *Understanding Your Users* by Catherine Courage and Kathy Baxter
- *Moderating Usability Tests: Principles and Practice for Interacting* by Joseph Dumas and Beth Loring
- *User and Task Analysis for Interface Design* by JoAnn Hackos and Janice C. Redish
- *Don't Make Me Think!* by Steve Krug
- *Observing the User Experience: A Practitioner's Guide to User Research* by Michael Kuniavsky
- *The Usability Engineering Lifecycle: A Practitioner's Handbook for User Interface Design* by Deborah Mayhew
- *Usability Engineering* by Jakob Nielsen
- *The Design of Everyday Things* by Donald Norman
- *A Practical Guide to Usability Testing* by Janice C. Redish and Joseph Dumas
- *User-Centered Design Stories* by Carol Righi and Janice James
- *Designing the User Interface* by Ben Shneiderman
- *Paper Prototyping: Fast and Simple Techniques for Designing and Refining the User Interface* by Carolyn Snyder
- *Universal Usability: Designing Computer Interfaces for Diverse User Populations* by Jonathan Lazar

The Usability and User Experience community of the Society for Technical Communication (STC) maintains a first-rate bibliography at `www.stc.org/usability/resources/bookshelf/index.html`. The STC's list is organized by such helpful topics as "usability testing," "inspiration and business support," and "user-centered design process."

Conferences and Seminars

There are now many conferences and seminars held "live" and "virtually." Some of the conferences and seminars can be pricey but are well worth the expense, considering the high-quality, intensive instruction offered. Some conferences and seminars are organized and sponsored by professional associations. Many universities put on small conferences, as do some corporations that have their own user research, user experience research and design, or usability groups. For a list of conferences and seminars, see the web site that accompanies this book at www.wiley.com/go/usabilitytesting.

Journals, Magazines, and Newsletters

When you are ready for meatier information, there are many usability-related publications to consult. The following all feature information related to usability, user-centered design, and user experience design. Those marked with an asterisk are more technical in nature.

Journals and newsletters

- *Behaviour and Information Technology**
- *Human Factors** (journal of the Human Factors and Ergonomics Society)
- *Interaction* magazine* (published by a special interest group of the ACM on Computer-Human Interaction called SIG CHI)
- *International Journal of Human-Computer Interaction**
- *International Journal of Human-Computer Studies**
- *Journal of Usability Studies* (published by the Usability Professionals' Association)
- *Technical Communication* (journal of the Society for Technical Communication)
- *UPA Voice* (a newsletter of the Usability Professionals' Association)
- *UX: User Experience* magazine (published by the Usability Professionals' Association)

Proceedings of Conferences of Professional Associations and Societies

- *Proceedings of CHI** (a special interest group on Computer-Human Interaction of the ACM)
- *Proceedings of the Human Factors and Ergonomics Society**
- *Proceedings of the International Professional Communication Conference*
- *Proceedings of the Usability Professionals' Association Conference*

E-Newsletters, Weblogs, and Other Resources

Many e-newsletters and blogs are free of charge. There are also many, many usability-related weblogs — so many that one group has published a "top

100." For the list, see `www.virtualhosting.com/blog/2007/top-100-user-centered-blogs/`. Dana writes a blog about usability testing to expand the discussion beyond this book at `http://usabilitytestinghowto.blogspot.com`.

You might also look into podcasts. Groups and individuals regularly publish podcasts of interviews with notable user-centered designers as well as discussions about tools, methods, and approaches to user research. Most are available through iTunes for free.

Usability-Related Societies and Professional Associations

As this book goes to press, the following associations and societies are concerned with usability testing as well as other elements of user-centered design. Each has local chapters in many cities throughout the world, which would provide you the opportunity to get involved with other like professionals within your community. And, each has a web site that includes its own list of links to additional resources.

- Usability Professionals' Association: `www.usabilityprofessionals.org`
- Society for Technical Communication: `www.stc.org`
- The STC offers a virtual community on usability and user experience: `www.stc.org/usability`
- Human Factors and Ergonomics Society: `www.hfes.org`
- Association for Computing Machinery's Special Interest Group on Computer-Human Interaction (ACM SIGCHI): `www.sigchi.org`

Become involved by attending presentations at a society's annual conference, or, better yet, make a presentation about your efforts and what you have learned.

Start Slowly and Conservatively, Get Buy-In

As mentioned earlier, user-centered design is a complex undertaking within an organization, and there is a danger in just simply "jumping on the usability bandwagon" in an unskillful way. It is important to build a usability program slowly, success upon success, rather than suddenly trying to reinvent the organization. Usability, like its counterpart, *quality*, cannot simply be mandated from above. It needs the support of everyone in the organization so that it can enter the organization's bloodstream, rather than existing as some superficial "user-friendly" flag that everyone waves, but that produces very little results.

Consider an approach of gradual infiltration of the organization, rather than simply an all-out attack on usability problems. As mentioned in an earlier anecdote concerning the premature implementation of a fully equipped usability lab, beginning *too* ambitiously can undermine a long-term program. Initially, usability may be seen as a threat and loss of control by those you would like to help. On the other hand, usability's most vociferous adversaries will often turn into its most ardent supporters, once they see that the user-centered process makes sense as a logical, cost-effective way to conduct business, and that it is not a threat.

Volunteer Your Services

While you need to proceed slowly, do not be a shrinking violet either. Usability is "hotter" than ever right now, and there has never been a better time in which to assert yourself. Look for opportunities to leverage your efforts. For example, if you are assigned to test the documentation for a product, that is an opportunity to positively affect the user interface as well. In your test report, include, as a "courtesy," problems originating from sources other than those directly tested, if they come up, such as the product's software interface or an inaccurate characterization of the end user. Offer to expand on these findings personally and to help with overcoming them.

Take on *any* usability project, even if it is one that occurs very late in the life cycle, with limited benefits. While a test conducted very late in the life cycle may have little bearing on the current release of a product, it will have effects on the next release some weeks or months from now. Therefore, keep the long-term vision in mind. Even for small projects, go the extra mile by creating a well-thought-out, professional report that will be acceptable and usable in your organization. Your methodology and approach will be scrutinized by others wishing to learn what this "usability" stuff is all about.

Create a Strategy and Business Case

How you begin, in terms of setting expectations and establishing an overall philosophy will go a long way toward determining ultimate success. Even if you are just starting to work with usability issues, it behooves you to think of the long term at the very start. Therefore, begin by developing a usability plan that extends over a two to three-year period. Sit down with management, and talk about the long-term vision of the organization as it pertains to usability. Jointly ascertain where you see the organization moving in the future, the types of user-centered design techniques and methods that need to be implemented, hiring needs, capital expenses, modifications and additions to the product life cycle, types of usability tests and evaluations to be performed, awareness-building within the organization, educational opportunities to be pursued for both yourself and the organization, and outside services required, such as recruiting or market research firms, usability consultants, and so forth. The plan can suggest guidelines for projects, such as usability checkpoints in the life cycle, when to develop usability objectives, and types of tests to conduct at different phases.

Develop the plan for either your own use or to show others, depending on your position and the amount of responsibility you are given within the organization. Why this emphasis on a plan at such an early stage? Because without a plan, usability, as with any other organizational and cultural change, will sputter and languish. As the organization becomes more serious about implementing a usability program, it will need to grapple with and address many of the issues in your plan. Even though you may be starting from scratch, assume that the techniques you implement will be successful and have people clamoring for more. It is important to stay one jump ahead and be prepared for success.

Your plan should take into consideration the political realities of the organization and management's commitment or lack thereof. In other words, find the right balance of stretching the organization, yet not proposing impossible endeavors. Also, remember that any plan is revisable as circumstances change. It's a living document.

Build on Successes

Resist the temptation to go for the home run. Instead, go for singles and doubles. Opt for steady, incremental progress on both specific products and on the overall program. You will be amazed when you review a product at a later date and see how all the "minor" revisions add up to a greatly improved product. By taking a more small-scale approach, you can try to avoid setbacks or resistance, which, during the early stages of developing a usability program, can create doubt in the program itself.

As you proceed from one project to the next, focus your efforts on earlier and earlier involvement, for that is where the greatest usability benefits can be shown. More on that later.

Set Up Long-Term Relationships

Consider a combined top-down and bottom-up strategy to establish long-term relationships within your organization. Work from the bottom up and from the top down simultaneously. Usability needs commitment from both the troops *and* management. Work "bottom up" by conducting actual projects and showing results. Work "top down" by educating management about the benefits of usability testing and user-centered design and by getting management involved. Obviously, you will need to enlist the help of any usability champions to take on such a comprehensive effort.

Sell Yourself and What You Are Doing

Tell people what you do and how what you are doing helps the organization and its customers and users, whether those are internal, external, or both. In the course of a week, you might have dozens of conversations with people in your organization. View these as opportunities to plant seeds and educate people about the benefits of user-centered design. Eventually, two or three seeds will take root, and you will find people requesting you to help them out.

Especially at the beginning, you need to *sell, sell, sell* at every opportunity. Expect it. Take every opportunity to make presentations or hold short training sessions for those with a vested interest and those who are simply interested. An obvious presentation to make is one comprising usability test results. Such presentations could include video excerpts of a test; sort of a "greatest hits" tape with emphasis on the most dramatic, cost-saving, embarrassment-preventing events that occurred (which may be different from a highlights tape that specifically documents findings). Nothing is as effective in bringing home the reality of and need to address usability deficiencies as seeing actual customers or representative users struggle. Never be defensive about modest test results. Five "minor" inconsistencies can equal one big headache to a user.

But there is a balance to be struck. Professional subtlety may also play a part in convincing people to incorporate user-centered design practices in your organization. Blatant evangelizing or door-to-door missionary zeal may put some people off.

Strategize: Choose Your Battles Carefully

Initially, usability is often an uphill effort, as you attempt to overcome old habits in the organization. If you are doing your job properly as a usability specialist, you *will* find yourself in adversarial positions. Expect it. The key is in how you handle these situations. Save your energy for major issues, such as getting access to real customers and conducting iterated tests, and do not get caught up with petty controversies. Bring in a vendor to conduct a test if there is a need for greater objectivity or a special skill that you don't have yet. This is one of the characteristics of an experienced usability specialist: he or she knows the issues that are worth fighting for and when to give in on minor points. Then you can properly frame your budget and business case for expanding further into user-centered design.

Formalize Processes and Practices

Once your initial seeds begin to bear fruit and you begin to establish the benefits of user-centered design, begin to formalize the process. Create both physical and organizational structures to support UCD.

Establish a Central Residency for User-Centered Design

It is important how you position user-centered design support in the organization. There are two major approaches you can take:

- Usability support can reside at the project level with a dedicated usability specialist working on a single project and reporting to the same project manager as everyone else.

~ OR ~

- Usability can be centralized with one or more specialists supporting multiple projects and reporting to a centralized manager. The former approach is often used by "usability-mature" organizations that employ many usability specialists, with each one assigned to a specific project and reporting to that project's manager.

While both approaches can be successful, for the organization that is new to usability, we recommend the centralized approach for two reasons:

- Usability advocacy can be a very difficult and lonely position, with the usability specialist often placed in an adversarial position on a project. Because support by others is so crucial for one's confidence, outlook, and success, it helps when one has a manager who has usability as a major concern. In addition, if there are multiple usability specialists reporting to the same manager rather than separate ones, then the reporting structure enables them to help support, reinforce, teach each other, and develop a genuine *espirit de corps*. This is very important in organizations new to user-centered design.

- When a usability specialist reports directly to a project manager on a specific project, it is easy to become unduly influenced by the goals of the project team, which may conflict with usability goals. One may find it difficult to be honest about a particular design because revising it may cause more work for the developer(s), your very close peers. This hesitation eventually threatens one's autonomy and user advocacy. Reporting to a manager outside the project, as well as working on multiple projects, can help to retain one's autonomy and objectivity, and especially one's user advocacy because there is less peer pressure associated with this reporting structure.

Once you have established some momentum, with usability tests occurring regularly, then it makes sense to commandeer or construct a permanent space. We are not necessarily recommending that you construct a fully equipped lab. Doing so isn't always the best thing. It can be expensive and isolating; it may not even be appropriate for your products' customers. For example, conducting usability research with people who run small businesses may be best done at the participant's work site, because asking them to come into a lab could put the person out of business for several hours that he or she cannot afford. Or, for customers who have disabilities, you may not be able to adequately mimic the very customized setup these people often have in the place where they normally interact with your product.

A lab should be the tool of a well-organized program and not the program itself. If it is set up before it can be used on an ongoing basis or before usability has gained widespread acceptance, management may find other uses for it or even question the value of a usability program altogether when times are tough. It is better to be too late with a full-blown lab than too early.

Remember that the lab can be extremely simple or it can even be portable; the main requirement is that it be available to conduct studies as required. (For a detailed discussion of testing setups, see Chapter 6.) Alternately, if you work for a company with a household name, you may want to arrange to have a secondary laboratory setting off site from which to run "anonymous" studies. Do consider setting up a physical space where you can archive recordings and reports, a place you can think of as a research "workbench" and that others in your organization can identify as the "Center for Usability Truths Revealed." Whether testing per se goes on there or not, there should be resources available to everyone in the organization that further the goal of user-centered design as an accepted practice.

Add Usability-Related Activities to the Product Life Cycle

To succeed beyond the superficial level, usability has to become incorporated into the fabric of the organization's development process. Ultimately, it should be viewed as a completely ordinary activity, much as any other development activity. It needs to be seen simply as the appropriate way to develop and build a first-class product.

Therefore, beware of developing a *separate* life cycle; one for the usual development activities and a different one for usability activities. To the degree that usability is thought of as being separate from other activities is the degree to which it can be undermined. When activities such as establishing usability objectives, formally characterizing the user, conducting a task analysis, and establishing testing checkpoints simply become the way to conduct business, you will know that usability has arrived, and it will be difficult to sabotage.

Educate Others within Your Organization

This suggestion is multifaceted. Here are some specific ways to spread the word about usability, as well as to expand your own horizons:

- Use data from usability tests (and other research) as evidence to explain usability decisions to colleagues at every turn, for example, why one

design is potentially better than another. When making recommendations, do not just expect developers to respond to your title or greater
sense of what is better for users. Instead, take the time to explain your
proposed changes and their benefits, as well as the dangers that exist if
such changes are not implemented. It may help to supplement your findings and recommendations with support from other published reports
of studies that were similar. Listen to their concerns and address them in
your recommendations.

■ Hold seminars on user-centered design concepts, methods, and practices. But make sure that they are appropriate and tailored to the audience. Not everyone needs to know the details of usability testing — some
just need to understand the benefits and the appropriate time to conduct
a test or other research. Others need to hear about success stories, what
the process involves, or expected cost/benefits and return on investment. Bring in professionals to conduct short presentations on a particular subject of interest to the troops or management for added credibility
and a less insular approach. This could range from a simple lunch-time
meeting to a full-blown seminar.

■ Start a usability resource area consisting of a library of books and articles
on usability, as well as project-related usability materials. Set up such a
space, even if it is merely one cubicle in an area, where anyone is free to
go and borrow materials. The project-related materials can be test plans
and test reports that can be used as reference materials and templates by
others who are testing.

Start a bulletin board and post articles of interest from newspapers, journals, magazines, product reviews, and so forth. Post product reviews
that highlight usability as a key issue, either negative or positive.

Encourage everyone to donate materials of interest, especially on success
stories.

Send articles and reports to those who require education, both advocates and adversaries.

■ **Place an article in your company's in-house newsletter espousing the
virtues of usability testing.**   Better yet, report the results of the most
recent test including the implications for the customer/user. Focus on
benefits that go beyond just the product tested and that have implications for other related products and the overall customer experience as
well. Many organizations are composed of groups that develop similar products for similar customers, yet because of politics, do not take
advantage of each other's research efforts.

■ **Publish your own newsletter.**   Findings from one usability study can
be applied to similar products under development.

Identify and Cultivate Champions

Who in the organization will benefit from usability testing? Who is chafing at the bit to get at usability information? Find out the answers to these questions. For those projects without formal usability support, use your influence to establish a usability champion on each project team; someone whose job it is to watch out for the customer/user. An advocate would at minimum be responsible for raising usability issues at meetings, ensuring that usability is included in all design documents and specifications, and helping — if only with the administration — to perform specific user-centered design methods such as testing. Without such champions, progress is slower, and "business as usual" continues.

As appropriate, find a way to unite these champions, as a task force or advisory board, for example. The task force should hold periodic meetings to compare notes on how work is progressing on the different usability fronts, and should exchange ideas and support each other's efforts.

Publicize the Usability Success Stories

Take advantage of the natural competitiveness of different departments and product lines with each other to publish usability success stories of internal departments or even competitors. No department wants to feel that someone else in the organization or an outside competitor has an edge. In particular, let others know if you are falling behind your competition.

Link Usability to Economic Benefits

Whenever possible, establish and report on the cost benefits of studies and tests that you perform. Take the attitude that UCD should at a minimum pay for itself. One way to establish this link is to use a particular economic-based objective within the organization as the basis for a user-centered design project. For example, an objective might be to "cut down on the number of usability-related hotline calls currently received." That means you would have to begin with research about the nature and frequency of calls to see how many are caused by usability-related issues. Then you need to determine what the hotline calls are costing the company and what proposed savings might be in terms of lost sales, additional customer support, and the need to send out "fixes." Here's such a calculation.

Suppose that you know that each hotline call costs the company about $45 in salary, phone costs, fixes sent to the field, and so on. You also know through some stellar detective work that of the 65,000 calls taken each month, about 30 percent (or 19,500) are directly attributed to usability issues. Therefore, about $877,500 of hotline costs are directly attributed to usability problems. If you can reduce usability-related calls *by 50 percent, you can save the company about $438,750 dollars per month or more than $5 million per year.*

This type of analysis will go a long way toward establishing the benefit of user-centered design in everyone's mind, and will create a very specific target. You can analyze the nature of the problems that are causing the calls and why they are occurring, and develop a strategy for solving them.

As an alternative, you might also pursue more indirect economic benefits. Propose as an objective to raise customer satisfaction ratings or cut down on the number of pages in documentation or on an information web site without loss of effectiveness.

Once you begin to approach problems in this way, you will be amazed at the treasure chest of problems that exist within the organization just waiting to be mined and analyzed. Pool the efforts of marketing and research and development to work on solving a specific problem. Quite often, this may be the first time these departments have worked together to address a specific usability issue or objective.

Review reports of product problems from all groups with a vested interest in the product, for example, marketing, training, and so on. Data and information about problems can come from the organization, such as hotline reports, warranty cards, letters and emails from customers, and marketing surveys, or can come from external sources such as product magazine reviews, beta site reports, and the like. With just a little emphasis on collecting and categorizing problem information, you can move from a shotgun approach to a more pointed, focused approach to usability.

More specifically, begin projects that consist of a "follow-on" product to an existing product by first gathering information about any usability problems of the existing product. Then address these problems by incorporating their improvement into the usability objectives for the new product. For example, if you know that the current product has online error messages that are cryptic and also lack clear explanations of the errors in the user guide, then cleaning up the error messages should be an automatic usability objective for the new project. While this seems like the most basic common-sense logic, it is amazing how often politics gets in the way and prevents such an analysis from happening.

Expand UCD throughout the Organization

After usability has begun to take root and there are many champions within your organization, you can extend yourself further, knowing that your efforts will not be threatened by a single setback.

This is a fruitional phase and the point at which things really become interesting and fun. It is also the point at which we end this book. Once your organization reaches this level of acceptance of the value of user-centered design in developing products, further efforts will be limited only by your imagination and by what the future will bring in the form of new technology. For example, user-centered design need not be limited to the product development life cycle, but can be expanded to include the entire product *ownership* life cycle, the whole customer/user experience. Much value can be achieved by taking a user-centered approach to these prepurchase and postpurchase phases, and how different aspects of a company work together (or don't) from the point of view of the customer. For example, say someone orders furniture from a web site but wants to pick it up at a local store location for that retailer. Are the two venues equally friendly, responsive, efficient, and service-oriented? Are the inventory systems of the two venues compatible so the order moves smoothly from one to the other? And so on.

Pursue More Formal Educational Opportunities

If you are serious about user-centered design as a career and do not have a formal education in the discipline, we would suggest pursuing a degree program in one of the behavioral sciences (such as psychology or sociology), industrial design, or human factors, or human-computer interaction. Alternately, there are also certificate programs being offered in human factors at some universities, or through private groups. Take advantage of the workshops and tutorials offered at the professional conferences mentioned earlier in this chapter.

Also, work with an experienced usability specialist who can serve as an advisor and help on the more technical aspects of projects. If you are a lone practitioner in your company, you may want to set up regular calls with a colleague at another company to talk over ideas, approaches, and progress (without revealing company secrets, of course).

Standardize Participant Recruitment Policies and Procedures

Formalize your relationships with your different sources of participants, such as recruiting agencies or market research firms as discussed in Chapter 7, so that recruitment is easy to carry out. Create and refine a database of participants, listing the who, what, where, and when of their participation. Remember that you may want to use people more than once if you require experienced participants. As the need for participants grows, you may want to assign one person to be in charge of acquiring them and maintaining the database.

Align Closely with Market Research and Industrial Design

If your organization is large enough and fortunate enough to have a market research and/or an industrial design function, work closely with these disciplines during the life cycle. There is a natural alliance of the three disciplines of usability/human factors, market research, and industrial design. For example, work closely with the marketing organization to characterize the user. Or, use marketing to help line up participants and acquire or conduct field research. The industrial design specialist(s) can help with solutions for user interface issues, graphic design, and an overall user-centered approach.

Evaluate Product Usability in the Field after Product Release

This evaluation expands the usability life cycle beyond the typical product life cycle which ends at product release. Conduct studies of the usage of your company's product out in the workplace and outside the lab. This could take several forms. You could observe the product being used and question users directly. Or, you could gather information on how the product is being used via either telephone or written surveys, or you could conduct remote usability tests. Fold this information back into the development of the next product by making it widely available to the follow-up product's development team.

So often a development team simply moves to another project as soon as the team completes and releases the current product. This creates a major gap in the feedback chain, since new ideas and implementations, while tested in the lab, are never seen in the light of day-to-day usage. Consequently, any problems experienced by users are simply carried over to the next product. There are many books, reports, and workshops on how to do field studies of various kinds. For a list, see www.wiley.com/go/usabilitytesting.

Evaluate the Value of Your Usability Engineering Efforts

To ascertain the effects of user-centered design, conduct "before" and "after" studies. First, conduct studies in the field of a current product — how it sizes up on ease of use, satisfaction, and so on. Then conduct a similar study on the next-generation product that has been subjected to usability testing or other techniques, and compare the results. This is an excellent way to establish a real foothold for usability within the organization and to find out which techniques are most effective. Of course, publicize your results, and refine your process based on what's working and what's not working.

Develop Design Standards

This activity certainly need not wait, but many organizations have great difficulty standardizing prior to the development of an ongoing program of user-centered design. The standards here refer to consistent methods for representing operations of the user-interface design or standards for documentation formats or the layout of a control panel; *within your own organization*. The idea is to ensure that similar design principles are being implemented in identical ways across all product lines. While standards cannot account for every situation, they certainly can account for the most common situations, which frees developers to worry about the more creative aspects of new product development.

Focus Your Efforts Early in the Product Life Cycle

Without question, the greatest benefits can be reaped by early involvement in the product life cycle. Always strive to influence products at the earliest possible moment, although typically one needs to prove the value of user-centered design in the later stages before this is possible. Focus on early exploratory tests of multiple design concepts. Take the time to interrogate users about the validity of your usage assumptions. For example, have as one of your objectives for an exploratory test to document how users perform specific tasks on the job. This is a very different objective from merely seeing if your design is usable. This early research has many times the payoff of a test conducted after much of the design is frozen. Do not be put off by developers who insist that there needs to be a more tangible product before research can take place. It is never too early in the product life cycle to consider usability. A very low-fidelity prototype can be tested. For a discussion about testing prototypes, see Chapter 13.

Create User Profiles, Personas, and Scenarios

Characterize and describe the users of your product and the tasks they perform and make this information widely and easily available. This might be the most important research you conduct, with the most impact on your organization, and, if you can do it sooner, by all means do so. There are many ways to do this research, and you can be extremely creative.

Visit customer sites, observe users in their workplace, and analyze and document the tasks they do. While many organizations do this, it must be performed systematically and consistently. For instruction and tips on how to do this research, check out *User and Task Analysis for Interface Design* by JoAnn Hackos and Janice C. Redish, *Contextual Design: Defining Customer-Centered Systems* by Hugh Beyer and Karen Holzblatt, or *The Field Study Handbook: A Common Sense Approach for Discovering User Needs* by Kate Gomoll, Ellen Story Church, and Eric Bond.

Then present your results in a compressed accessible format. Usually, it is not a lack of necessary information, but information that is in a form that makes people's eyes glaze over, that sabotages this process. Let's face it — reviewing a typical task analysis can put anyone to sleep.

One of the ways to overcome this obstacle is to use personas. Personas are evidence-based character sketches of archetypical users. They represent typical behavior patterns and goals of larger groups of users as they relate to your product. Personas get names, photos, and stories that help designers and developers relate to users as *people*. If you incorporate personas as members of the team, soon everyone in the organization will be asking "What would our personas do?" There are a dozen or so resources available about researching, developing, and using personas, including seminars from Cooper design, User Interface Engineering, and others, and great books such as *The User Is Always Right: Making Personas Work for Your Website* by Steve Mulder and *The Persona Lifecycle: Keeping People in Mind Throughout Product Design* by John Pruitt and Tamara Adlin.

Afterword

When the first edition of this book was published, we expected that automated usability evaluations would be built directly into software products. These evaluations would provide feedback about customer usage, preferences, and difficulties, gathered more quickly and on a much larger scale than ever before. This hasn't happened the way Jeff envisioned it, but analytics and automated usability testing of web sites and web applications come close.

The first edition also predicted a "continued demise of manual programming skill as a prerequisite for designing software interfaces." While many prototyping tools have made the development of mocked-up interfaces quick and simple, and it is possible that comprehensive programming skills are now unnecessary, delivery methods and outputs have changed greatly, so new programming languages and tools have been invented. The idea that the writing of program code would be completely automated, with developers needing only to specify desired design parameters and the computer automatically writing the code to implement the design, has come to pass for some platforms and applications but not for others.

However, over the last decade and a half, usability and communication skills *have* become *requirements* for developing interfaces *along* with technical skills for all of the roles on any given product team. The importance of cross-discipline cooperation on interdisciplinary teams is greater than ever.

Now we can expect to see usability research expand further into experience design as more firms assign resources to exploit the economic advantages of usable products (money talks) and the overall relationship that organizations have with their customers. Regardless of how the future unfolds and how tools and technology evolve, we can take heart that the following time-tested tenets of user-centered design in all their wonderful simplicity will remain inviolate:

- Analyze and understand the user's skills, knowledge, expectations, and thought process.

- Analyze, understand, and document those tasks and activities performed by the user which your product is intended to support and even improve.

- Design your product in iterative phases based on your analysis of users and usage. Evaluate your progress at every stage of the process.

Any organization that truly takes these principles to heart will be well on its way to successful products and a host of satisfied customers.

Index

A

accessibility, qualities of usability, 4–6
accuracy statistics, performance data, 249–250
activity component, Bailey's Human Performance Model, 7
actors, end users as, 118
ambiguity, moderator comfort wit, 50
analyzing data. *See* data analysis
assessment (summative) tests, 34–35
  for first-time users, 201
  iterative testing in development lifecycle, 41–42
  methodology for, 35
  objectives of, 34–35
  when to use, 34
assistance
  how to assist participants, 211–212
  when to assist participants, 211
associations, sources for participant selection, 137
attention span, of test moderators, 51
attitudes
  discovering with pre-test questionnaires, 175–177
  mental preparation for test sessions, 218
audio recordings, debriefing sessions, 236

B

background questionnaire, 162–164
  administration of, 163–164
  ease of use, 163
  focus of, 163
  overview of, 162
  participants filling out preliminary documents, 220

  pilot testing, 163
  purposes of, 162–163
Bailey's Human Performance Model, 7
"bare attention", test moderators practicing, 61
behavior
  performance data, 165–166
  rationales for, 208–209
behavioral measurements, of product usability, 13
benchmarks
  as means of developing user profile, 119
  for measuring usability, 4
  profitability and, 22
  test plans and, 80–82
  validation tests and, 36
"best case" testing, 133
between subjects design, for test plan, 75
"big picture" view, of test moderators, 51–52
biometric data, gathering, 112
blueprint, test plan as, 66
body language, of test moderators, 203
branching questions, 198–199
BRD (business requirements documents), 118
bugs, assisting participants and, 212
business requirements documents (BRD), 118

C

card sorting, for findability of content or functionality, 18
catastrophe, validation tests as, 36
categorizing user profiles, 124
cause-and-effect relationships, in experimental method, 23
checkbox questions, 198